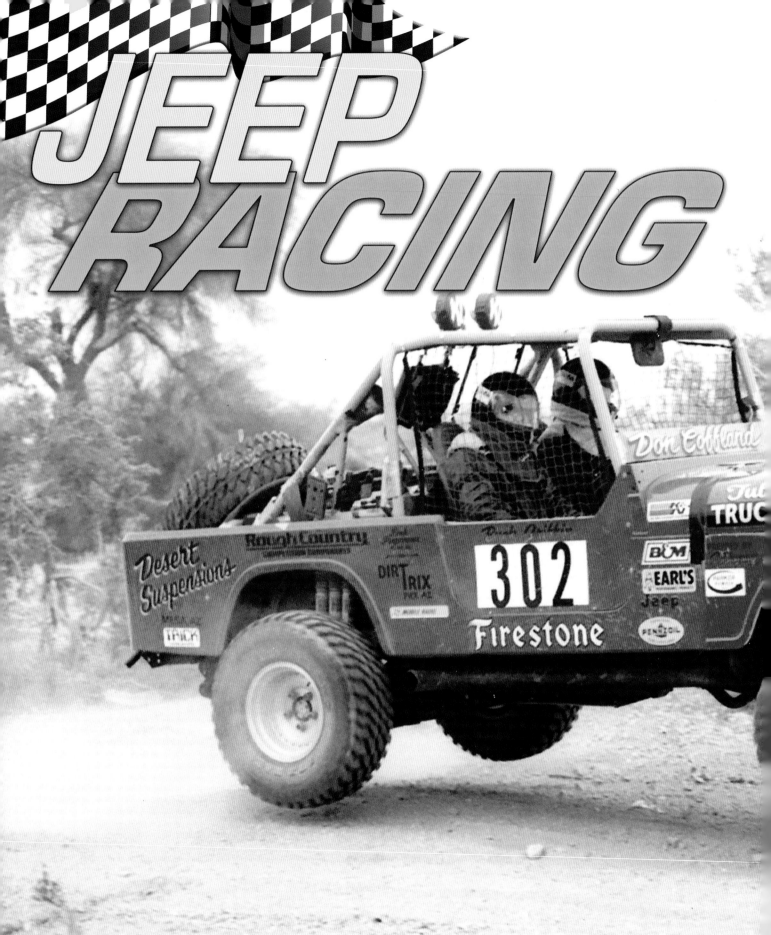

JEEP RACING

John Elkin

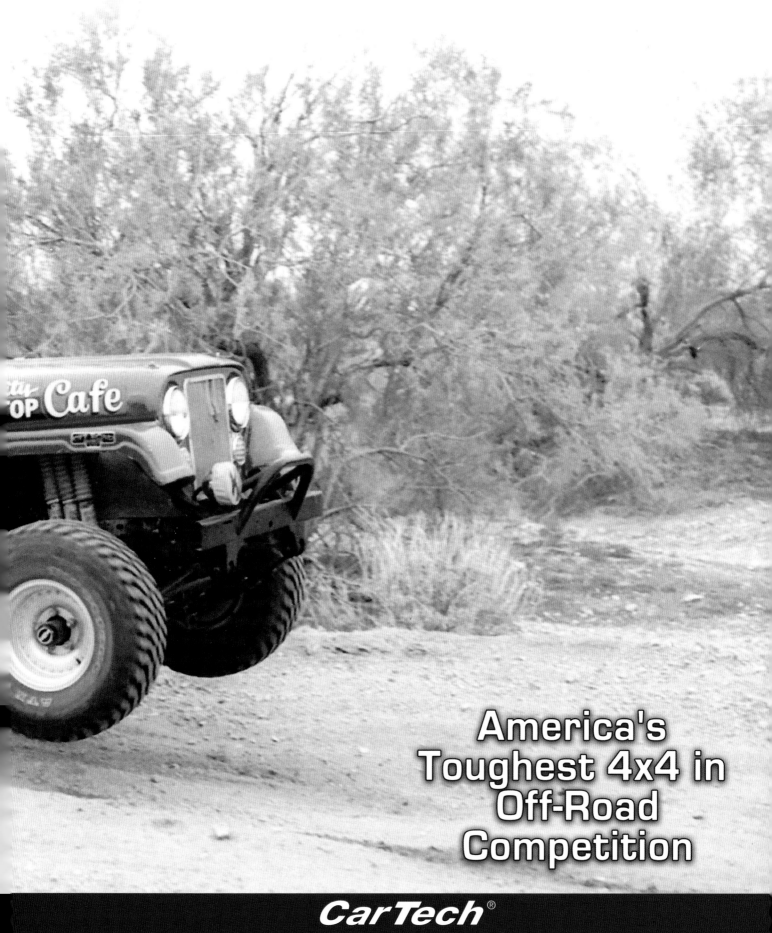

America's Toughest 4x4 in Off-Road Competition

CarTech®

CarTech®, Inc.
6118 Main Street
North Branch, MN 55056
Phone: 651-277-1200 or 800-551-4754
Fax: 651-277-1203
www.cartechbooks.com

Edit by Wes Eisenschenk
Layout by Connie DeFlorin

ISBN 978-1-61325-775-3
Item No. CT693

Library of Congress Cataloging-in-Publication Data Available

Written, edited, and designed in the U.S.A.
Printed in China
10 9 8 7 6 5 4 3 2 1

CarTech books may be purchased at a discounted rate in bulk for resale, events, corporate gifts, or educational purposes. Special editions may also be created to specification. For details, contact Special Sales at 6118 Main Street, North Branch, MN 55056 or by email at sales@cartechbooks.com.

Front flap photo: (Photo by Jere Alhadeff, Courtesy Lou Hart)

PUBLISHER'S NOTE: In reporting history, the images required to tell the tale will vary greatly in quality, especially by modern photographic standards. While some images in this volume are not up to those digital standards, we have included them, as we feel they are an important element in telling the story.

DISTRIBUTION BY:

Europe
PGUK
63 Hatton Garden
London EC1N 8LE, England
Phone: 020 7061 1980 • Fax: 020 7242 3725
www.pguk.co.uk

Australia
Renniks Publications Ltd.
3/37-39 Green Street
Banksmeadow, NSW 2109, Australia
Phone: 2 9695 7055 • Fax: 2 9695 7355
www.renniks.com

Canada
Login Canada
300 Saulteaux Crescent
Winnipeg, MB, R3J 3T2 Canada
Phone: 800 665 1148 • Fax: 800 665 0103
www.lb.ca

TABLE OF CONTENTS

DEDICATION

To my friends who I lost to cancer while writing this book:
Fred Ankeny
Dan Hook
Mark Ridler
Emily Skeen
Melissa Stiles
Matthew Sweeney
Willie Stroppe

ACKNOWLEDGMENTS

Things that are difficult to create can't be made without the support of good people who are willing to help. The writing of this book was a collaboration of many people from all walks of life and time periods of Jeep racing history. To each of these people, I owe a great debt.

First, a huge thanks goes to J. M. and Peggy Bragg for packing 14 boxes of memorabilia with results to read and photos to scan as well as for some mighty fine glasses of iced tea. Carl and Mendy Jackson invited me into their home and allowed me to take photos and go through boxes of Carl's magazines and results. I spent a wonderful afternoon with David Bryan at his home and came away with many stories about racing off-road for more than 20 years. Larry and Sandy Minor have worked with me since my previous book, *Bronco Racing: Ford's Legendary 4x4 in Off-Road Competition*, and they continue to be valuable assets and dear friends. Mike Randall likes my phone calls. He gets to remember a time when his family was king of the desert.

Thanks to Roger and Carol Mears, who selflessly put together the foreword for this book and endured many phone calls, texts, and emails about a certain red *Honcho* pickup. Roger and Carol sent me to Tom Blattler, who was an amazing asset to me.

The Off-Road Motorsports Hall of Fame (ORMHoF) is a valuable resource for everything off-road racing. ORMHoF is where the entire run of *Dusty Times* is available to view along with Judy Smith's photo collection and stories about every inductee. Visit ormhof.org for more information.

Trackside Photos has chronicled the history of off-road racing from 1970 through 2015. Original Owner Jim Ober spent 50 years in the desert and in the mountains taking off-road racing photos. Ober passed away unexpectedly in 2023 at the age of 76. He had the foresight to pass along the entire Trackside catalog to Art Eugenio (getsomephoto.com), who continues to keep the website (tracksidephoto.com) going so that everyone can enjoy Ober's legacy.

A special thank you to the celebrities who took valuable time to speak with me about their adventures and misadventures racing Jeeps: Larry Wilcox, James Brolin, Ruth Buzzi, Catherine Bach, Ted Nugent, and Vikki Carr. A special thank you goes to the staff members who connected me to them. A special thanks to Elizabeth Bassin, who helped with super secret projects.

One of the original Jeep clubs in the United States, the Hemet Jeep Club, opened its archives to me. This club can rightfully boast that it produced more Baja-winning racers than any other club.

Other former and current Jeep racers have been helpful as well. Thanks to Sandy Cone, Tim Casey, Doug Robinson, Evan Evans, Walker Evans, Curt LeDuc, Jerry Kirkpatrick, Dick Sasser, Rob Herrington, and Brad Russell (the son of Ray Russell). Dennis Sletten endured so many intrusive direct messages from me. I salute your patience. Mike Lesle, Larry Maddox, Chuck Johnson, Steve Kelley, Mark McMillin, Eric Heiden, Brain Stewart, Rob and Amber MacCachren, Jim Bell, Don and Harley Coffland, Don German, and Al Unser Jr. deserve kudos for providing help.

Warren Baird was there to witness the racing careers of Ray Russell and Don Adams. Baird built Jeeps alongside Ray Russell, worked on the pit crew, occupied the right seat, and even did some driving. Through Baird, I got to know John Libby, who was Baird's assistant for many years. Thank you for the photos.

Former Jeep Motorsports Manager Jim Rader was very helpful in clarifying the Jeep Celebrity Challenge years from 1978 to 1980. Rader also had the copilot duties for J. M. Bragg for thousands of miles.

Former General Tire Motorsports Manager Olga Vernon provided insight into her first-time co-driving for the late Mike Schwellinger. Rally truck drivers Roger Hull and Jeff Hendricks helped with photos and results. John Gabrial helped with results, advertisements, and entry lists. Mike Pearlman helped straighten me out regarding some National Off-Road Racing Association (NORRA) history. A special thanks to Jeff Furrier for his knowledge of the *Budweiser Jeep Honcho* vehicles as well as the cover photo.

Thanks to Bob Holcomb, my photography guru. Holcomb took old, scratched-up photos and made them new again. Anything that came up with photography, he was there to help for the duration of making this book.

Without my family, there would be no support for me to undertake this project. My wife, Mary; my son, Robert; my mother, Adrienne; and my mother-in-law, Jean, are all responsible for supporting me in one way or another.

Finally, thank you to CarTech for your faith and patience in the writing of this book. Wes Eisenschenk was my editor, and he never yelled at me—even when he could have.

FOREWORD

by Roger Mears

During my racing career, I drove a variety of machinery. Everything from IndyCars, Sprint Cars, Midgets, and Stock Cars to Buggies, Mini Trucks, and more. However, one of the most exciting and fun trucks to race was the legendary *Budweiser Jeep Honcho.*

Competing in off-road races was and still is my favorite form of racing. Off-road racing features a lot of seat time driving a race car or truck for many hours through terrain changes, weather changes, and other challenges that come with racing in the desert.

The Mears gang began with my father, Bill, winning Stock Car titles in Kansas. We moved to Bakersfield, California, where he started a backhoe business, but my brother, Rick, and I wanted to race like our dad. We began riding motorcycles and moved to buggies (sprint and desert), and I had opportunities to drive in the Stock Car, Midget, and Sprint Car categories as well.

(Photo Courtesy Centerline Images)

More opportunities came my way when Texas oil man Mike Moore asked if I was interested in racing for the desert racing team that he was forming with a Jeep Honcho truck. I said that I definitely would, and I knew that the funding was there to win races. That addressed my main concern in racing, which was, "Can I win with the machine?"

Moore went to off-road legend Walker Evans to build the first Jeep for the team, and we worked with Jeep's Jim Rader to produce the first Jeep in 1978. The rest is history.

We won almost everywhere with that *Budweiser Jeep Honcho,* including the Parker 400, Mint 400, Baja 500, Baja 1000, and Riverside World Championships. We competed in Southern California Off Road Enthusiasts (SCORE) and High Desert Racing Association (HDRA) races and took the SCORE Class 3 series title in the Jeep, which was the same machine that won 12 of 22 races in a three-year period.

To be honest, I had to learn to drive the 4x4 truck after racing with a 4x2 for many years. That new Jeep was fast and a complete blast to drive. When I look back on my racing career, I think of the wonderful experiences that I had with Moore, the team, and those Jeeps. There are so many great stories.

One of the more memorable stories dates back to 1980. At Ascot Park, I flipped a midget and broke both arms. Doctors advised me to rest, but the Baja 1000 was coming in a few weeks and I was battling for the series title. The doctors decided to perform surgery and install plates in my arms. I began the race and recruited my dad to finish for us. We took second place in the race and won the series title.

When I look back on my career, I laugh about the great times with the *Budweiser Jeep Honcho* and Moore. Moore was a tremendous guy to work with and drive with in the desert. We had national Budweiser and Jeep advertisements on television and in magazines. I think that we helped put the Honcho on the map in those days.

Maybe the funniest thing about the *Budweiser Jeep Honcho* was that we weren't actually sponsored by Budweiser. I asked Moore, "Why are we running Budweiser on the Jeep when we don't get any money for it? He replied, "I like Budweiser, and it looks good on the Jeep."

I think that we received some money from Budweiser later, but that was Moore. He was one of the best guys that I ever worked with in my racing career. I thank him for those experiences with that Jeep Honcho.

CHAPTER 1

BIRTH OF THE JEEP

The legendary Jeep line that has been known to produce off-road racing champions and race winners had an interesting start. To better understand the machine that wins races, let's get to know the machine that helped the Allied Powers win World War II.

I will briefly touch on the genesis of the Jeep brand and the high points that led it down the road to becoming the Baja-winning machine that is known today.

In 1938, the United States military was keeping a close eye on Nazi Germany's European occupation as well as the tension between Japan and China. A decision was made to start modernizing many aspects of the US armed services. From airplanes and ships to weapons and vehicles, everything was con-

From the photo of the Bantam CRV prototype to this photo of J. M. Bragg in 1984, the Jeep came a long way from being a war-fighting machine to a championship-winning off-road racer.

sidered for a complete redesign.

One of the vehicles that was called for was designated as a Command Reconnaissance Vehicle (CRV). The US

TOP: This is one of the first prototypes of the Bantam CRV. While the front end looks different, the body from the A-pillar to the rear of the vehicle has definite Jeep styling.

This undated Bantam prototype photo shows a subtle difference from the previous prototype (mainly in the headlights and front grille). It was still a long way from the Jeep that soldiers began using in 1938. Surrounding the prototype are executives and leaders from the Bantam factory in Pennsylvania.

The unique styling of the Bantam Model 60 roadster inspired Walt Disney to design Donald Duck's car after it.

Army mandated strict guidelines on weight, size, engine power, and performance. The unit also was required to have four-wheel drive. One of the companies that submitted a prototype was American Bantam.

American Bantam was founded in 1935 when the American arm of British automaker Austin went bankrupt. One of the Austin salesmen, Roy Evans, purchased the bankrupt company. He renamed it American Bantam and began a subtle redesign of the American Austin. By 1937, production was rolling at the factory in Butler, Pennsylvania, which is a small town located north of Pittsburgh. The company produced several bodystyles from light trucks and sedans to a wood-sided station wagon. In 1938, Walt Disney was so taken with the Model 60 roadster that he modeled Donald Duck's car after it.

When the opportunity to vie for a government contract came up, Bantam had Karl Probst and Harold Crist

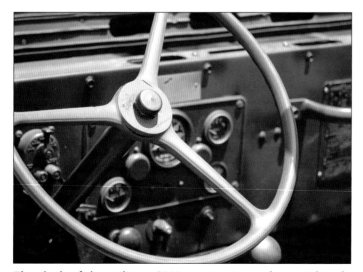

The dash of the military CRV was spartan at best with only the necessary gauges and switches. Note the size of the steering wheel, as there was no power steering.

The Jeep, which helped win World War II, housed the gutsy, little 134-ci inline 4-cylinder Go Devil engine.

The Willys MB was the evolution of the Bantam Prototype with the taller grille that Ford made popular.

design the vehicle. At the heart of the design were live axles at each end with leaf springs all the way around. This concept was the basic design for four-wheel-drive suspensions for decades moving forward.

By 1940, American Bantam was awarded the contract based on design and the engine's fuel economy, even though it fell a little short on torque. Both the Willys and Bantam prototypes used the Willys Go Devil engine. The 134-ci, 4-cylinder engine featured an L-head design, which meant that the valves were parallel to the cylinders. The engine produced 60 hp and 105 ft-lbs of torque in its final design. The reason that Bantam achieved better mileage was due to the unit being lighter overall.

The US Army quartermaster corps claimed that Bantam did not have the production facilities to meet the quantities that were demanded, so the plans for the Bantam design was given to Ford and Willys-Overland. Bantam retained the manufacturing of the trailers that the Command Reconnaissance Vehicle (CRV) towed.

Willys-Overland refined the engine design and increased the torque to satisfy the US Army. Spicer supplied the drivetrain parts, and what was initially known as the Bantam Reconnaissance Vehicle (BRV) found its final form. The Willys-Overland-produced units were called Willys MBs, and the Ford units were known as GPWs.

World War II

Sooner than anyone imagined, the US found itself in a war on two fronts half of the world away. BRVs were produced in great numbers and were shipped to American and English military bases. Some were also shipped to the Soviet Union, but that was done to a lesser extent.

There are many theories as to the real story of how the vehicle picked up the "Jeep" moniker. The leading story is that the Ford-built GP designation morphed from "Gee Pee" to "Jeep." Others believe that since the BRV was small and nimble and could fit between objects, it was like Eugene the Jeep, which was a character in the King Features animated short films. Either way, the name stuck.

The Jeep was more than a general-purpose vehicle. It was called upon to do much more than it was originally designed to do. Jeeps could be outfitted with special wheels to travel down railroad tracks. Because they were so capable, Jeeps were used for a variety of tasks, including laying communications cable, as ambulances, as machine-gun platforms, as firefighting pumpers, and as towing vehicles for everything from trailers and guns to airplanes.

The Ford-built GPW featured a lower hood line and short grille.

Soldiers in the European Theater utilized the Jeep in many capacities, including as a mail courier, makeshift ambulance, and compact troop carrier. The vehicle did whatever was asked of it.

Army nurses used the Jeep during their daily duties. Photos such as this increased support for the war effort.

Raybestos Products knew what consumers wanted to see in its advertisements: soldiers in a Jeep.

Above all, the Jeep was designed for one main purpose: to be an amazing off-road-capable vehicle. It served with distinction in battle from acting as a miniature troop carrier to carrying the most famous generals. By the time that the Axis powers surrendered, Ford and Willys-Overland had contributed 640,000 Jeeps to the war effort.

With an eye toward the end of the war, Willys-Overland submitted paperwork in February 1943 to copyright the Jeep design. Bantam immediately protested the trademark, and by May 1943, the trademark for design was restored to Bantam. Willys-Overland continually received citations from the Federal Trade Commission for advertising that it designed the unit.

End of the Military Jeep

The Jeep went through many changes over the years, as it continued to serve in the Korean and Vietnam wars. Jeeps were lengthened to become makeshift ambulances. The platforms were strengthened so that large-caliber automatic weapons could be mounted on them. Suspension changes made them faster and safer than the original design. No matter the configuration or purpose, they served faithfully for 50 years.

The need for something new was highlighted during the Vietnam War. The Jeep was not ideal for the heavily forested highlands in which the war was fought. Many new designs were tested and introduced in the 15 years following the Vietnam War.

In 1989, the faithful Jeep was phased out of the

United States military. The replacement was the Humvee, which was built by AM General. It gained respect after it was deployed to Panama for Operation Just Cause, and its legend grew in the deserts of Kuwait, Iraq, and Afghanistan.

Future off-road racing legend Kurt Strecker (driver) served in Vietnam and experienced the military version of the Jeep. Note the extra armor plating that was added above the window line of the body. (Photo Courtesy Kurt Strecker)

It took a big vehicle to fill the shoes of the CRV in military duty for the armed forces. American General designed the its replacement with extra protection and increased power from a diesel engine. As with the Jeep, the Humvee found its way into civilian driveways and garages (albeit big ones).

Civilian Introduction

By August 1945, World War II was over and the military downsized to a peacekeeping force. Many items used in the war effort were auctioned off to the public to help recoup the $288 billion ($4.7 trillion when adjusted for inflation in 2022) that World War II cost. Soldiers who returned home were thrilled to see the little Jeeps become available as war surplus.

For many years after the war, surplus Jeeps rolled back to the United States shores in waves. Independent sellers auctioned them off as quickly as they became available. Willys-Overland was not done yet with trying to capitalize on the design, legacy, and name. To sidestep the issue, Willy-Overland designed a civilian 4x4 called the Universal Jeep and copyrighted the name Jeep.

Adventurous civilians and war veterans discovered that the Jeep provided a freedom that conventional sedans did not. If the Jeep could conquer the Pacific Theater, North Africa, Italy, France, and Germany, why would it not be able to conquer the Mojave Desert, a forest, or a mountain?

A family with a spare $200 ($2,600 in 2022) or so could find itself going where most crowds could not. When those with Jeeps came across another Jeep in the backcountry, friendships were often forged. As Jeeps flooded back to American shores, great numbers of people enjoyed them and sought out others who were doing

Through the late 1940s and 1950s, newspapers and magazines featured advertisements, such as this one, for surplus Jeeps. These advertisements launched the recreational off-roading lifestyle, which launched an industry of aftermarket parts and accessories.

Postwar, many Jeeps such as this one were used as transportation through inhospitable terrain. With a catchy slogan, this owner lets you know that this is the way to travel on mountain trails.

At any typical club event, many Jeeps (such as this 1959 CJ-5) were entered in hill climb, obstacle course, and sand drag events. The driver is Carl Jackson from the Hemet Jeep Club. He went on to be the winning driver of the National Four-Wheel-Drive Grand Prix multiple times. (Photo Courtesy Carl Jackson)

the same. By 1948, clubs were formed around Jeep ownership. In some cases, existing car clubs changed their charter to become Jeep clubs. When two or more people in the same vehicle meet, can racing be far behind? Soon, people were using their Jeeps to drag race in the sand, race up sand dunes, conquer obstacle courses, and perform a motorized version of barrel racing.

Modifications

Driving a military-spec Jeep on paved roads was challenging at best. The military-spec Jeep was not designed with pavement in mind. The original 2.2-ci, 4-cylinder engine (the Go Devil) could only produce 60 hp. However, it did make 105 ft-lbs of torque, which was more than 20 percent over what the US Army required. It was plenty good for fighting a war but not so desirable for recreational driving in postwar America with a top speed of 45 mph.

When Willys-Overland began selling as a civilian Jeep (CJ), the more-powerful Hurricane engine was installed. It was a modified Go Devil design with valve and intake modifications that made 72 hp and 112 ft-lbs of torque. It was better, but it was still not enough for Jeep owners with big imaginations and fabrication skills. This was not long before V-6 and V-8 engines were transplanted into Jeep engine bays.

The ride quality of the early Jeeps could be categorized as covered-wagon-like. It was a bone-rattling affair at best. With no doors on the military-spec Jeeps, soldiers and recreational users had to take care not to fall out of the Jeep on rough terrain. Postwar, Jeep owners began playing with spring rates and spring placement. Shock-absorber companies came up with units with better dampening capabilities. It was still a rough ride, but

at least the ride and top speed on and off the road were improved a little bit.

The basis for many of these early innovations was to better the competition in any one of the club events that were available at the time. Many club event weekends included sand drags, obstacle courses, and hill climbs.

Willys-Overland

Seeing the future, Willys-Overland did not go back to manufacturing its sedan. Instead, it went all in on the Jeep line. The CJ-2A was sold as early as 1945. It is commonly known today as a "flat fender" Jeep due its front fender design. Soon afterward, Willys launched the Jeep Station Wagon in 1946, the Jeep Truck in 1947, and the Jeepster in 1948.

In 1952, Willys tried to re-enter the sedan market with the Aero. The sedan was wildly unpopular, and Willys-Overland was unable to recover from the financial failure. In 1953, Willys-Overland was purchased by Kaiser Motors for $60 million. The company was renamed Willys Motors until 1963, when it was renamed as Kaiser-Jeep. At that time, the Jeep Gladiator pickup truck and the Cherokee were introduced.

In 1966, the Jeepster was reintroduced as the Commando and was offered in several configurations throughout its run. It was intended to be the contender to take

Before the CJ-5, many Jeep buyers purchased a 1955 M-38 model with some civilian upgrades. These crossed the Rubicon (California), the rocks of Moab (Utah), the dunes of Pismo (California), and the hardscrabble landscape of Death Valley (California) with adventuresome families. (Photo Courtesy Jeff Zurschmeide)

After the acquisition of the Jeep, Willys-Overland discontinued the Aero Eagle production to produce more of the increasingly popular 4x4s.

on the Ford Bronco. While it was a good unit, it could not put a big dent in Ford's market share. By 1973, the Commando was shelved.

American Motors

By 1970, Kaiser was losing money and looked to sell off Jeep. Along came American Motors Corporation (AMC), which was happy to relieve Kaiser of its burden. AMC had ideas to modernize the Jeep and appeal to people who saw that other 4x4s (namely the Ford Bronco) afforded more comfort. For $70 million, AMC now had its new Jeep division.

AMC saw steady growth with its handling of the Jeep line. In 1971, the government, postal, and military vehicles were spun into what became AM General. In 1976, AMC introduced the CJ-7. Previously, AMC made do with the CJ-5 and CJ-6 models that were designed by Kaiser.

The CJ-7 was a different unit altogether. It was bigger than the early CJs, a little more comfortable, and styled for the times. However, it still retained the rugged look of a Jeep.

By 1979, Renault invested heavily into AMC to allow Jeeps to be imported into Europe by Renault (instead of independent importers). Renault gained a foothold in the company throughout the early-to-mid 1980s.

Under the AMC reign, Jeep expanded into several different models. It upgraded the Cherokee in 1974 with new styling and powertrain options. By 1981, the mini truck ruled the young driver's sales preferences. To create the CJ-8 Scrambler, AMC lengthened the CJ-7 chassis and added a bed behind the cab. It had a short run and ended in 1985, but it made its mark in off-road racing at that time.

The year 1984 was a big one, as Jeep rolled out the new downsized Cherokee with a unibody platform. In the second year of production, sales surpassed 100,000 for the first time. The same platform had the Comanche mini truck supplant the Scrambler. The chassis was named the XJ, and it was produced until 2000.

At the 1986 Chicago Auto Show, AMC debuted the Wrangler YJ chassis to replace the CJ. Although it had slightly less ground clearance, the YJ featured a wider track, more comfort, and better handling. It retained classic Jeep styling with a modernized (yet still boxy) front end. The Wrangler YJ changed and evolved as it went through various iterations, calling itself a TJ, a JK, and most recently, the JL.

Chrysler

In 1987, Renault had major financial issues. The rapidly expanding Chrysler Corporation saw an opportunity to pull in the Jeep line under its wing. Lee Iacocca swooped in, and $1.5 billion later, Jeep had a new owner. Chrysler took what AMC started with the YJ and XJ platforms and introduced the Grand Cherokee and the Liberty. It then took a stab at a full-sized SUV called the Commander, which flopped.

Even though Chrysler has changed hands many more times, the Jeep family has remained under the Chrysler banner and has flourished. Through it all, each corporation embraced the tough nature of the Jeep name and supported its efforts in off-road racing.

CHAPTER 2

JEEP CLUBS LEAD TO
COMPETITION

O rganized in 1946, Sareea Al Jamel (Fast Camel) was the first recorded Jeep club. It was based in the desert community of Indio, California, and was well-known for its Fast Camel Cruise, which started in 1954. It drew hundreds of off-roaders and was held annually from 1946 to 1991 until land closures forced the club to dissolve. Many other clubs popped up in California after the war, and a culture began to take hold.

Jeep clubs followed a protocol that included monthly meetings, a short cruise (once or twice a month), and one large event, which was followed by its big signature event. It was customary to open these larger meetings to other clubs. Some events of note garnered up to 400 entries. Competitions occurred amidst the potlucks, campfires, and cruises. Hill climbs, sand drags, and obstacle-course events were common for these weekends.

Through the late 1940s and into the 1950s and 1960s, Jeep clubs were created in nearly every state and Canada. Since there was no organized off-road racing until the late 1960s, competing at club events was the only way to build a reputation as an off-roader.

Other clubs of note in the Southwest in the early days included the Yucca Valley Cactus Jumpers, Auburn Jeep Club, Tierra del Sol, Prescott Jeep Club, Ukiah Jeep Club, Sidewinders Jeep Club, and the Jeepsters Club—just to

TOP: Jeep Club events, such as obstacle courses, instilled a sense of competition in Jeep owners. This led to modifications, faster Jeeps, and an increased competitive desire. All of these things were the nucleus of what is now professional off-road racing. (Photo Courtesy Hemet Jeep Club Archive)

After each event, most club newsletters featured a photo collage that highlighted the weekend's events. This is from the 1963 Afton Canyon Jeep Junket. (Photo Courtesy Carl Jackson)

Jeep clubs still exist today, but many became 4x4 clubs so that they wouldn't be tied to one brand. Some still stay true to their Jeep roots.

Some clubs are specific to a cause or a charity. This TJ participates in a trail run by the Veteran Overland group, which uses off-roading and the group dynamic to help veterans through the healing power of connection. (Photo Courtesy veteranoverland.org)

name a few. Due to land closures and encroaching civilization into their beloved canyons and valleys, not all clubs survived.

It was not long before drivers from one club began to dominate club events. The Hemet Jeep Club drivers were always among the favorites. Eventually, they became sought after when off-road racing was in its infancy.

Hemet Jeep Club

No Jeep club that is still in existence has been around longer than the Hemet Jeep Club. Unofficially, there were documented Jeep trips in 1947 to the Truckhaven Hills next to the Salton Sea in California. The official club history started in 1948 as the Hemet Cavalcaders. Not long afterward, the name was changed to reflect the Jeep culture that grabbed hold in Hemet, California. Many legendary off-road drivers came out of the Hemet Jeep Club, most notably Jim Loomis, Larry Minor, Rod Hall, Carl Jackson, and Jim Fricker.

The first official event of the Hemet club was the DeAnza Cavalcade. The event started in Hemet, ran 30 miles through Coyote Canyon south of Anza, and then went south to Borrego Springs. The reason for the run was twofold: 1) it was fun and challenging and 2) it brought to light the need for a proper road to connect Hemet to Borrego Springs. Jeeps came from all over the Southwest to take part in the Cavalcade. Participation sometimes numbered in the hundreds.

Bud Jackson

Bud Jackson is the father of Carl Jackson, who had a prolific off-road racing career with Jeep, Ford, and Nissan, and he was one of the founding members of the Hemet Jeep Club. While he was never a club president, he was known as the undisputed leader of the club, especially on trail runs.

A well-known mechanic in Hemet, Bud had the distinction of being the first off-roader to be ticketed by the Bureau of Land Management on a trip looking for new trails for club events. He was instrumental in the building of a concrete dance floor at Afton Canyon, which was 40 miles from anywhere.

Every club has a behind-the-scenes force that gets things done, and Bud was that for the Hemet group. He passed away while on a trail run near Wickenburg, Arizona. He was only in his mid-50s.

Before being renamed as the Hemet Jeep Club, the organization was called the Hemet Cavalcaders. The group kept the goat as its mascot, which is fitting for off-roaders. (Photo Courtesy Hemet Jeep Club)

LOCAL AID PROJECT — Sign explains how the large work crew was recruited for Hemet Jeep Club's fifth annual Afton Canyon Junket, Nov. 11-14. They're completing a concrete dance floor 40 miles from anywhere.

Bud Jackson and his crew poured a concrete slab at the base of Afton Canyon to serve as a dance floor. It was the social hub of the group's massively successful Afton Canyon Jeep Junket. (Photo Courtesy Carl Jackson)

Afton Canyon Jeep Junket

The DeAnza event was joined by what became Hemet's signature event: the Afton Canyon Jeep Junket. Afton Canyon is located about 40 miles east of Barstow, California. It is known as the Grand Canyon of the Mojave. The road through the canyon runs parallel to the Mojave River and crosses it several times, and it is a fun trail for off-roaders. The Mojave River is mostly an underground river. It makes its only appearance on the surface at Afton Canyon. However, Afton Canyon offers much more, with sandstone canyons, slot canyons, natural sandstone caves, and abandoned mines. Because the river flows year-round, it is a great location for watching wildlife.

The first Afton Canyon Jeep Junket was in 1960 and was a wildly popular event. Before long, the Hemet Jeep Club was widely known for hosting one of the most popular weekends of the year. More than 400 entries regularly crowded into the canyon area to enjoy the trails through and around the canyon. A highlight of the junket was the 50-mile trail run that traversed the canyon, rocky hillsides, and sand dunes.

The competitions drew most of the interest. These included obstacle-course races, hill climbs, and sand drag racing for men and women. In those early years, some of the names that were at the top of the results were destined to change off-road competitions forever, including Ray Harvick, Larry Minor, Carl Jackson, Rod Hall, and Jim Loomis. Most made their reputation right there in Afton Canyon, where a win carried a lot of weight with other clubs.

Jeepers Jamboree

In 1952, some local men wanted to start a get-together to financially benefit the Georgetown Divide area in the Sierra Nevada mountain range. Since the area is the gateway to the famous Rubicon Trail, it made sense to plan a gathering of off-roaders to spend a few days in the area and tackle the toughest 17 miles in the Sierra Nevada. They came up with the name Jeepers Jamboree and began planning.

According to the official history of the Jeepers Jamboree that was published in the July 28, 2017, issue of the *Mountain Democrat* newspaper, this was how the route was planned.

"These local men spent time devising the perfect route and trip itinerary," the newspaper article stated. "They crossed the Rubicon River to the Rubicon Valley, which was a lush green meadow with a perfect camping

The 1957 Jeepers Jamboree was the fourth-annual running of that event. The numbers grew every year as participants returned with tales of the previous year's event.

area. In the middle of the meadow were the remnants of the old Rubicon Hotel to add a bit of history to the camping area. To get backing for the trip, it was presented to the Georgetown Rotary Club and the Georgetown Rifle and Pistol Club. They were thrilled with the idea of reviving the economy and helped back the trip."

There were 55 vehicles with a total of 155 passengers who attended the first event in the summer of 1953. The participants enjoyed the hospitality of the area and spent some cash with local merchants along the way. By the third year, the Jeepers Jamboree became the event that the organizers hoped that it would be.

As the popularity grew, Jeep clubs from across the country gathered for the social event of the year at the campsites. The Rubicon became the trail of the year because it's a bucket-list trail that every competent off-roader needs to complete.

The organizers of the jamboree kept raising the stakes to ensure that no other gathering would surpass it for hospitality and experiences. The jamboree is completely catered with three meals a day, entertainment, and raffles. It even supplies 20 mechanics to help keep your rig in top shape. You may have to pay for some parts, and a tip is always welcome to the mechanic, but it is worth it to many of the attendees.

"THE WAY WE WERE"
A LOOK BACK THROUGH OUR HISTORY
OCTOBER 2016 – ISSUE #41 By Diane Boss, Co-Historian

While looking through the old Hemet Jeep Club photo books, I came across these cool photos of the 1950 Cavalcade through Coyote Canyon to Borrego Springs. Take a look at the folks in the top right photo. Can you name any of these jeepers?

It's easy to name the
fellow in the jeep below

Jeep clubs, such as the Hemet Jeep Club, cherish the past and often run these photo collages in club newsletters. It's important to maintain the club archive and make the new members aware of the club's history. (Photo Courtesy Hemet Jeep Club Archive)

In 1962, Dave Ekins and Bill Robertson Jr. wrote themselves (and Honda) into the record books with their journey from Tijuana to La Paz. (Photo by Walt Fulton Sr./Courtesy Dave Ekins Family)

The jamboree celebrated its 72nd anniversary in 2024 and shows no signs of slowing down. From gatherings like this, off-road racing organizations learned that off-roading, whether racing, sand dragging, or motoring down a trail is like a family event. Even in the largest races, such as the Baja 1000, there is an undeniable family feel to it.

Big-Time Off-Road Racing

Local trail runs, Jeep clubs, sand drags, and mud-racing competitions were the primeval ooze from which off-road racing as it is known today was born. The next step in off-road racing began in 1962, when Honda sponsored a record-establishing run down the length of the Baja Peninsula from Tijuana to La Paz.

Dave Ekins and Bill Robertson Jr. were the riders hired to make the run. Honda provided two of its CL72 Scramblers for the journey.

The peninsula was so primitive in 1962 that it was decided that the official timing would consist of sending a Western Union telegram from the start in Tijuana. If they finished, another telegram would be sent from the Western Union office in La Paz to establish a finish time. The first attempt took 40 hours. Once it was official, people began planning how to break that record.

There was a lack of fuel for great distances, so the team was supported by an airplane. The best maps they had were 30-year-old maps from the Auto Club. They used celestial navigation at night, but a thick fog rolled in and obscured the stars during night two.

There were many incidents along the way, including crashes, mechanical issues, and insufficient lighting. Ekins and Robertson became lost near San Ignacio when Ekins noticed that he was following his own tracks. They quickly realized that their 36-hour target was going to need to be recalculated to 40 hours. While Robertson nursed his Honda that was running on 1 cylinder, Ekins clocked in to La Paz in 39 hours and 58 minutes.

That trip and the ensuing advertising and news articles about it contributed toward 89,000 Scramblers being sold between 1962 and 1968.

Action like this at the inaugural Brian Chuchua National Four-Wheel-Drive Grand Prix brought the crowds and kept them coming back. This shows Rod Hall blasting through one of the many creek crossings. (Photo Courtesy Carl Jackson)

Off-Road Racing for the Masses

As various automotive and motorcycle brands ran up and down the Baja Peninsula and lowered the record several times per year, it was fun to hear about, but there was no way for spectators to watch it. Off-road driving was exciting, and Orange County Jeep dealership owner Brian Chuchua thought that the lack of spectators should change. In 1965, he did something about it.

With the help of the Jeepster Club and the Rubio Jaycees, Chuchua found a section of the Santa Ana River bottom between Riverside and Corona, California. There, he carved a course into the sandy, rocky riverbed. There was a bluff on one side where spectators could see the action without being too close to the course or posing a safety concern.

Chuchua named it the National Four-Wheel-Drive Grand Prix and made sure everyone knew about it to

Carl Jackson starts his Stock-class winning run at the 1965 National Four-Wheel-Drive Grand Prix. (Photo Courtesy Carl Jackson)

secure a good entry and gate. The inaugural races ran from July 3 to 5. Dune buggies, trucks, 4x4s, and motorcycles ran in separate classes.

This event and the next couple that followed were the launching point for a new kind of off-road racing that was more of an adventure than anything that had previously been done in North America.

The National Four-Wheel-Drive Grand Prix ran from 1965 until 1972. There is more about this event in chapter 3.

Baja

Record attempts were commonplace in Baja. Every manufacturer wanted to be the fastest from Tijuana to La Paz. Not all were successful. AMC and Chevrolet aborted attempts after accidents or weather issues put the records out of reach.

These record attempts, and the Brain Chuchua Grand Prix events, led to the formation of the National Off-Road Racing Association (NORRA) and the Mexican 1000—a rally-style race that started on Halloween in 1967.

Feeder System

Every big-time system needs a feeder system. The National Football League has college football and Major League Baseball has the minor leagues. In the beginning of off-road racing, there were Jeep clubs. Although, many clubs allowed other brands of vehicles so that they could expand.

By the 1970s, smaller off-road-racing organizations supplanted the club feeder system. People with an itch to take their chances in a battle against the desert and the competition could begin with these smaller races in southern Nevada, Arizona, and California.

David Bryan competes at the 1978 Southern Nevada Off-Road Enthusiasts 250 in his CJ-7 to keep his skills sharp and promote his sponsors. (Photo Courtesy Judy Smith Collection/Off-Road Motorsports Hall of Fame)

CHAPTER 3

THE 1960s

Brian Chuchua (right) and Dennis Sletten inspect the Holy Toledo *Jeep that Chuchua's shop built for him in 1969. (Photo Courtesy Dennis Sletten)*

Even before the Mexican 1000 or the National Four-Wheel-Drive Grand Prix, there was no shortage of Jeep adventures. The entire Southwestern United States was riddled with trails that had not seen much traffic since covered wagons trundled west. Mexico revealed itself as an off-roader's paradise in Baja and on the mainland. With a Jeep, the known limits of vehicular travel were stretched further than before.

By 1965, club events took place everywhere from the Borrego Desert to the mountains of Washington state, the state of Colorado, and down into Texas. Individuals took it upon themselves to tackle great distances. Maybe none were more adventurous than Brian Neal Chuchua.

Brian Chuchua

Chuchua was born and raised in Southern California. He was exposed to the car culture that had been permeating the greater Los Angeles area since before World War II. At the age of 15, his father, who ran a steel mill, bought him a Jeep. Soon afterward, Chuchua found a Jeep that opened a whole world of freedom and adventures for a restless young man.

TOP: *Many Jeep club events include mud races, which are good, dirty fun. Family-oriented fun and healthy competition laid the groundwork that was picked up by organized off-road racing. That same community feeling still exists today.*

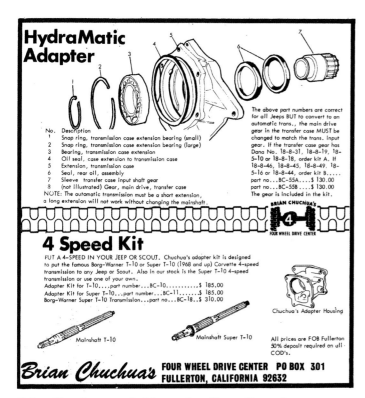

HydraMatic Adapter

No.   Description
1   Snap ring, transmission case extension bearing (small)
2   Snap ring, transmission case extension bearing (large)
3   Bearing, transmission case extension
4   Oil seal, case extension to transmission case
5   Extension, transmission case
6   Seal, rear oil, assembly
7   Sleeve transfer case input shaft gear
8   (not illustrated) Gear, main drive, transfer case
NOTE: The automatic transmission must be a short extension, a long extension will not work without changing the mainshaft.

The above part numbers are correct for all Jeeps BUT to convert to an automatic trans., the main drive gear in the transfer case MUST be changed to match the trans. Input gear. If the transfer case gear has Dana No. 18-8-31, 18-8-19, 18-5-10 or 18-8-18, order kit A. If 18-8-46, 18-8-45, 18-8-49, 18-5-16 or 18-8-44, order kit B....
part no...BC-55A....$ 130.00
part no...BC-55B....$ 130.00
The gear is included in the kit.

4 Speed Kit

PUT A 4-SPEED IN YOUR JEEP OR SCOUT. Chuchua's adapter kit is designed to put the famous Borg-Warner T-10 or Super T-10 (1968 and up) Corvette 4-speed transmission to any Jeep or Scout. Also in our stock is the Super T-10 4-speed transmission or use one of your own.
Adapter Kit for T-10...part number...BC-10...........$ 185.00
Adapter Kit for Super T-10...part number...BC-11.......$ 185.00
Borg-Warner Super T-10 Transmission...part no...BC-18..$ 310.00

Mainshaft T-10   Mainshaft Super T-10

Chuchua's Adapter Housing

All prices are FOB Fullerton 50% deposit required on all COD's.

Brian Chuchua's FOUR WHEEL DRIVE CENTER PO BOX 301
FULLERTON, CALIFORNIA 92632

Brian Chuchua made his mark selling off-road accessories just as much as he did selling Jeeps at his Orange County, California, dealership. (Advertisement Courtesy Dennis Sletten)

By 1954, after he graduated from high school, Chuchua had already attended the second Jeepers Jamboree. He drove the first Jeep that successfully climbed the infamous Devil's Slide at Pismo Beach. That summer, he entered his first race at a Chuckwalla Jeep Club event in Borrego Springs and won. By 1959, he graduated from junior college and was considered to be a very experienced off-road driver.

By 1960, at the age of 23, Chuchua left La Habra, California, and drove through Mexico and Central America to see the Panama Canal. Surely, that journey could be a book in and of itself.

Brian Chuchua Jeep

In April 1963, Chuchua and his partner Doug Olsen opened a Jeep dealership in Orange County, California. The dealership quickly became the premier Jeep dealership in the United States. It was among the first to offer aftermarket Jeep parts, roll bars, and V-8 conversion kits. The same year that Chuchua opened his dealership, he joined the Specialty Equipment Manufacturers Association (SEMA) as a charter member. Chuchua quickly got into the habit of being on the ground floor of almost every major off-road innovation as well as drag racing.

Brian Chuchua takes a few moments to replay his time in off-road racing in his mind. His significant impact in the sport landed him a home in the Off-Road Motorsports Hall of Fame. (Photo Courtesy Dennis Sletten)

All Roads Lead to Baja

By 1965, Chuchua wanted to bring off-road racing closer to major population centers to entertain off-road fans and pick up some new enthusiasts. Thus, the National Four-Wheel-Drive Grand Prix was born. Chuchua found a piece of the Santa Ana River bottom between Riverside and Corona that fit his needs perfectly.

At the inaugural NORRA Mexican 1000, he backed three Kaiser Jeeps in the race. By 1969, he backed 12 different entries in NORRA competition. At one time or another, he backed drivers such as Rod Hall, Carl Jackson, John Ulfeldt, Dick Dahn, Orrin Nordin, and Cam Warren along with American rallyists Ken Adams and Erik Hauge.

The World Cup Rallies

By 1970, the challenge of the World Cup Rally events caught Chuchua's attention, and he took on the massive financial obligations himself. The first event that he entered was the London to Mexico City Rally. In 1974, he ran the London to Munich rally (via the Sahara Desert and Turkey) and then the London to Sydney rally.

Later Years

Chuchua stayed active as a driver in many kinds of racing through 1982. He eventually sold his dealership in 1994 and took up politics on a local level in Orange County. He was inducted into the Off-Road Motorsports Hall of Fame in 1978 as a pioneer of the sport.

The National Four-Wheel-Drive Grand Prix

Chuchua advertised the first National Four-Wheel-Drive Grand Prix events in many local newspapers. It brought out all of the local hot-shot drivers in 4x4s, motorcycles, and dune buggies. They gathered at the Hidden Valley Gun Club along the Santa Ana River west of Riverside, California.

The course was a figure-eight design. Competitors started side by side but split off onto their own courses at the start. Each traversed one side of the figure-eight and then crossed over and raced on the other side. Basically, the first one back to the start was the heat winner (since they traveled the exact same distance).

Being that the course was a river bottom, there was lots of sand, rocks, and standing water. Because the water cut through the sandy bottom, there were hills to climb and descend. The course had a little bit of everything.

A Short but History-Altering Run

The National Four-Wheel-Drive Grand Prix ran from 1965 to 1972 until Mickey Thompson started his short-course event at the Riverside International Raceway in 1973. These river-bottom runs spawned the formation of NORRA, Mickey Thompson's two short-course series, and advanced off-road racing technology the same way that World War II advanced aviation.

At the inaugural race in 1965, Jeep earned four out of a possible seven class wins. Donnie Beyer made the trip from the city of Truth or Consequences, New Mexico, to win the E Stock class. He had the fastest lap of the weekend with a 4-cylinder Jeep Universal. Rod Hall was the winner in B Modified with a Jeep Universal that was fitted with a 327-ci Chevrolet engine. In C Modified, Orrin Nordin took his 283-ci Chevrolet-powered Jeep

Wins at the 1966 National Four-Wheel-Drive Grand Prix were good padding for a driver's resume. An enthusiastic checkered-flag wave for Carl Jackson capped a successful and profitable weekend. (Photo Courtesy Carl Jackson)

Universal to a win. In F Modified, Virgil Garrison and his 4-cylinder Jeep Universal triumphed for the last Jeep win of the event.

By 1966, the number of entries was much larger and there were 3 more classes for a total of 10. Jeep earned 6 of those class wins. That year was also important because the new kid on the block, the Ford Bronco, made its debut at the event. Bill Stroppe's drivers took two class wins in the stock divisions. This was the beginning of the Jeep-versus-Bronco war.

Rodney Hall and Orrin Nordin were repeat winners in B and C Modified, respectively. Nordin took the fastest lap of the weekend and edged the upstart Broncos. Vic Wilson won E Modified with a Jeep Universal that was fitted with 163-ci 4-cylinder engine. F Modified was won by Art Archer in a 4-cylinder Jeep Universal, and Roy Davidson took his homebuilt Jeep-based creation powered by a 301-ci Chevrolet engine to a win in G Modified. Carl Jackson was the big winner of the weekend with the F Stock win, which was the biggest class of the weekend.

Chuchua is the true founder of short-course off-road racing. His efforts are directly responsible for the birth of that sport and desert racing as we know it today.

Carl Jackson, in his 1959 Jeep CJ-5, won the biggest class of the weekend during the 1966 event. It was the beginning of a string of impressive wins that launched him into several factory rides from 1968 into the 1980s. (Photo Courtesy Carl Jackson)

Don Francisco (left) and Ed Pearlman (right) are the founders of the National Off-Road Racing Association (NORRA). (Photo Courtesy NORRA Archive)

Ed Pearlman (right) confers with Saab driver Ingvar Lindquist before the 1968 Mexican 1000. (Photo Courtesy NORRA Archive)

NORRA

Chuchua got the ball rolling, and his events were the catalyst for the formation of the National Off-Road Racing Association (NORRA), but desert racing came from the adventurous mind of Ed Pearlman.

Ed Pearlman

Pearlman was no stranger to promoting Jeep racing. During World War II, while serving with the US Marines in the Pacific Theater, he organized Jeep races in Guam to raise morale. Upon returning from the war, Pearlman and his wife, Shirley, opened a chain of flower shops in Southern California. As with many former soldiers, he purchased a surplus Jeep. Since Pearlman was an avid fisherman, he spent three months in Baja and recorded prime fishing spots and got to know the desolate peninsula.

By the mid-1960s, Pearlman started to participate in Chuchua's events in the Santa Ana River bottom. They were fun, but he could not help but think that there was more of an adventure out there for those looking for a challenge. Europe had rally events that covered great distances across Europe and Africa, so his beloved Baja came to mind.

With the news about new speed records being recorded from Tijuana to La Paz, he nurtured an idea about a rally-format race. Initially, the event was known as the Mexican 1000 Rally. There was a transit run from Tijuana to Ensenada, then after a few hours' layover, the speed section of the rally took place in one stage all the way to La Paz.

By 1966, in partnership with Don Francisco and a group of other Southern California–based off-roaders, NORRA was formed. Francisco was a pilot who enjoyed the peninsula. He even went as far as modifying his aircraft to run on the lower-octane fuel that was available in Baja. Francisco used his airplane to plot a basic course and estimate where fuel stops were needed down the peninsula to La Paz.

The word went out about the NORRA Mexican 1000 rally that was going to start at the bull ring in Tijuana on Halloween in 1967. Unbeknownst to Pearlman, Francisco, and others, off-road racing would be transformed due to their efforts, and one of the greatest automotive adventures in the world was born.

Pearlman ran NORRA from 1967 to 1974. He, his partner, and their associates grew NORRA to include a second Baja race, a race in Parker, Arizona, and some one-off events. A political shift in Mexico spelled the temporary end of NORRA in 1974, and it was mothballed for 36 years.

1967

As a tumultuous 1967 began, there was a significant buildup of forces in Vietnam. The Apollo space program suffered a setback as Apollo 1 astronauts Gus Grissom, Ed White, and Roger Chaffee were killed in a launchpad fire. In England, the Beatles released the *Sgt. Pepper's Lonely Hearts Club Band* album.

This was the keystone year for off-road racing, as it saw the birth of desert racing as we know it today and added factory support. The inaugural Mexican 1000 exposed millions of people to the sport through newspaper articles and magazine reports.

Carl Jackson is yelling at his CJ-5 to go even faster, as he felt Larry Minor breathing down his neck in the finale to the 1968 National Four-Wheel-Drive Grand Prix. (Photo Courtesy Carl Jackson)

National Four-Wheel-Drive Grand Prix

The third-annual version of this fast-growing race had a new course design. It included four river crossings, more jumps, deep ditches, hairpin turns, and a straight where speeds reached 90 mph. There were 46 entries from 5 states that competed.

This flyer was distributed to all four-wheel-drive clubs and was used as an advertisement in many magazines of the day. (Advertisement Courtesy Carl Jackson)

The new course added more attrition to the mix, as some of the early favorites had misfortune and were spectators instead of racers. Rod Hall set a fast time for Friday that earned him some money. However, early on Saturday, he became stuck and was out of the race. Jim Loomis had a similar fate as he became bogged down in the riverbed and was eliminated.

The final came down to Larry Minor in his 1966 CJ-5 with a Buick 225-ci V-6 engine versus Carl Jackson in his 1957 CJ-5 with a stock F-head 4-cylinder engine. Minor recorded the fastest time for the event with an 8:44 lap earlier in the day. Jackson had a best time of 8:45. So, despite the displacement advantage to Minor, Jackson proved to be a crafty driver.

The much-anticipated Top Eliminator Final was lined up and ready to go. The green flag dropped, and both men dumped their clutches. Minor shot off the line, as did Jackson. As they went into the very first corner and Jackson downshifted, his pressure plate shattered and the clutch slipped terribly. Stuck in second gear, Jackson decided to keep going—because you never know what will happen.

On the other side of the course, Minor, unaware of Jackson's misfortune, kept pushing hard as the crowd cheered him on. As he neared the halfway point where the Jeeps were to cross over to the other side of the course, Minor suffered a flat tire. There were now two limping Jeeps that were attempting to traverse the course. Jackson feathered his throttle with a light touch. Any more would allow the clutch disc to slip. Minor tried to muscle his way through with only three inflated tires.

As Jackson motored around the course, he tried to keep the clutch engaged and sometimes took three attempts to climb hills leading up to the dike-road part of the course.

Minor got stuck. Jackson had no idea why the crowd was going so crazy. He could hear them over his struggling engine. When he arrived at the finish, Minor was not there. Jackson won what must've been the slowest final in National Four-Wheel-Drive Grand Prix history.

Jackson won a pile of money and a brand new 1967 Ford Bronco. He sold the Bronco to help fund his racing program and repair the clutch assembly that he destroyed.

Inaugural Mexican 1000

In world news, October 1967 was known for a lot of things. People talked about Air Force Major Pete Knight, who piloted an X-15A-2 to the new speed record of Mach 6.72 (over 4,520 mph). The final animated film that Walt Disney supervised before his death, *The Jungle Book*, premiered. The Beatles put the finishing touches on the *Magical Mystery Tour* album. What history glossed over was that off-road racing (as it is known today) was born on October 31, 1967.

There were 68 teams signed up for the inaugural Mexican 1000. The entry fee included fuel because there were no established gas stations past Ensenada. Fuel was available at each of checkpoints that were located in Camalu, Santa Ynez, El Arco, La Purisima, and Villa Constitución. It also included full insurance coverage, accommodations for two in La Paz (for three

Record Attempts Continue Before the Inaugural

The timed runs down the Baja peninsula increased, and the official time was down to 31 hours. The new record was set by renowned automotive journalist Spencer Murray and photojournalist Ralph Poole. The vehicle was a 1967 Rambler American with a 199-ci straight-six engine. The uneventful nonstop run was accomplished with the help of a half-dozen carrots, a box of crackers, four apples, a jar of cheese, and a gallon of water.

This record run, which was authenticated by NORRA, helped spotlight the appeal of the upcoming Mexican 1000 on Halloween. Since it was officially timed and verified by checkpoints along the way, any time quicker than 31 hours would be an official record.

NORRA founder Ed Pearlman made a run at the record with a trio

This recent photo shows Ed Pearlman's Toyota Land Cruiser, which was refurbished by his son Mike. Why is there a Toyota in this Jeep book? It's because this Land Cruiser was the key ingredient in the founding of NORRA. (Photo Courtesy Mike Pearlman)

of Toyota Land Cruisers. His personal Land Cruiser was powered by a small-block Chevy. In his biography on the Off-Road Motorsports Hall of Fame website, the feat was described as following:

"The race consisted of three teams, with one team doubling as the press corps to cover the event. Pearlman and Dick Cepek drove a Toyota Land Cruiser with a Chevy engine, as did Claude Dozier and Ed Orr. Bruce Meyers donated a Meyers Maxx buggy for the press vehicle,

driven by Drino Miller and John Lawlor, a journalist.

"The racers faced a multitude of technical difficulties, yet all completed the course. Orr and Dozier crossed the line into La Paz first with a time of 41 hours and 45 minutes. Pearlman and Cepek came across the line in 56 hours. It took Miller and Lawlor an additional 10 hours to finish, with a time of 66 hours. During the course of the race, Pearlman came to the conclusion that there needed to be a more organized form of off-road racing."

days and two nights), and a banquet for the finishers.

The event was classified as a rally. Therefore, the leg from Tijuana to Ensenada started in the bull-fighting ring with a ceremonial start. Teams had a certain amount of time to arrive in Ensenada without incurring extra penalty time. From Ensenada, the gloves were off and the all-out speed section ran all the way to La Paz.

There was every kind of four-wheeled vehicle imaginable—from stock 4x4s, foreign sedans, and dune buggies to two-wheel-drive pickups and big American sedans. There were motorcycles too. Most of the entries had never been to Baja before, and most had not been beyond Tijuana. Many had an Auto Club map of Baja from the 1940s and a handheld compass. La Paz was southeast, so head south by southeast, or south, or east.

The Jeeps Prove to be Dominant

The Jeep drivers were already in a rivalry with Ford's newcomer, the Bronco. Three Broncos were entered in the race. One met an early demise with a broken front differential, one finished (but after the official time limit expired), and the last one officially finished far down the order. It was not the last time that Bill Stroppe and his Broncos battled Jeep. There was a huge struggle ahead for both manufacturers.

Mexican 1000

Repairs on the side of the trail are common in off-road racing. This front-end repair was completed during the record attempt from Tijuana to La Paz in early 1967. (Photo Courtesy NORRA Archive)

Jeep Takes a Stab at the Record

Kaiser Jeep didn't want to be outdone by AMC (who bought Kaiser Jeep three years later) and took a contingent of five Jeeps down to Baja to set a new record. It hired current record holders Spencer Murray and Ralph Poole to drive one of the Jeeps. Notable names in the other four vehicles were Dick Cepek, Rod Fish, Charles Coye, Speed Boardman, and "Wild" Bill Hardy (the San Diego–area sales manager for Kaiser).

The attempt was ill-timed. As the Jeeps started down the peninsula, Hurricane Katrina bore down. With 100-mph winds and record rainfall, Hurricane Katrina took aim at the five Jeeps. Oddly, one Jeep reported that it was okay at Guerrero Negro, on the west coast of Baja (477 miles south of Tijuana). The other four Jeeps were stranded near Bahia de Los Angeles (the Bay of Los Angeles) with the road washed out in front of and behind them. The Jeep on the west coast could not make it across the peninsula due to extensive road damage. That crew made its way back to the United States safely.

The rest of the Jeep drivers agreed that they needed to help. They traveled a treacherous washed-out road and headed north toward San Felipe, where they learned there was great need of help. In that area, 155 homes were lost, 24 fishing vessels were sunk, and the highway north of San Felipe was washed out in 20 places, which cut them off from Mexicali.

Dick Cepek led the new mission to aid the Mexican residents. The men used their two-way radios to help direct aircraft over areas that were desperate for help. They also gave their food and water supplies to help people who had lost everything until more aid came from America. The Mexican government praised the men for their efforts in the emergency.

Larry Minor Recounts His Winning Run

The following text is an excerpt from *Bronco Racing: Ford's Legendary 4x4 in Off-Road Competition*:

In a March 2020 interview, Larry Minor recalled the first Mexican 1000.

"So, the race started, and gosh that was a long race! We saw the sun come up twice. So, people were passing us, we were passing people who were broken down on the side of the road. We got to El Arco, which was about the halfway point in the race about midnight, and Rod asked the checkpoint guy, 'How far is that Bronco ahead of us?'

"He said that it was two hours ahead of us. 'Holy crap,' we said. 'How are we going to catch that Bronco?'

"So, Rodney and I decided, 'Let's go racing like we do.'

"We took the ice chest out, the tool chest out, and left them with the checkpoint crew. We aired our tires down like we would running an obstacle race, and we took off and drove the crap out of that Jeep."

"Just as the sun came up, we were in the silt beds down around San Ignacio, and we were just heading south in these deep ruts. All we knew was that La Paz was south, and a cheap compass was all we had to go by. So, we were going along and here came Stroppe and Harvick going the wrong way, so we waved them down to talked. That was really the first time I met Bill Stroppe, I had known Ray Harvick for a long time because he was from the beach area, and we went down there to street race all the time.

"So Stroppe says, 'You guys are going the wrong way.'

"We said we weren't and that *this* is south. Stroppe said something about a magnetic field interfering with the compasses.

"I said, 'I don't know about you, Bill, but we're going to keep going this way.'

"So, we took off and left them. What we didn't know when we left them was that the ruts they were in were really deep, and when they went to take off, they high-centered and got stuck."

It was not until well after Minor and Hall arrived in La Paz that Stroppe and Harvick finally made it to the finish. It was then when Minor heard the rest of the story. Stroppe and Harvick had to wait until someone came along to pull them out of the ruts. The Bronco, with Stroppe driving, took off and looked to catch the Jeep. Due to over-exuberant driving, the Bronco rolled and crashed four to six times. The exact number depends on who you ask. Different people have different answers.

It took 32 hours, but Minor and Hall etched their names in the record books as the first winners of the pro-duction four-wheel-drive class. It was not the last time for either man to win in Baja, but those other wins were not with a Jeep product.

Two More Class Wins

Before there was a Mexican 1000, Orrin Nordin used a Jeep to compete in club events and several Four-Wheel Drive Grand Prix events. He drove for Brian Chuchua and was paired with Chuck Owen for this first-of-its-kind event.

Their mount was a 1966 Kaiser Jeepster. It had two-wheel-drive and a 225-ci Buick V-6 with 160 hp and 235 ft-lbs of torque. The engine was mated to a 3-speed manual transmission, and at the end of the driveshaft was a Dana 30 differential. It was probably the lack of four-wheel drive that allowed the Jeepster to run in the production car class.

Nordin and Owen took 30 hours and 5 minutes to complete the drive to La Paz and reported no major issues with the Jeepster along the way. They beat *Hot Rod* magazine editor Ray Brock and Ak Miller in their Ford Ranchero to La Paz by 4 hours.

The third of the class wins was in the non-production unlimited class. Farris E. Hightower and Ed Venable from Blythe, California, used a 1946 Willys Jeep truck with a 283-ci Chevrolet V-8 to win the race in 32 hours and 2 minutes. Two hours and 16 minutes later, Andy Dever-celly and Dick Archibald took second place with their Volkswagen. Jeep also took third place, as Monte Carlton and Chuck Hoyland brought a 1965 Kaiser Jeep, which was also fitted with a Chevrolet engine, home in 42 hours.

The Jeep brand dominated the race with the most class victories by winning three of the five classes. Jeep had vanquished the Bronco challengers, and, as 1968 dawned, it felt good about its chances at the new events in Las Vegas and for the rematch in Baja.

Split Loyalties

Not long after the Mexican 1000, Ford's Bill Stroppe contacted Larry Minor to ask if he would come to his team and drive a Bronco. Minor accepted the offer. Rod Hall wanted to remain loyal to Jeep, so the friends went their separate ways. Minor went to Ford and Hall went to Brian Chuchua's Jeep team. Both were among the favorites at every race they started in 1968.

1968

As 1968 began, the Green Bay Packers enjoyed their second Super Bowl win in a row. Johnny Cash prepared for a live concert at the Folsom Prison that was recorded for an album. On January 7, George Harrison of the Beatles traveled under the name "Mr. Brown" and flew to India to record with local musicians for his *Wonderwall* film score.

For off-road racers, word spread quickly about two new events in Las Vegas that would test the reliability of man and machine. The first Mint 400 was scheduled for late March with a brutal 355-mile loop from Las Vegas, Nevada, to Beatty, Nevada, and back. In June, the Stardust 7-11 would use almost the same course but would run two laps from the Silverbird Raceway outside of Las Vegas to Beatty and back. The Mint 400 was self-promoted by the Mint hotel and casino, while the Stardust 7-11 was sanctioned by NORRA.

The Mint 400

The Mint hotel and casino had been a fixture on Las Vegas's Fremont Street since it opened in 1957. Del Webb bought the Mint in 1961 and began an expansion that included a 26-floor hotel and a 6-level parking garage.

By 1967, with the popularity of the Mexican 1000 and off-roading in general, Norm Johnson, the Mint's promotions director had an idea to promote the hotel and casino's annual $10,000 deer hunt. Two dune buggies set off from the Mint to establish a record from Las Vegas to Lake Tahoe. The team of LeRoy Wickham and John Sexton completed the run in six days.

For 1968, the idea was to make an actual race out of the former publicity stunt. A grueling nearly 400-mile racecourse was laid out from Las Vegas to Beatty, Nevada,

and back. The course had three pit areas, where cars could be refueled or repaired and drivers could change positions.

Kaiser factory representative Russ Smith attended the race by the order of Kaiser executives to report back regarding what was happening. Kaiser and Jeep were well

The race vehicles are lined up in front of the Mint hotel and casino. It was the beginning of the parade to the start line. A variety of vehicles attempted the first 400-mile race. (Photos Courtesy Carl Jackson)

The first attempt of the Mint hotel and casino to use off-road hijinks was a record speed run from Las Vegas to a sister property in Lake Tahoe, Nevada. It was tied to the annual deer hunt that the casino sponsored. (Clipping Courtesy Carl Jackson)

Carl Jackson splashes through the Santa Ana River to victory over Don Crofts. This placed Jackson back in the finals against his old friend Larry Minor, who competed in a Bronco this time. (Photo Courtesy Carl Jackson)

On the way to overall victory, Carl Jackson defeated powerful competitors, including the Baja Boot. *The legendary creation was always fast but had issues with reliability. (Photo Courtesy Carl Jackson)*

some gains in spectator attendance and prize money. The 3,000 spectators bought tickets to see 30 entries battle in 7 classes. The low entry numbers were most likely due to the race's timing after the Mint 400. This was the first year that a class was available for dune buggies, and it was the first time that the event was sanctioned by NORRA. Previously, Brian Chuchua self-sanctioned and insured his events. With the sanctioning by NORRA, Chuchua had access to better insurance, timing, and scoring.

Having won the last two Top Eliminator races, Carl Jackson was the man to beat in his stock CJ-5 4-cylinder. The usual suspects hunted for him as well. Now that there was a non-production class for the custom-built vehicles, the *Baja Boot* was there with Bud Ekins at the wheel. Ekins was an exceptional off-road motorcycle racer. This

was his first time on four wheels.

Jackson went up against Portland, Oregon, driver Don Crofts in the B Stock final and easily dispatched him to move into the four-wheel-drive final. Rod Hall won A Stock by defeating another Portland-based driver, Jim Murphy. Both drivers were in CJ-5s with the Buick V-6. Larry Minor beat Jim Loomis to move into the four-wheel-drive finals. Minor was now a Stroppe team driver in a Ford Bronco. Minor beat Rod Hall, so the final was yet another rematch with Jackson.

Minor got the jump on Jackson at the start and was visibly ahead until Minor got out of shape on the fenced ridge and lost a few seconds. Pushing to make up for the error, Minor almost turned over the Bronco on a jump but recovered. At the crossover, Minor had a scant lead over the consistent Carl Jackson, as the men switched courses. Jackson continued to set a blistering pace while Minor tried everything to take the win. Heading into a soft sandy corner, Minor got out of shape and lost precious seconds regaining the course, but it was too much. Jackson set the fastest time of the entire weekend with a 5:41.59, beat Minor again, and took his 1959 Jeep home with a nice check.

Jeep was very happy with the win and hoped that the momentum from the Grand Prix weekend carried over to upcoming events. Those were long, grueling desert races that favored the Bronco.

The Stardust 7-11

The Mint 400 got the jump on starting organized off-road racing in Nevada with its independent sanctioned event. NORRA, looking for a foothold in racing north and south of the border, wanted a piece of the Nevada desert.

After talks broke down between NORRA and the Mint hotel and casino, NORRA moved on to the Stardust Hotel. NORRA was keen to go up against the Mint event with an even tougher challenge. While the Mint used the nearly 400-mile lap once, the Stardust 7-11 used a slightly

Stardust International Raceway was the site of the start and finish of the longest and toughest race in United States off-road racing history. A total of 137 entries started the race, but only 24 entries were listed as official finishers. (Photo Courtesy Carl Jackson)

modified lap of 355 miles run twice. Instead of running right out of town, the race started and finished at the Stardust's own short-lived racetrack west of Las Vegas in what today is known as the city of Spring Valley.

June in Nevada comes with its own special challenges, and all of them are centered around the heat of the Mojave Desert. However, a stout prize of $25,000 was a tempting carrot that was dangled in front of the starting field. That clouded the vision of what you were signed up for.

While the Mint 400 garnered 98 entries, the Stardust profited on the success of the Mint 400 and started 137 entries. All of the era's heavy hitters were present. There were the mighty Stroppe Broncos with names such as Larry Minor, Parnelli Jones, and Jim Loomis. In addition, there were a handful of Toyota Land Cruisers, the Chuchua team, the Beyer family, and a half-dozen other powerful Jeeps.

Race Days

In the early morning, as teams rolled into the Stardust Speedway, it was obvious that it would be a hot day. By 11 a.m., when all of the teams were already well into the desert, the conditions were bordering on miserable. In interviews with racers who were there and went on to extensive off-road racing careers, every one of them stated that this was the single roughest race in which they ever competed.

Production Four-Wheel-Drive Class

The Bronco continued its string of wins with Larry Minor and Jack Bayer taking the win by more than 4 hours. Yes, 4 hours. The anticipated battle between Larry Minor and Rod Hall never had a chance to materialize when Hall's Jeep CJ-5 broke early during the first lap.

A Ford Military Utility Tactical Truck (MUTT) finished in second place and was followed by the first Jeep of Lonnie Beyer, which was another 2.5 hours behind. It was obvious that every single entry encountered some kind of issue. The difference was that the Bronco had fewer issues.

Donnie Beyer had a year's worth of trouble in the Nevada Desert, but there was a reason that Beyer was known as "Diehard" Donnie. A double endo, a broken front axle, numerous flat tires, and getting stuck were all overcome to win the modified class. (Photo Courtesy MotorTrend and Petersen Museum Archive)

Modified Four-Wheel-Drive Class

Most of the finishers came in close to the 40-hour cutoff. A few finished the race after the cutoff and were recorded as a non-finishers. For example, the #22 Jeep of Russ Smith, who after 40 hours and 36 minutes of struggle and repairs arrived at the finish line but did not get counted as a finisher.

As with the production class, it was a race of attrition, as the conditions of the Nevada desert were difficult for the vehicles and drivers to handle. What did it take to win the modified class? Let's follow the near super-human exploits of class-winner Donnie Beyer.

On the first lap, as competitors struggled with the sand dunes south of Beatty, four cars came over a dune but found that the opposite side of the dune was straight down, so there were four rollovers. Beyer came flying over but did not stick the landing. He went end over end at least twice. When he came to a stop, a quick inspection showed that the entire front end of the Jeep was caved in.

Undeterred and about 20 miles from the Beatty pit, Donnie hitched a ride (unknown with whom) to Beatty. He located his pit crew, and they scavenged an entire front end from

the Jeep wagon, loaded it up, and went out to find the racer in the dunes. Once his vehicle was located, they set about to replace the front end. It took hours.

Eventually, the Jeep was racing again. "Diehard" Donnie was off again in hot pursuit of a Blazer, another Jeep, and a Bronco that had passed him while in the dunes. There were a few flat tires and a rumor that he got stuck for a short amount of time.

It was with great relief that he came over a hill and saw the lights of Las Vegas and the speedway finish line. Thirty-five hours and 54 minutes had elapsed since he started the first lap. Upon arrival, he was astonished that he was the winner. Fourteen minutes later, the Blazer

Rod Fish and Russ Smith took third place in the modified class at the Stardust event. Two of the top three class finishers drove Jeeps. (Photo Courtesy MotorTrend *and Petersen Museum Archive)*

Even though Donnie and Ronnie Beyer's Jeep won the modified 4x4 class, Jeep chose to highlight a different vehicle in its advertisements. The Bill Janowski and Roger Gamut Jeep Wagoneer took fifth place in the production 4x4 class and barely finished in the allotted time limit. However, the team completed the entire course without any downtime, which Jeep's advertising department thought was more appealing. (Advertisement Courtesy Carl Jackson)

For the 1968 NORRA Mexican 1000, Rod Hall and Carl Jackson were entered in a 1969 Kaiser Jeep that was equipped with the Dauntless V-6 and an automatic transmission. The Chuchua team felt that provided an advantage over the Stroppe Broncos. (Photo Courtesy Carl Jackson)

arrived in second place. After another 9 minutes had passed, the Jeep of Rod Fish came roaring in to claim third place. More than 3 hours later, the last official finisher, a Bronco, took fourth place.

The Stardust 7-11 never again took place. The hotel was not keen to renew the event, and the organizers knew that there had to be serious changes to the course. It was laid to the side of the road like so many race cars between Las Vegas and Beatty.

NORRA Mexican 1000

By November, all eyes looked south of the border, as it was time for the second NORRA Mexican 1000. The first event, which took place the previous year, had 68 entries. In the second year, it attracted 254 entries and ABC's *Wide World of Sports* with Jim McKay as the commentator.

Jeeps were entered in the production four-wheel-drive, production passenger cars, production utility vehicles, and non-production four-wheel-drive classes. The roughly 832 miles of Mexico Highway 1 tested competitors and machine in every way. While the Stardust and Mint races were rougher, Baja was still far more primitive, help from pit crews was less available, the navigation was far more crucial, and there were more unknowns on the peninsula than in the Nevada desert.

A New Racer for Rod Hall

After the disappointment of Rod Hall's early exit at the Stardust 7-11, the Jeep team that Brian Chuchua fielded did whatever it could to fight the Bronco contingent. The drivers and co-drivers took extended time to pre-run the best routes around known hazards, especially the silt beds that were south of Punta Prieta.

Rod Hall wanted a new co-driver and pressed fellow Hemet Jeep Club member Carl Jackson into service. Jackson had been behind the wheel for the James Garner AMC team and the *Baja Boot* team of Vic Hickey. He was a proven driver with many wins at Chuchua's Riverside events and many club events. The pair ran a Jeepster with a 225-ci V-6 and an automatic transmission.

Jeep versus Bronco versus Baja

Exactly one year earlier, Larry Minor and Rod Hall partnered to win the inaugural Mexican 1000. The friends now found themselves in competition with each other but in separate brands in the production class. To date, the scoreboard was Larry 3, Rod 0. Going into the biggest race of the year, Rod looked to end the season on a high note.

The Bronco pulled the number 3 starting position, while Rod went number 27 off the line. At 1-minute starting intervals, that meant that they were 24 minutes apart on physical time. It also meant that Rod Hall had to deal with the dust of more cars and motorcycles.

Don't Worry about the Bronco

At the first checkpoint, which was a scheduled pit stop, Carl Jackson asked where Minor and Jack Bayer were.

"Don't worry about the Bronco," a crewmember said. "They came in here overheating and were pouring in stop-leak. They'll never make it to La Paz."

Slightly skeptical, Hall and Jackson pushed on.

At the next checkpoint, they again asked about the number 3 Bronco.

"Oh, don't worry," a crewmember said. "They came in here blowing steam and running 240 degrees. They can't make La Paz." Yet, they still had not caught them. Just in case, they kept the pressure on and thundered down the road.

Just past Cataviña, Mexico, about one-third of the way down the racecourse, in the world-famous Boojum forest, the Jeep sputtered to a stop. Jackson leapt out and opened the hood to survey the problem. He jiggled

In a rare aerial photo, Rod Hall and Carl Jackson attempt to chase down the Bronco of Larry Minor. (Photo Courtesy Carl Jackson)

The First All-Women Mexican 1000 Team

Aletha Patchen and Carol Bryan were two accomplished off-roaders from the desert community of Indio, California. Their husbands, Marv Patchen and Bill Bryan, were stalwart members of the local off-road club and proven racers. During a casual conversation with friends about the upcoming 1968 Mexican 1000, the conversation turned to how there were some male/female teams, but no all-woman teams.

Aletha and Carol looked at each other with a knowing glance that people get when they are about to do something eccentric. Their husbands agreed to let them use Marv's Jeep and prepared it for competition. Brian Chuchua agreed to let the ladies pit with his team.

In the two months before the race, Carol took a two-week mechanics course at the College of the Desert. The editors of *Desert Magazine* were approached about writing a story about the women's exploits. They agreed with one stipulation: "Okay, but don't kill yourselves."

Two weeks before the event, Chuchua asked Rod Hall and Carl Jackson to let the ladies ride along on their pre-run of the course.

"If it hadn't been for Brian's offer, I know we would never have finished," Carol said. "There are just too many wrong turns to make if you don't know the right turns."

Marv and Bill supplied aid to the ladies and the rest of the Chuchua team via two airplanes. The planes followed the Jeeps. Then, they flew ahead and landed at the checkpoints to service the team.

Aletha took the wheel at the start and took the paved road south out of Ensenada. They were finally racing in the Mexican 1000.

Near Laguna Chapala, Mexico, which is 280 miles

Althea Patchen (driving) and Carol Bryan start the 1968 NORRA Mexican 1000, which included incredible highs and lows for the ladies. In the end, they were the first all-female team to complete the race. (Photo Courtesy David Bryan)

from Ensenada, the first problem surfaced in the form of a broken steering stabilizer. While Carol held the flashlight, Aletha made the repair in good time, and they continued south to the next pit stop at El Arco. A quick stop to clean the points when the engine died was the only other issue, which happened often in off-road racing at the time.

Aletha and Carol arrived at the El Arco at 6:45 a.m., which was right on time. Bill and Marv made some minor adjustments to the engine, gassed up the Jeep, and sent them on to the next pit in San Ignacio.

a suspicious-looking spark plug wire, and the Dauntless V-6 roared to life. It was a heart-stopping moment that luckily did not repeat itself for the rest of the race.

Jackson asked the same thing at the next checkpoint. He was told that the Bronco's engine was burning up. However, if Minor's engine was so bad, why hadn't they caught him yet?

Spare Tires Are so Overrated

Before the race started, Hall and Jackson had inspected their new Jeepster. In the back was a double spare tire mount. Jackson did not like that J-hooks were used to hold the straps that were holding the tires. The mechanics said that it would be fine and that they had used them before. Jackson figured that they knew what they were talking about and went along with pre-race preparations.

Somewhere after Checkpoint 1, they heard rattling and bumping behind them. The spare tires were loose. As Jackson had feared, the J-hooks stretched. They made a quick stop to readjust and retighten the straps that were holding down the tires. However, it happened again by the next checkpoint and again farther down the road.

Near El Arco, the spare tires came loose while climbing a steep hill along a canyon wall. They bounced out and rolled down the canyon side a long way down inhospitable terrain. Hall had (just a year ago with Larry Minor) dumped the spares at a checkpoint in an effort to gain some speed. With that in mind, Hall pressed onward without the spares and bet that he would be fine.

Sitting in the post-race impound yard is the number 109 Jeep entry of Patchen and Bryan. It took 47 hours and 55 minutes, and 7 of those hours were spent getting out of a mud bog. In Baja, finishing is winning. (Photo Courtesy David Bryan)

At 11:20 a.m., the ladies arrived right on time, with the Jeep running well.

A few miles south of San Ignacio, a driver in a buggy warned them about a nasty stretch of sand that was too soft to cross. Carol walked up to the sand wash, dug her heel into the sand, and figured that it was no worse than the sand washes near Indio that she crossed often. Back in the Jeep, she pulled around the buggy, gunned the engine, and easily crossed the sand.

As the 32nd hour came (since starting the race), the ladies made an error at a marked shortcut and turned right instead of left. Several miles from the turn, Carol got a feeling that they had made an error. As she realized they had to turn around, they crested a hill and landed in a lagoon of soft mud near the ocean. The Jeep was stuck up to the hubs.

According to Carol's tide tables, they didn't have long before high tide. As luck had it, a large deposit of salt was not far from the Jeep. Using bags from their personal belongings, the ladies made trips back and forth and spread salt under the tires. It was an agonizing process to make 5 feet of progress backwards to hard ground. Seven hours later, the Jeep was free.

Disheartened that they lost so much time, the ladies drove at a moderate pace to the pit stop at Villa Constitution. There, they discovered that they could still make the finish before the time limit. The last 130 miles of pavement was a breeze compared to what they had gone through.

The ladies rolled into La Paz in 47 hours and 55 minutes, which was 2 hours and 5 minutes under the 50-hour time limit. They secured the title as the first all-female team to finish the race.

Just outside San Ignacio, California, with a dusty Carl Jackson at the wheel, Rod Hall is bundled up for the chilly Baja night, as he takes a well-deserved break. (Photo Courtesy Carl Jackson)

The Punta Prieta Incident

Pre-running is an important ingredient in the success of any off-road racing team. It is as true today as it was then. The main difference is that today's racers have an array of electronic aids, including a global positioning system (GPS), pinpoint weather forecasts, and more modern communications and roads than what existed in 1968. All of these differences contributed to what was possibly the difference between first and second place in the production 4x4 class.

Team manager Cam Warren had a decision to make at the Punta Prieta fork in the road. The first option was to go straight and take on the deep silt beds. The second option was to go right and take the road to the coast, which could be faster under the right circumstances, but it was longer. Go right at the wrong time, and the tidal pools are a muddy quagmire. If the tide is in, the beach becomes impassable. Warren believed the beach was the way to go.

Hall and Jackson were right where they wanted to be when they arrived at Punta Prieta. Crews told them that Minor's Bronco went toward the silt beds. Not far down the road, Rod and Carl realized that they were lost. They missed a turn somewhere not far into the loop. They turned around a few times and looked for the road but soon decided to return to Punta Prieta and take the silt beds. They met a motorcycle racer along the way and helped guide him back to the main road.

Now 60 to 90 minutes behind, a determined drive was underway to beat the Bronco to La Paz. In the dark, as they came into the last part of the race near Villa Constitution, the Jeep ran into a nasty ground fog.

"It was so strange," Jackson said. "You couldn't see ahead at all, but if you looked up, you could see the stars."

To further complicate issues, crews told them that there was a broken-down hay wagon somewhere in the fog, which made them take extra time to get through the fog.

The Finish

In the predawn darkness, Rod Hall and Carl Jackson arrived at the finish line. Ahead of them and off to the side was the Bronco. Hall and Jackson were 90 minutes late and in second place. Minor and Bayer came to congratulate their Hemet brothers on the finish. Upon seeing Minor approach, Rod Hall exclaimed, "Tomorrow we are going to race you back up!"

Hall and Jackson were the only top-five production class Jeep finishers.

In the pre-dawn hours, Rod Hall and Carl Jackson crossed the finish line in second place in the production 4x4 class. The 22 hour and 43 minute drive was 3.5 hours faster than the third-place finisher. (Photo Courtesy Carl Jackson)

Other Classes

In the production utility class for two-wheel-drive trucks, Jim Taylor and Manuel Ayala (driving for the Brian Chuchua team) took a strong second place in class and were nearly 2 hours ahead of third place. It was a strong showing for the Jeep DJ-6 half-cab soft top.

In the non-production four-wheel-drive class, the winner entered their vehicle as a "Buick Mite" (more commonly known as a "Mighty Mite"). In reality, it was a 1946 Jeep prototype called the M-422. It was designed by a team of four former Bantam engineers as a lightweight aerodynamic military quarter-ton vehicle. It only saw duty with the United States Marine Corps.

The vehicle was driven by John Ulfeldt and Terry Weir down the peninsula in 31 hours and 43 minutes. In second place was the Chevrolet V-8-powered Jeep CJ of non-production winners Gene Hightower and Ed Venable. They were 50 minutes behind the Mite. In third place was another Chevrolet-powered Jeep driven by Bill Haddad and Michael McConathy, which completed a Jeep-built 1-2-3 sweep of the class.

Finally, in production passenger-car class, a Jeep took a third-place class finish 2 hours behind the winner. Francisco Duret and Ignacio Costonans spent 32 hours and 27 minutes making their way down the peninsula and trailed a rally-built Saab and a Volkswagen sedan.

In another Chuchua entry, Jim Taylor and Manuel Ayala chased Ak Miller and Ray Brock down the peninsula for a strong second-place class finish. (Photo Courtesy MotorTrend and Petersen Museum Archive)

Gene Hightower and Ed Venable, winners of the 1967 modified 4x4 class, settled into a second-place finish for 1968 in their Chevrolet V-8-powered Jeep. Hightower and Venable enjoyed successful careers in off-road racing, with Hightower in a variety of Jeeps and Venable in a Volkswagen. (Photo Courtesy MotorTrend and Petersen Museum Archive)

1969

The turbulent 1960s were coming to a close, and America achieved great success in getting humans into space and eventually the moon. A rash of high-profile assassinations divided the country and created a rift between age groups. The sociological issues did not seem to be present in the off-road racing world, as horsepower transcended it all.

The Jeep crews knew the Bronco contingent was making some big gains. It was time to step up the preparation and driving styles. The Jeep was tougher overall than the Ford, and teams were going to exploit that in the rougher races.

NORRA had a new race for 1969. The Baja 500 was an abbreviated race in Baja California that looped the northern state of Baja Norte.

Mint 400

Much like the second running of the Mexican 1000, where there was a large bump in the entry numbers, the Mint 400 attracted more entries. The organizers learned from the inaugural event that the long, single-loop format was too difficult to organize, too difficult on the teams' logistics, and allowed the field to get too spread out.

Carl Jackson and Kent Horning chase a Volkswagen Beetle in the two-wheel-drive Jeep Cherokee. The Cherokee was, on paper, a possible favorite to win. However, the desert decides if it is your day, and there was little that Jackson and Horning could do but smile and take fourth place. (Photo Courtesy Carl Jackson)

the finish line but had exceeded the time limit to be considered an official finisher. The class was scored through 350 miles. A trio of Volkswagen Beetles nabbed the first three spots, but Jackson and Horning were able to get the battered Jeep home to earn fourth place.

"The truck was so badly bent that the team salvaged the parts they could before cutting it up and throwing it away," Jackson said.

National Four-Wheel-Drive Grand Prix

The fifth-annual visit to the Santa Ana River bottom proved to be wetter, rougher, and sandier than the previous four events. The minds of Brian Chuchua and Tex Carter came up with a course that led to the demise of many favorites.

Returning two-time champion Carl Jackson received an early exit after he got off line in the wrong area and became mired in thick mud. Ray Harvick was behind the wheel of "Wild" Bill Hardy's Jeep and was shown the door in an early eliminator round. Sherman Balch, in his CJ-2A known as *Moby Grape* with a Chevy V-8, was comfortably ahead of the Bronco of Jim Loomis, when he got fender-deep in the mud and was eliminated.

While the Jeeps were shut out from the Top Eliminator competition, there were some highlights. In the A Stock final, Rod Hall nipped the Chevy Blazer of Johnny Diaz with his Jeepster. Hall won $1,045 for the weekend.

In the end, sponsorships tell the world how good a product is. Rod Hall and Spike Cooper were the top dogs in production 4x4 class, and Champion Spark Plugs told the whole world about it through advertisements such as this. These advertisements built the reputation that the Mint 400 maintains to this day.

Rod Hall charges into one of the many water crossings during the 1969 National Four-Wheel-Drive Grand Prix. (Photo Courtesy Dennis Sletten)

In the E Modified class, two Archer Brothers Jeeps went head to head for the win. Ray Cronin and Bill Bollenbacher were neck and neck throughout the figure-eight track. It looked like it could be a dead heat when they headed toward the finish. After doublechecking the clocks, it was a win by a hair for Bollenbacher in his Universal Jeep V-6.

The 1969 National Four-Wheel-Drive Grand Prix marked the end of Carl Jackson's streak of wins in the Santa Ana River bottom. The axle-high mud was more than the stock 4-cylinder could overcome. (Photo Courtesy Carl Jackson)

Rod Hall is on his way to the A Stock class win over a Chevrolet Blazer. Hall didn't make it any closer toward the Top Eliminator prize, but he earned $1,045 for his efforts. (Photo Courtesy Carl Jackson)

Baja 500

With the cancellation of the Stardust 7-11, NORRA looked for another option to expand its schedule. Since Baja is what Mike Pearlman and Don Francisco knew best, they decided to run a loop event concentrated in Baja Norte. The Baja 500 ran 558 miles and followed the Mexican 1000 route until south of Santa Inez before it turned north and followed the coastline to San Felipe. Then, the trail went northwest back to Ensenada.

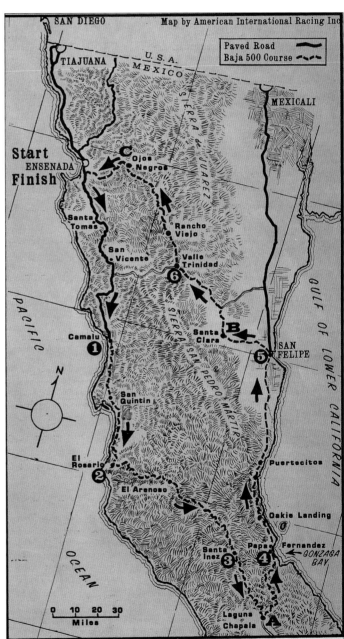

The inaugural NORRA Baja 500 course took competitors on a long loop around Baja Norte. Some believed that the loop was more challenging than the Mexican 1000 in some ways. This course was used annually until 1972. (Course Map Courtesy Carl Jackson)

Prior to the race, there was a driver shakeup at Brian Chuchua Jeep. Rod Hall was disgruntled with the situation concerning tires. Hall and Chuchua could not come to an agreement, so they parted ways.

Hall found a new ride with the new James Garner Racing team and drove AMC Ramblers. The team was ill-fated and did not last long enough to make it to the Mexican 1000 a few months later. Hall broke down in a remote and difficult-to-get-to section of the course. He said that it was the coldest night of his life waiting to get rescued.

The Race

For the first loop race in Baja, NORRA received 163 entries for the inaugural Baja 500. For the first time, most racers had their first look at the eastern side of the peninsula. While the mileage was certainly shorter than the race to La Paz, the eastern side of the peninsula contains rocky hills, boulder-strewn canyons, and sandy washes.

The trail had conditions ideally suited to the tough Jeeps, as they took the first four places in the production class. John Ulfeldt and George Elliot stormed to a commanding 1 hour and 36 minute lead over Rod Fish and Wally Smith, who took second place. Both entries were in Jeepsters, The winner Ulfeldt was in a Chuchua team rig, while Fish was in a private entry.

In third place, which was only 1 scant minute behind second place, was Spike Cooper and Richard Lee in a Jeepster. Completing the Jeepster sweep was Bill Ramsey and Mike Chuchua exactly 40 minutes behind third place.

Leading the four-Jeep sweep of the production 4x4 class was John Ulfeldt and George Elliot in their Chuchua-prepared Jeepster. (Photo Courtesy MotorTrend and Petersen Museum Archive)

Mexican 1000

The Mexican 1000 was now a major motorsport event that garnered the attention of the mainstream media. For many drivers and car builders, it was a thing to be conquered. For aftermarket manufacturers of tires, lights, shocks, motor oil, and many more items, it was a race to

Prior to the start of The 1969 NORRA Baja 500, Brian Chuchua's fleet of racers sit on display in the impound yard. (Photo Courtesy MotorTrend and Petersen Museum Archive)

Ready to go at the impound yard for the 1969 Mexican 1000, the Chuchua team of 12 racers was larger than it had ever been. The Jeep fleet was ready to take on an equally formidable fleet of Ford Broncos. (Photo Courtesy MotorTrend and Petersen Museum Archive)

market their products with Baja-proven durability.

For Jeep, it was a time to ride the momentum of its Mint 400 and Baja 500 successes to beat the Bronco again in the biggest race. The Bronco team was reloaded with Larry Minor and Rod Hall, who reunited in a brand-new build and looked to beat the motorcycles to La Paz.

The Race

The race to La Paz started on 8:01 a.m. Thursday, October 30, 1969, from Ensenada. The Chuchua Jeepster entry of John Ulfeldt and George Elliot was the first vehicle off the line. In fact, the first 12 entries off the line were all Chuchua vehicles. Only three of the Chuchua

team's vehicles were non-Jeep products, as it also serviced a pair of buggies and one Chevrolet pickup.

As this was a NORRA race, there were two four-wheel-drive classes: one for production-based stock rigs and one for modified rigs.

Modified Class

Out of the 11 entries in the class, an astonishing 9 made it to La Paz within the 48-hour time limit. The pre-race favorite was the *Baja Boot* of actor Steve McQueen. However, off-road racing does not care if you are a celebrity. Ninety miles into the race, near the first checkpoint at Camalu, McQueen got lost for a time. Then, at 238 miles from the start, at Santa Ynez, the *Baja Boot*'s engine blew. Game over.

The bulk of the field (all 10 other starters) met various mechanical gremlins. Some that tried the coastal

John Ulfeldt and George Elliot are about to open the road for the 1969 Mexican 1000. Early in the race, they fell from the lead due to steering and electrical issues. (Photo Courtesy MotorTrend and Petersen Museum Archive)

With Oldsmobile power under the hood, Bob Seivert and Dan Weidner arrived first in the modified 4x4 class in La Paz. Second place was more than 5 hours behind them. (Photo Courtesy MotorTrend and Petersen Museum Archive)

route instead of the silt beds south of Punta Prieta were stuck for hours in the tidal pools. It was, as many off-road races become, a race of attrition.

Starting 73rd off the line, the Oldsmobile-powered Jeep CJ-3A of Bob Seivert and Dan Weidner went with a bold choice of a Gates high-flotation tire over an all-terrain tread, such as the Commando. It must have been the right choice, because 23 hours and 36 minutes after they started, they arrived in La Paz and were nearly 5 hours ahead of the second-place finisher.

A few Toyota Land Cruisers with Chevrolet engines took the next two spots before a Jeep finished in fourth place. A Chevrolet-powered, flat-fender Jeep CJ sponsored by Camper World Jeep Center came in after 31 hours on the trail.

Production Class

Even with a relatively dust-free road in front of them, John Ulfedt and George Elliot had some issues with the steering and electronics that dropped them back early. The Bronco of Minor and Hall smoked the entire field in all classes. It took almost 3 hours longer for Ulfeldt and Elliot to arrive in La Paz.

The Finish

It was a Bronco day, as Minor and Hall made the finish in La Paz in 20 hours and 48 minutes and beat the first motorcycle by 47 minutes. They beat the first open-wheel car by 20 minutes.

Jackson can only wonder what would have been if things had not gone so sideways. He and Cooper had taken third place, an agonizing 7 minutes behind their teammates. It was another 16 hours before another production Jeep crossed the finish line in 11th place.

In the end, the dust you make is equal to the trophies you take.

The 1960s ended, and amid the turbulent times that they spawned socially and politically, it was an adventurous time for a bunch of dusty off-road racers. Together, they built a sport and a legendary chapter of Jeep history.

Flying past the cacti, John Ulfeldt and George Elliot pushed hard to make up for early mechanical issues. (Photo Courtesy MotorTrend and Petersen Museum Archive)

Sometimes you get Baja, and sometimes Baja gets you. Doug Hunt removes the dust from the distributor somewhere in Baja. Bill Bryan and Hunt pressed onward for hours until the rear end failed just past halfway into the race. That is Baja racing. (Photo Courtesy David Bryan)

The Adventures of Cooper and Jackson

Spike Cooper and Carl Jackson were old friends from the Hemet Jeep Club. Cooper and Jackson teamed up in one of the Brian Chuchua Jeepsters. Each had been down the peninsula enough times that they decided to run solo to save weight and take every advantage of their number-3 starting position.

Cooper started the race in Ensenada, while Jackson waited in El Arco, which was the traditional halfway point of the race. To Cooper's chagrin, as he arrived at the Jeepster the morning of the race, he saw used tires on the racer and two used tires for spares. He was assured that the pit crew had new tires in Santa Ynez, 230 miles into the race.

Not far from the Santa Ynez checkpoint, Cooper smacked a rock hard enough to bend the tie rod and flatten two tires. All alone, Cooper changed the two tires and nursed the Jeepster into Santa Ynez to find no tires. The crew was not there either. It took a while for Spike to find a welder in the town, but when he did, he made a back-country repair. With no choice, he repaired the steering and plodded onward to El Arco and hoped that Jackson had tires.

Carl Jackson did not have tires. The checkpoint crew did not make it to El Arco, either. This was either a mistake by the Chuchua pit crew or by the NORRA checkpoint crew that was in charge of transporting the teams' spares and fuel. When Cooper came in to El Arco to hand off the Jeepster, he showed Carl the repair to the steering. The remaining four tires looked good enough to try for the finish. Jackson took off and minded the tires. He knew they were way behind, as Minor and Hall had been through hours earlier, and Ulfeldt had a half hour on him.

In the dark, in the middle of a dry lake bed, Jackson saw a parked Jeepster watching the cars go past. He pulled over and asked the gentleman if he could borrow his spare. It turned out he was working his way to La Paz and said he would get his spare tire back in a few days. They strapped the spare down, and Jackson sped off. Minding his tires, Jackson made a valiant drive to finish the race. Two days later as Jackson was at the hotel, the gentleman from the dry lake showed up, collected his spare tire, and went on his way.

In third place off the start line, Spike Cooper took the first leg to El Arco, where Carl Jackson waited to bring the Jeepster home. There were time-consuming adventures for both men. (Photo Courtesy Carl Jackson)

Early in the race, Spike Cooper hustles the Jeepster down a nicely graded road. Nice roads were the rarity in 1969, and you had to take advantage of them before the terrain changed to something less friendly. (Photo Courtesy Carl Jackson)

A dusty and tired Carl Jackson arrives in La Paz for a well-deserved third-place finish. He ran the entire race on the same used rubber that he started with because the spare tires that he expected never appeared in El Arco. (Photo Courtesy Carl Jackson)

CHAPTER 4

THE 1970s

A cultural shift in America took place in the 1970s. Late 1960s assassinations and high-profile murders robbed the country of an innocence that was enjoyed through much of the 1950s and 1960s. The Vietnam War was still raging, teenagers were protesting, and the Beatles broke up.

In off-road racing, the 1970 season began much the same as the late 1960s, but it would change radically. Technology from the National Aeronautics and Space Administration (NASA) space program and the Indianapolis 500 changed the way that men and women raced off-road.

Parnelli Jones and Mickey Thompson were in a war to build the fastest, meanest, and toughest machine to get to La Paz faster than anything had in the past. As the men stretched the limits of machinery, the Jeeps were content to concentrate on class wins.

1970

In the first year of the new decade, the Apollo program paused sending men to the moon after the near disaster of Apollo 13. That same spirit of ingenuity and cooperation is often how an off-road racing Jeep gets to the finish line.

The new year also saw the Brian Chuchua team expand to 12 entries at the bigger races of the year. A crop of new drivers and Jeeps helped sculpt the Jeep legend and make it successful.

Mint 400

With a $50,000 purse (about $400,000 in 2023) up for grabs, the four-wheel-drive vehicles entered the 1970 Mint 400 in droves. The Chuchuas, Stroppes, Beyers, and others competed in the eight-lap, two-day race. Overall, 293 participants entered the race, and only 13 completed the entire 400 miles. Of those, only two were 4x4s.

The Nevada desert took aim at the 4x4 class. Early favorites, such as Parnelli Jones, Larry Minor, Bill Bryan, Spike Cooper, and Carl Jackson, all became spectators early in the race. One by one, the Stroppe entries fell to the side of the road—except for one that chased the New Mexico–based Jeep CJ-5 of Donnie Beyer and Don Richardson.

In Nevada, if you are not in the rocks, you are in the sand and silt. This Jeep entry is working hard to stay afloat. (Photo Courtesy tracksidephoto.com)

TOP: In the three short years that off-road racing (as we know it) was formed, the Holy Toledo *Jeep of Brian Chuchua was the most well-known Jeep to the general public. (Photo Courtesy tracksidephoto.com)*

A steady pace over inhospitable terrain was the winning combination for New Mexico's Donnie Beyer and Don Richardson in their CJ-5. (Photo Courtesy tracksidephoto.com)

Despite having to stop and repair the rear end, John Ulfeldt and George Elliot pressed onward for second place in the production Class. (Photo Courtesy tracksidephoto.com)

Donnie Beyer is one of many Beyers that raced in Jeep events in the Western regions of the United States. He started at age 12 and rode with his father at events. By the time that he was 16, he won his first race in Denver, Colorado.

At the end of the first day's four laps, Beyer and Richardson held a slim lead in the extreme conditions. The 50-mile laps were strewn with boulders and had deep sand and silt deposits. Broken cars and trucks were another obstacle, especially with low visibility. A Bronco lurked about 10 minutes behind, and no one else was close.

On Day 2, the Bronco closed the gap to 6 minutes but could get no closer. Beyer, who was only 23 years old at the time, finally won the Mint 400 on his third try. Unfortunately, no other Jeep vehicle was among the 13 finishers.

Baja 500

The 1970 Baja 500 was the second-annual 558-mile trek around Baja Norte. It was popular with the racers because it offered all of the Baja experiences without the massive return trip from La Paz. Back in the early days, once you made it to La Paz, there were two choices to get home: 1) retrace the racecourse or 2) take the ferry over to mainland Mexico, drive paved roads up to Nogales, Arizona, and enter the US that way. Therefore, this race required less financial strain and less vacation time from employers.

Even though the race was 300 miles shorter than a La Paz run, it was more difficult and technical to drive. For the four-wheel-drive crowd, it meant that the advantages of four-wheel-drive wouldn't come into play until the second half of the race at Laguna Chapala, which was the southernmost point of the race.

In the production 4x4 class, Jeep favorites John Ulfeldt and George Elliot started 150th, which meant that there were a lot of cars to pass and a lot of dust. There was also a large contingent of Broncos in front of and behind them. The Jeepster held its own late in the race and kept pressure on a hard-charging Larry Minor in a Stroppe Bronco.

Just south of San Felipe, after the tortuous run over the rocky Three Sisters area, the rear end failed. Ulfeldt and

Jim Taylor, who finished in third place overall, was the first of the production-based modified 4x4s to finish. The first- and second-place cars were hand-built specialty cars. (Photo Courtesy trackside photo.com)

Elliot quickly removed the rear driveshaft and brought it into the pits at San Felipe with front-wheel-drive. Repairs were made to the rear end, and they were back in the race (albeit about an hour down). The drive into Ensenada was uneventful, and the Jeep settled into second place after 14 hours, sandwiched between two Broncos.

In the modified 4x4 class, it was stacked due to the machines that were entered and the talented pool of drivers. Jeep was shut out of the top two places by Doug Fortin's tube-frame 4x4 buggy and one of the *Baja Boots*, which were separated by 18 minutes. Jim Taylor in his CJ-5, finishing 21 minutes behind second place, earned the final podium spot.

Mexican 1000

In the fourth annual run to La Paz, there was a loaded field in the four-wheel-drive classes, as drivers competed for their share of the $110,000 in prize money. In total, 271 race vehicles were launched from Ensenada. All participants looked for the quickest way to La Paz, but only 145 finished.

NORRA ran two classes for four-wheel-drive vehicles, production and modified, and there were a few Jeeps scattered in the two-wheel-drive utility class. One of those was the newly finished *Holy Toledo* Jeep, which was driven by Brian Chuchua.

In the late 1960s, the Jeep team built a Jeep Commando, similar to what it had done before. However, this certain Commando was for Chuchua. It didn't debut until the 1970 NORRA Mexican 1000 in the two-wheel-drive utility class, which was known at the time as Category 2. This was for pickup trucks, vans, and any utility vehicle with two-wheel drive only.

The *Holy Toledo* did well as it neared the halfway point and earned a top-five class finish. Somewhere after El Arco, a wrong turn cost the team about half an hour. This was not uncommon in the early days of unmarked racecourses.

Several stops were made to clean the dust out of the distributor and change at least one flat tire. It was not a clean debut for the iconic yellow Jeep, but it finished with a respectable run. In the end, it came into La Paz with a fifth-place finish in its class.

Holy Toledo was built well and accounted for every type of terrain and water crossings. (Photo Courtesy tracksidephoto.com)

After a quick pit stop late in the race, Sandy Cone and Gene Hightower were solidly in first place. (Photo Courtesy tracksidephoto.com)

In 1970, being a favorite was not the way to go in the production class. Many of the odds-on favorites came to grief before the halfway point, including all but one of the Stroppe Broncos. In the southern end of the course, it was a mixed bag of Jeeps, a Chevy Blazer, a lone Bronco, and a Toyota Land Cruiser running for second place.

Sandy Cone and Gene Hightower drove a charmed race in the Brian Chuchua–sponsored Jeepster. Prior to the race, two new parts fell into their lap. First, Brian stopped by with a preproduction power-steering unit that could be fitted to the Jeep's Dauntless V-6 without any major modifications. The second part was something new for the time: take-apart shock absorbers. This allowed you to customize your rebound and dampening. It's common today, but it was new at the time.

Cone and Hightower's trip to La Paz was not without some issues. It wouldn't be Baja if there were not. But for all the little issues, some things worked in their favor. Coming out of San Ignacio, you have a choice to take the beach route and risk the tide pools and the tide itself. Smart racers take tidal schedules with them. Cone and Hightower decided to take the interior route, which was quite rocky and had a fair amount of silt. It was the right choice.

Baby, It's Cold Outside

"The worst thing that happened in that race (besides some flat tires) was in the last part of the race—it got really cold," Cone said in a recent interview. "This ground fog made it very difficult to see, but if you looked up, you could see the stars. Gene already had his jacket on, and I decided that it was time to put mine on. Reaching down between the seats, it was wet. The water jug cracked, and the water pooled right on my jacket. At times I thought that I was going to freeze to death."

The Finish

The freezing 20-year-old Sandy Cone and the 40-year-old Korean War veteran Gene Hightower roared into La Paz in 19 hours and 2 minutes. It was a new record for the production 4x4 class by almost 2 hours.

Bob Sievert and Dan Widner took their Oldsmobile-powered Jeep CJ-5 to a commanding 3-hour margin of victory and won the modified class handily, although it was still 2.5 hours behind the winning production 4x4 time. A Jeep Wagoneer took a second-place class finish, piloted by Nick Lusich and Don Ohnstad. The Reno, Nevada–based team finished 3 hours and 3 minutes later but only 3 minutes in front of a Toyota Land Cruiser.

After 19 hours and 2 minutes, the winners of the production class were mobbed at the finish line in La Paz. (Photo Courtesy tracksidephoto.com)

Brian Chuchua drove thousands of miles in Holy Toledo *through this central Baja scenery. (Photo Courtesy track-sidephoto.com)*

*H*oly Toledo was built for racing from the start. It had a stock 1969 Commando frame and a beefed-up stock suspension with an added Gabriel shock at each corner. The body and hood were fiberglass to reduce weight.

This meant that the stock 225-ci Dauntless Buick V-6 had less drag on it. The engine was mostly stock except for a set of Hooker Headers. Power got to the rear wheels via a Turbo Hydra-matic 400 automatic transmission with a manual valve body and Art Carr shifter. A trussed Dana 30 axle was the final piece to get power to the ground.

The interior was gutted and caged, and a sheet-metal dash was fabricated to hold some fuse panels, gauges to monitor temperatures and electric systems, and a Halda rally odometer. A speedometer and tachometer were not needed. Stock Jeep high-back seats and stock seat belts held Brian and

The 225-ci V-6 known as the "Dauntless" powered the Holy Toledo. *Its current owners are Dennis Sletten and Rick Barfield. (Photo Courtesy Dennis Sletten)*

The dash may not look complicated by today's standards. However, in 1970, it was everything that you needed and more. Simple gauges indicate how the engine is running, and the box in the center was a scroll onto which you rolled a Baja map. This scroll could be moved as you went to indicate the next landmark. (Photo Courtesy Dennis Sletten)

his co-driver in place for races ranging from 6 to 24 hours. After a few races, the belts were replaced with five-point harnesses.

The Change

Starting in 1973, *Holy Toledo* was modified and refitted with four-wheel-drive. The utility two-wheel-drive class was mostly longer-wheelbase pickup trucks with V-8 engines. The right thing to do was to race the other Jeeps on an equal footing.

Life after Chuchua

Brian Chuchua drove the *Holy Toledo* for 10 years: 3 in two-wheel drive and the remaining in a four-wheel drive. However, *Holy Toledo's* life was much more involved than its 10-year run with its builder.

For a time, Chuchua rented out *Holy Toledo* to whoever needed it, so it went through many drivers and adventures. When it was time for *Holy Toledo* to move onward, Chuchua sold it to Tom Barnett, owner of T&J Off-Road Center. *Holy Toledo* was renamed *Herbie* and repainted white with red- and blue-striped livery that resembled the famous Volkswagen Beetle from the

Disney movies. The Barnetts drove it, as did Rock Bradford (for some events), and then Janet Hickey was behind the wheel.

After it sat for a while, Dennis Sletten and Rick Barfield bought it without knowing that they had purchased the famous *Holy Toledo*. While sanding down the current paint on the body, a certain shade of yellow showed up, along with other telltale signs. As of this writing, it is still owned by Sletten and Barfield.

After Brian Chuchua sold Holy Toledo, *it was painted in the colors for T&J Off-Road Centers. (Photo Courtesy Dennis Sletten)*

Bob Sievert and Dan Widner used Oldsmobile power under the hood to nab the class win by a gigantic 3-hour margin. (Photo Courtesy trackside-photo.com)

Mint 400

The fourth edition of the Mint 400 featured changes to the format. Instead of two days of racing and four laps of 50 miles, all eight laps were run in a single day. The motorcycles raced on the day before the cars raced for safety reasons. This allowed some adventurous types to compete two days in a row.

Out of 264 entries, only 50 were classified as official finishers. Out of those 50, there were no Jeeps that had a remarkable or noteworthy finish. The high point for Jeep fans came from a sixth-place finish by New Mexico's Donnie Beyer and Don Welch. The pair in a CJ-5 kept the Jeep together enough to reach the finish. Another New Mexico team, R. K. Blackman and Tom Moore, managed a 15th-place finish in their propane-powered Jeep.

Sandy Cone recently remembered the 1971 Mint.

"[On] the first lap, John [Ulfeldt] broke all of the bolts that held on the steering box," he said. "We didn't know where he was. There were no radios or GPS in those days.

The best finish so far recorded by a Jeep Cherokee went to Nick Lusich and Don Ohnstad from Reno, Nevada. (Photo Courtesy trackside-photo.com)

1971

In the second year of the new decade, America was out of the turbulent 1960s, and social norms were turned on their heads. On January 12, America met Archie Bunker with the debut of a new kind of television sitcom called *All in the Family*. Apollo 14 took Alan Shepard to the moon successfully and overcame the issues faced by Apollo 13. In addition, a new kind of low-cost air carrier called Southwest Airlines began flying between three cities in Texas: Dallas, Houston, and San Antonio.

In the off-road-racing world, more innovations arrived with shock absorbers, tires, lighting, and suspension travel. Speeds went up, as did entry numbers and cash prizes.

New Mexico was proud of the highest-placing Jeep in the Mint 400. Donnie Beyer finished in sixth place. (Photo Courtesy trackside-photo.com)

When John Ulfeldt and Sandy Cone moved, they looked spectacular. Even with the help of a helicopter to ferry parts, they could not beat the Nevada desert. (Photo Courtesy tracksidephoto.com)

But they had helicopters, so I rented one and found John. We flew back, went to the farm supply near to the start line, got some bolts, flew back, and got going again! I got in the car, and I was in a hurry. The front end was already blown up, so I killed the rear end in the silt. It was really deep!"

Baja 500

The event began with 226 entries, and 114 were official finishers. NORRA followed suit with the Mint 400 and combined the four-wheel-drive vehicles into one class. Whether they were production, modified, or home-built, they all ran against each other.

The Race

This race was tough on the Jeeps, as none made it onto the podium positions, which was populated by Broncos and a GMC. However, John Ulfeldt and Sandy Cone's Jeepster missed the final podium spot by 1 minute. Rod Fish and Bob Dressler, in another Jeepster, took sixth place, 34 minutes behind Ulfeldt. Another 32 minutes back in seventh place was the Jeep CJ-5 of Dick Dahn and W. R. Janowski.

It was not a landmark event for the Jeep contingent, but it is worth noting that 9 out of the 20 official finishers were in Jeep products, compared to Ford's 6 finishers, and GM's 2 finishers.

In what was a forgettable weekend for the Jeep faithful, the high point was a fourth-place finish for John Ulfeldt and Sandy Cone. The pair was 2 hours behind the winners and 1 minute behind third place. (Photo Courtesy Sandy Cone)

Mexican 1000

The four-wheel-drive racing world returned to Baja five months later for the annual run down the Baja peninsula. The race to La Paz in the 4x4 class was the most heated of the event, as the top six finishers were covered by 1 hour.

The Race

John Ulfeldt teamed up with last year's winner, Sandy Cone, in a Jeepster AMX that was sponsored by Wolper Productions out of Los Angeles. Near El Arco, the team had a lead over the Bronco of Bill Rush. While cruising down a sandy two-track road, the right front wheel came off, including the hub, spindle, and brakes. Cone noted the direction in which the wheel bounced off as they ground to a halt.

After hiking about a half mile, they found the wheel assembly and carried it back to the Jeepster. They clamped off the brake line to save time trying to fix it and reattached the wheel well enough to limp into El Arco for repairs. Rush started well ahead of them, as did the *Crazy Horse* Bronco and the Chevy-powered Jeep of Al Brown and Ray Russell. They knew from prior checkpoints that they were their main competitors.

After a lengthier stop in El Arco, Ulfeldt and Cone were off to make up some time. The fact they were minus one front brake assembly made for some moments in the long, dark Baja night. At one point, they overshot a turn and slammed into a Saguaro cactus that fell over and landed on top of the Jeepster. It was a prickly predicament to get it off the Jeep.

Other stories

Brown and Russell, in their second Mexican 1000, got lost.

"I remember we stopped at a dead end and shut the engine off, hoping to hear the racers," Brown said. "We couldn't hear them but did hear a strange scratching sound. We turned

The Jeepster AMX is moving well early in the race. Things weren't always this smooth for Ulfeldt and Cone. (Photo Courtesy tracksidephoto.com)

It was a long day and night for J. M. Bragg and Jack Fiscus. They often repaired the little CJ-5. Steering-box issues, a tie-rod end repair, and getting lost were some of the problems that cost the team an 9 extra hours. (Photo Courtesy tracksidephoto.com)

Richard Bundy and James Hudson are featured here not for their racing prowess (although they did finish) but for their luck. The pair neglected to install an air filter in the Jeepster and ran 850 miles without destroying the Chevrolet engine. (Photo Courtesy tracksidephoto.com)

on the lights and saw that the cliff in front of us was covered with iguanas. [That was] spooky, so we got out of there. [We] found the track again and headed south."

Also in the running was J. M. Bragg and Jack Fiscus in a Buick-powered CJ-5 until they broke a tie-rod. Farther down the road, they had problems with the steering box. All in all, they lost 9 hours due to repairs and eventually finished in 14th place, less than 1 minute behind Richard Bundy and James Hudson, who came from Connecticut to race their Chevy-powered Jeepster. During the post-race inspection, it was discovered that there was no air filter in the housing. Bundy and Hudson looked at each other and accused the other of forgetting to install the filter. They could not believe their luck in racing 850 miles without an air filter and not ruining the engine with sand.

Back at the Front

Ulfeldt and Cone ran as hard as they could to chase down the Broncos and the other Jeeps. They were not sure how much time they lost, so the only thing to do was drive hard the rest of the way, which they did. They arrived in La Paz and saw the Broncos and the Brown and Russell Jeep already at the finish. How long had they been there? Since the race is run on elapsed time, the vehicles that were already there had started anywhere from 83 to 48 minutes ahead of them.

In the end, Ulfeldt and Cone finished in 19 hours and

31 minutes and beat the Broncos by 5 and 17 minutes, respectively. Brown and Russell brought home fourth place 43 minutes behind the winners.

1972

In a tumultuous election year, Richard Nixon made an unprecedented visit to China and then had a landslide win over George McGovern. Watergate didn't come to light until after the election. The last manned moon mission was launched at the end of the year. Apollo 17 was the last manned space flight beyond low earth orbit. The Middle East oil embargo was in full swing, and tragedy marred the 1972 Summer Olympics in Munich, Germany.

For off-road racers, the upheaval and change around the world did not matter much in the deserts of the American Southwest and Baja California. There were miles to travel, competitors to vanquish, and adventures to be had.

National Four-Wheel-Drive Grand Prix

The final race that was held in the Santa Ana river bottom had a 3.2-mile-long course. Jeeps competed in both the production and modified four-wheel-drive classes. The modified final came down to Sherman Balch in his 215-ci Buick V-8-powered CJ-5 versus Doug Fortin in a homemade 4x4 Corvair-powered buggy. Fortin kept his wheels on the ground more than Balch and took the win by a narrow margin. The production class the final came down to Jeff Wright, a Jeep executive, who was driving a Brian Chuchua Commando and wily veteran Dick Dahn. Dahn's vast experience overcame the Chuchua-prepared Commando, and Dahn notched his second production win in three years.

It was not quite the end of an era, as Mickey Thompson carried the short-course racing torch to Riverside Raceway for the next 15 years. In the eight years since Brian Chuchua organized the first of these races, his events spurred the beginning of NORRA and desert racing as we know it

Ulfeldt and Cone pushed hard where they could and flew the Jeepster to make up for some down time. It was the start of an impressive list of wins that the pair posted. (Photo Courtesy tracksidephoto.com)

The desert is tough, but Jeeps were often tougher in 1972. (Photo Courtesy tracksidephoto.com)

today. His events accelerated technology in the sport to deal with the challenging river-bottom terrain. Finally, Thompson's events helped drivers (such as Larry Minor, Carl Jackson, Sherman Balch and Rod Hall) make a name for themselves and gain "legend" status.

The Dam 500 and Cal 400

NORRA wanted to branch out and had another try at organizing a race in the continental United States. They came up with the Dam 500, out of Parker, Arizona, where a dam controls the Colorado River. The event was unique because it ran loops in two different states. It was billed as a Baja 500–style race of 544 very rough miles.

During pre-running, Bill Stroppe decided that the course was too demanding, with miles of volcanic rock among the obstacles. He pulled his team from the event. Others did as well, which had a mere 50 starters. After the race was completed, changes were promised for 1973. Sandy Cone and John Ulfeldt won their class in the Jeepster.

The American Recreational Vehicle Racing Association (ARVRA) was formed to promote racing north of the border. In January, they ran 11 laps of a 34-mile course outside of Barstow, California. There were 91 entries, and 24 finished. This event was instrumental in bringing off-road racing to the Barstow area, where it flourished for decades. Ulfeldt and Cone also won this race by completing the 11 laps in 12 hours and 20 minutes.

These events garnered little media coverage, but they are mentioned due to their significance to the future of the sport.

Mint 400

It was time again for a return to Tule Springs, the Mint Gun Club, and the tortuous laps around some of Nevada's most inhospitable terrain. This year, instead of the four laps of a 50-mile trail format, organizers extended the lap to 67 miles on some less-challenging terrain. However, it was still tough for everyone.

The Race

Sherman Balch and Arthur Archer had their Jeep CJ-5 running so well that they won the race by more than 2 hours. It was a $7,000 payday for Balch (about $56,000 in 2024), as he clicked off all six laps without relief in a tidy 10 hours, 51 minutes, and 27 seconds. Spike Cooper and Mike Zeller were able to nail down second place to give Jeep a solid 1-2 finish.

Racing in the Mint 400 means that you do not spend a lot of time with all four wheels on the ground. Sherman Balch and Art Archer show their form on the way to a commanding win in the CJ-5. (Photo Courtesy tracksidephoto.com)

Spike Cooper and Mike Zeller took their CJ-2A, which was powered by propane, to a second-place finish. The pair drove without a co-driver to save weight. (Photo Courtesy tracksidephoto.com)

Baja 500

It was June, and that meant that it was time for the Baja 500, a 558-mile trek through the north of Baja that started and finished in Ensenada. It had been 10 weeks since the Mint 400, and most everyone had licked their wounds and were ready to go racing again.

You wouldn't think weather would be a big factor in Baja in June, but the West Coast was experiencing an unseasonable rainstorm and foggy conditions. Racers were caught in this weather pattern outbound from Ensenada and again coming back to the finish. It was warm and toasty eastward from the center of the peninsula.

John Ulfeldt and Sandy Cone blasted their way down the Baja roads to a heartbreaking second-place finish. (Photo Courtesy tracksidephoto.com)

The Race

Baja racing makes for interesting friendships both on and off the racecourse. John Ulfeldt and Sandy Cone had a good plan. Each would drive the Jeepster solo for half the race. It worked beautifully, and when they changed drivers at the halfway point, they had a half-hour lead

over the Bronco of Bill Rush. Cone handed it off to Ulfeldt and was confident they were in a good position.

As he headed back into the rainy side of the peninsula, Ulfeldt lost the road and took a wrong turn without realizing it. Ulfeldt knew that Rush was close behind, as the nearest competitor for third place was three hours behind them. So, he turned around and drove as fast as he could in the opposite direction. The Jeep arrived first

Dick Dahn and Vern Roberts were in a tough battle with a Bronco for third place but prevailed in their CJ-5. (Photo Courtesy tracksidephoto.com)

at the finish, but where was Rush? Rush started behind the Jeep and could still finish the race and beat him on elapsed time. With just over a minute to go, Ulfeldt heard the sickening sound of a Ford V-8 closing in for the win. Rush was friends with both Cone and Ulfeldt, so the pair figured that if you have to lose, lose to a friend.

Dick Dahn and Vern Roberts motored their Jeep CJ-5 into another close battle for position with the Bronco of Airey and Rossi. Since the Bronco started almost 2 hours later than the Jeep. it took a while to see if they could hold third. It took 125 minutes, but as the 126th minute passed and no Bronco showed up, they claimed third place. Seconds later, Airey and Rossi showed up and were deflated when they found out that they missed the podium.

In the Passenger Car class, Brian Chuchua brought the *Holy Toledo* Jeepster home in sixth place. Mechanical issues dropped him out of the top three, which is where he ran early.

Mexican 1000

Hurricane Joanne blew up from the south and ravaged the west side of the Baja Peninsula from the tip to the US border in late October. Many of the roads used for the Mexican 1000 were now washed away or so badly rutted that they were rendered impassable.

NORRA had to scramble for an optional route. The Baja government had been looking for a way to bolster the economy in Mexicali, a border town to the east. This seemed like an excellent way to save the race and infuse much-needed funds into the area.

The implication of this was that the race distance was

longer, so there would be no record-breaking runs. The hurricane had an impact on some of the roads on the eastern side between Mexicali and San Felipe because of water run-off from the mountains.

The Race

Pre-race favorites John Ulfeldt and Sandy Cone received a 401-ci engine for their Jeepster from AMC and picked up some bigger tires from Firestone. The combination of those two changes put a strain on the 28-spline axles in the Jeepster. Twenty miles from the first checkpoint in El Crucero, the axle failed, and the Jeepster flipped three times. Ulfeldt had two broken kneecaps, and Cone had multiple cuts and contusions. The pair was rushed to El Centro for medical care.

The Jeeps did not have anything for the Ford contingent this time around. Broncos swept the first three places.

1973

As Watergate dragged on through the media and the houses of Congress, OPEC flexed its muscles to the oil consuming world. The Vietnam War was finally winding down, and the United States launched Skylab, its first space station.

Parker Dam 500

Organizers from NORRA kept their promise and avoided areas of the desert that cost them entries during the previous year. As promised, those that left returned and brought friends. There were 118 entries that started the race, and that was 68 more than the previous year.

Each entry drove two laps each in California and Arizona for a total of 484 miles. The California loop included racing through areas where General George S. Patton trained his tank troops before they were shipped off to North Africa.

The Race

Out of 16 official finishers, 13 were Jeep vehicles. First and third place eluded the brand, but otherwise it was an excellent showing for Jeep. Gene Hightower and Dale Frahm were able to take their Chevy-powered Jeep CJ-5 and sandwiched it on the podium between two Broncos. They kept Ford from sweeping the class with a time that was 17 minutes behind first place and 18 minutes ahead of third place. Spike Cooper in a CJ-2A and an open-wheel 4x4 rounded out the top five in the class.

Mint 400

It was a year of great changes for the Mint 400, as the racecourse was moved from Tule Springs, (north of Las Vegas) to Jean, Nevada (south of Las Vegas). Encroaching civilization was the reason for the move.

The geographical change allowed for a lap of 200 miles that wound through four counties: two in Nevada and two in California. The course was not spectator friendly. Some called it more remote than the Mexican 1000.

The new area meant that there were fewer rocks and less silt. That did not mean the course was easier. To top that off, Mother Nature intervened with her own challenge. The race day was cold and windy with heavy, dark clouds in the air. Many prepared for rain at some point in the day, which is troublesome in the desert because of flash-flood dangers. What happened was the temperature plummeted. At higher elevations, there was a fair amount of snow that collected later in the day.

Another challenge was faced by the competitors. Nefarious individuals stole a 5,000-gallon tanker truck filled with fuel that was meant for the racers. As a result, racers were diverted to a fuel station in Jean, Nevada, to refuel like anyone traveling on the highway.

The Race

Jeep had occupied the winners circle since 1969 and shut out Ford, Toyota, Chevrolet, and International. Maybe they were cocky, or maybe the roads south of Las Vegas suited the competition better. Former Jeep racer Rod Hall and Jim Fricker won the race in a Bronco.

For some, the race ended early. In the case of Ray Russell, his front axle housing broke on the first lap. He

Gene Hightower and Dale Frahm wait for the signal to go. In 484 miles, they took second place with their Chevy small-block-powered CJ-5. (Photo Courtesy NORRA Archive)

It was a hard-fought day with the weather and a few mechanical issues. In the end, Bragg helped fill the top 10 with a few Jeep entries by taking sixth place. (Photo Courtesy J. M. Bragg)

limped the Jeep to a nearby highway, but it was fenced off with no gates anywhere. When his crew arrived, they had to cut the fence to get the Jeep out. The crew repaired the fence to not get the organizers in trouble.

There were some great drives by Jeep entries. Fred Bear and Gary Highman in their CJ-5 had a great run for second place and finished 45 minutes behind the winner. J. M. Bragg earned a sixth-place class finish with his Buick-powered CJ-5.

Baja 500

NORRA ran the show in Baja for six years and had a very good record of dealing with the government and the people of Baja. Racers brought supplies for orphanages and hospitals and handed out extra treats to kids. Things seemed to be going well. If anyone in the local government or NORRA knew this would be the last race in Baja, they did not show it.

This was ironically NORRA's largest entry to date with 333 teams at the start. This was also the longest Baja 500 on record with a total of 610 miles instead of the usual 558. The reason for the change was to avoid some newly laid pavement. The weather was typical for a Baja 500: cool and cloudy on the west side and hot on the east side. Some checkpoints recorded temperatures of 111°F.

The Race

Jeeps had extra incentive to do well in this race. American Motors provided an additional $5,500 in contingency prizes. A large chunk of that would go to the Jeep product with the lowest elapsed time. It was a hefty carrot to dangle in front of the Jeep racers.

A pre-race favorite was John Ulfeldt and Sandy Cone, which wasn't a surprise. This time, they had a new weapon: a highly modified Jeepster that was lighter and more powerful. Things were going well as Cone took the first half of the race down the Pacific side of the peninsula. At about the 130 mile mark, the Jeep lurched, and Cone watched a wheel roll off into the desert. Game over.

Gene Hightower and Dale Frahm took their CJ-5 with a Chevy engine and had a marvelous battle with Rod Hall and Jim Fricker in a Bronco for nearly 610 miles. Hightower left the starting line as the 89th vehicle on the road, while Hall pulled a bad number and was 298th on the road. This meant that they were separated by 3 hours. They didn't even know they were racing each other until

The Jeeps competed against the Bronco contingent all day and into the night. In the end, Gene Hightower and Dale Frahm earned the win by 9 minutes. (Photo Courtesy tracksidephoto.com)

Hightower was over halfway done and Hall had just cleared a few checkpoints.

All other competitors were more than 1.5 hours behind the lead pair. Hightower and Frahm could only shoot for the best time while racing back to Ensenada. It was a 3-plus hour wait to see if Hall and Fricker made it back. The three-hour mark came and went. It wasn't until 9 minutes after the target time that the Bronco crossed the finish line. Hightower earned the win, but because he ran a Chevrolet engine, he was not eligible for the AMC bonus money.

Ray Russell and Warren Baird were in the next Jeep to cross the finish line and took fifth place. In a recent interview with Baird, what he remembers most about that race was the heat.

"I remember it was midnight when we arrived at the checkpoint at Gonzaga Bay, and it was still 100°F!"

The AC Delco Off-Road Spectacular by Mickey Thompson

The first official race under the Short Course Off-Road Enterprises (SCORE) banner was a 7.5-mile-long short-course event at the world famous Riverside International Raceway. Mickey Thompson had been enchanted with off-road racing since the beginning. He desired to bring that exciting driving style to the general public because not everyone was willing to travel to Baja or the wilds of Nevada to watch cars and trucks fly by one at a time.

Thompson said that no one (other than the rattlesnakes and jackrabbits) was able to see his 100-mile wheel-to-wheel duel with Parnelli Jones in Baja. Brian Chuchua organized an event similar to this this in the nearby Santa Ana River bottom, but Chuchua's format did not have cars running wheel to wheel.

Thompson, ever the showman, was determined to bring off-road excitement to venues closer to major population centers. This event set into motion many years of off-road racing innovation by Thompson.

The Race

In the beginning, competitors were not sure that they wanted to race their desert machines wheel to wheel until Thompson announced a $150,000 (more than $1 million in 2023) prize fund. Every big off-road racing name entered.

Sherman Balch was fast enough to take second place in the 4x4 race, and he sandwiched himself between a Chevy and a Ford to make the podium diverse. (Photo Courtesy tracksidephoto.com)

The Win that Wasn't

If you were there in 1973, you probably saw the wild-looking Jeepster painted red, white, and blue that ran away with the modified race. Sandy Cone and Phil Incikaya had a challenging weekend. While qualifying the Jeep, they got into a wreck that ruined the front suspension and driveline. They loaded up the Jeep, took it home for an overnight fix, and made it to the race the next day.

During the repairs, it became apparent that they could not restore the four-wheel drive to the front axle. Everything else was ready to go, so racers being racers, they decided to run in two-wheel drive. Despite the muddy conditions, they were able to outrun the competition and take first place.

During the post-race technical inspection, one competitor noticed that Cone and Incikaya could not use the front axle and protested the win. The rules stated the vehicle must be able to drive through all four wheels. The protest was ruled upon, and the win was reclassified as a disqualification.

Most other racers thought that it was wrong to win on a technicality. The protester barely got out of the racetrack without being beaten by other teams—but not by Cone and Incikaya. They accepted the ruling and moved on to fight another day.

It was an up-and-down weekend for Sandy Cone and Phil Incikaya. First, they dominated in practice and qualifying until they crashed. Then, it was back home to make repairs and return to the track early. They won the race, but then they were disqualified. (Photo Courtesy Sandy Cone)

Central California's Ray Russell fought hard all weekend in his CJ-5 to find speed. It came together in the race when he was able to score a second-place class finish. (Photo Courtesy Brad Russell)

Thompson and his SCORE crew decided that the 4x4 trucks should be divided into two classes: Class 3 was for production-based 4x4 trucks, and Class 4 was for modified 4x4 trucks. Jeeps with non-AMC engines ran in Class 4. The manufacturers were in favor of the change and kept the pure production builds separate from the Frankenstein creations.

Another change was to split some classes into a Sportsman division. Class 3 was one of these classes. SCORE allowed some of the less-professional entries to not have to battle the mighty Chuchua, Stroppe, and Hickey teams. J. M. Bragg took the Sportsman win followed by his friend Fred Bear, both in Jeep CJ-5s, who skunked the Fords.

Lonnie Woods and his Chevrolet Blazer outran Sherman Balch in the high-flying Archer Brothers Jeep to take a big win. Balch had a Bronco grille in his mirrors for much of the second half of the race and was able to keep it behind him, as he took second place. A bevy of Fords and Jeeps finished behind the Chevrolet-Jeep-Ford podium.

In the modified class, the *Crazy Horse* Bronco drove past the rest of the field for the win. This left Ray Russell in a Jeep CJ-5 and Steve Mizel in a Stroppe Bronco to fight for second place.

The wily Russell was an off-roader from New York before he moved to California, so slop was a second home to him. Russell kept up his pace over Mizel and earned second place.

Baja Sports Committee Baja 1000

In the time between the Baja 500 and the traditional 1,000-mile race from Ensenada to La Paz, there was a bloodless coup of sorts. The Mexican government was convinced that NORRA and Ed Pearlman made an extremely large amount of money at the expense of the Mexican people, and they were ousted from sanctioning events in Baja. The Mexican government formed the Baja Sports Committee (BSC), which was overseen by local business owners, to oversee the race and rake in all of the money that they thought Pearlman and NORRA received.

Ed Pearlman was decidedly miffed and organized a race out of Parker, Arizona. He called it the Big River 500. It was not a huge success, but it cost the Baja 1000 about 90 of its entries, which helped ease the pain.

To make a long story short, the BSC Baja 1000 was a disaster from the organizational side of things. Someone made off with much of the entry fees that were collected, and the race was short of volunteers which made for ill-managed checkpoints and timing issues. The BSC disbanded immediately after the 1974 Baja 500 race and brought in another sanctioning body to handle the race.

Due to the NORRA Big River 500 scheduling, a great many of the stalwart four-wheel-drive entries chose loyalty to NORRA. Therefore, there were only a handful of Jeeps, and none made a notable finish in the race for the first time.

Big River 500

While the race in Baja was taking place, NORRA was in Parker, Arizona, organizing a version of the 500-mile races that they set up in 1972 and earlier in 1973. It was a spiteful move by NORRA to cut the Baja Sports Committee entry, but all is fair in love and war. It was a short-lived war with no winners. NORRA tried to hang on and get back into Baja, but it never happened.

The Race

NORRA had never joined the Coordinated Council of Off Road Racing Directors (CCORRD), so it still ran the four-wheel drive vehicles in a single class. That bunched a lot of talent into one class that passed on Baja to support NORRA. Parker was a shorter race, but that did not mean it was any easier than Baja. Most who attended the race agreed that it was certainly rougher overall. It took a steady pace and conserving your vehicle to win this one.

Early in the race, the Jeepster of Sandy Cone and Phil Incikaya had a great battle with Gene Hightower and Dale Frahm in a CJ-5 throughout the Arizona side. Somewhere on the California side, Hightower had an issue that cost him 3.5 hours. This dropped him from being in contention for the win to taking seventh place. Cone and Incikaya had a very clean race and dusted the second-place Bronco by 34 minutes. Earl Colton took third place in a Jeep CJ-5 and was followed by Don Adams and Peter Fleck in another CJ-5.

In a few short years, Don Adams got the hang of getting to the end of off-road races. His steady pace kept him close to the lead pack, and he netted a fourth-place finish. (Photo Courtesy tracksidephoto.com)

The big Jeepster kept on running at the Big River. Sandy Cone and Phil Incikaya took a commanding 34-minute margin of victory over a Bronco. (Photo Courtesy tracksidephoto.com)

Earl Colton from Phoenix, Arizona, drove the CJ-5 the entire distance solo and was rewarded with a third-place finish. (Photo Courtesy tracksidephoto.com)

1974

The year 1974 was riddled with uncertainty for the entire automotive world, as the OPEC oil crisis threatened to bring many big-name races to a halt. It was only with strict rules on fuel usage that the Indianapolis 500 and the Pikes Peak Hill Climb were able to occur.

In the off-road racing world, the crisis hit hard and canceled the Mint 400 and Baja 1000. It was only with assurances from the Mexican government that the Baja 500 was able to happen at all. Some races cut mileage. For example, the Parker Dam 500 became the Parker 400 and the California 400 (a smaller event in Barstow) was shortened to 250 miles. However, this was only secondary to the biggest news in off-road racing of the year that reshaped the sport for years to come.

Mickey Thompson Steps In

One historical hot topic that is still debated to this day is the takeover of all off-road racing in Baja California in mid-1974.

After the failure of the BSC to organize the Baja 1000 and Baja 500 efficiently in 1974 and channel money to the youth of Baja, local businesses and the Mexican government looked elsewhere to save the races and the economic boost that the races brought to the entire peninsula. Mickey Thompson was a big deal in Baja. He became involved with charitable causes that improved the lives of citizens in Baja. Many racers did the same and continue to do so to this day.

Locals, along with concerned big-name teams in the United States, knew that Thompson had formed a

In 1974, Mickey Thompson went from competitor to owner and organizer of both Baja races. His reputation south of the border and his ability to put the right people in the right job made the Mexican government comfortable. So, the races were entrusted to him. (Photo Courtesy tracksidephoto.com)

sanctioning body, and they turned to him. Meetings were arranged in both countries, and a plan was soon in place for SCORE to take over all off-road racing in Baja California.

First and foremost, Mickey Thompson is a racer. He formed SCORE with the idea of starting it and then turning it over as soon as possible to someone else so that he could return to the driver's seat. It was with great reluctance that Thompson accepted the role of organizer. However, Thompson went into it full steam ahead and aimed to solidify the event for future generations of off-road racers to come.

Short Season

Despite the fuel crunch and the cancellation of some races, it was still a semi-full year of racing. Walt Lott took advantage of the Mint 400's absence and promoted two of his own races. The Bonnie and Clyde 350 replaced the Mint, and at the end of the year, the Oasis 400 helped fill the gap of the missing Baja 1000. There was another World Cup Rally on the calendar that Brian Chuchua took part in: the London to Munich Marathon.

The season began with the California 400, where a Bronco onslaught took the win. J. M. Bragg and his Jeep CJ-5 managed to wedge himself into second place behind John Baker's Bronco. Aside from Bragg's accomplishment, it was a forgettable weekend for Jeep fans.

Parker 400

SCORE's first desert race was in Parker, Arizona. It was shortened by one lap in consideration of the fuel crisis, and the event continued for decades as the Parker 400 and dropped the dam reference.

Twenty-two production rigs started the race. Sherman Balch and Steve Post were the quickest around the first Arizona loop in their 304-ci V-8-powered CJ-5, followed by about three Broncos and three Jeeps within a few minutes. The Jeeps in the running besides Balch were Don Adams, Dick Dahn, Brian Chuchua, and Larry Olsen.

The California lap (rougher than the Arizona side) separated the field, as a Bronco took the lead, followed by Dick Dahn. Balch lost more than an hour and a half for unknown reasons. Chuchua lost a couple of hours there as well.

Headed into the final lap, the Broncos stretched the lead to take the first two positions. Dick Dahn and Vern Roberts upheld Jeep honors in third place.

Out of the 20 entries in the modified class, 15 were Jeep products. The rest were Broncos. In the end, 9 of the top 10 finishers were Jeeps, including the top 8. The favorite, Sandy Cone, set a fast lap in Arizona. Then, in California, the Jeepster lost the front driveline, which punched a hole in the oil pan and ended its day.

Gene Hightower and Dale Frahm started 30 minutes in front of Cone and never knew of his "did not finish" (DNF) status until they headed back to the Arizona side for the final lap. They had a commanding lead over J. M. Bragg, who was driving solo. Two teams were fighting hard for third place. Richard Stumpfhauser and Jack Heitzman from Fresno, California, swapped lap times with another solo driver, Spike Cooper.

Hightower and Frahm brought home a comfortable victory by 1 hour and 3 minutes over Bragg. Stumpfhauser beat Cooper by 1 minute and 28 seconds. The remaining class finishers trickled into the finish over the next 3 hours.

Baja Sporting Committee 500

The Baja Competition Committee organized the race for the second year in a row. The Baja 500 was getting very popular and sometimes drew more entries than the Mexican 1000. The mishandling of the 1000, the late payments of prize money, and no payment at all for some caused a serious dip in entries. Only 80 entries cleared technical inspection.

Dick Dahn and Vern Roberts wheeled the CJ-5 well and broke up a potential Bronco first- through third-place sweep with their second-place finish. (Photo Courtesy tracksidephoto.com)

Most of the heavy hitters in the 4x4 classes made the trip south of the border and took their chances with the BSC.

The meat in a Bronco sandwich was the CJ-5 of Dick Dahn and Vern Roberts. They were 35 minutes behind winner Rod Hall and 34 minutes ahead of Dennis Harris. Hall and Harris both drove Stroppe Broncos. Dahn's CJ was the only Jeep in the top five.

Ray Russell chased the tube-frame Bronco of Bill Rush all day in his Jeep CJ-5. At each checkpoint, Russell found out that he was anywhere between 6 to 10 minutes behind Rush. At one point, Russell closed the gap to 4 minutes and stuck his foot into the firewall to catch Rush. In the last 100 miles of the race, Russell had an engine problem that dropped him to seven cylinders and second place.

Nineteen minutes behind Russell was the CJ-5 of Gene Hightower and Dale Frahm to claim the last podium spot. J. M. Bragg brought home fourth in another CJ-5 after some front-end issues.

The AC Delco Off-Road Spectacular by Mickey Thompson

The second version of the off-road races at Riverside International Raceway held September 28 and 29 were much improved from the inaugural event. The changes were popular with the racers and the ticket-buying public. The course was shortened from its original 7.5 miles down to 3.2 miles, and more of the action was in front of the grandstands.

The Jeeps came out in force for this one. In Class 3, 12 of the 25 entries were Jeeps. In Class 4, 24 out of the 31 entries were Jeeps. Broncos were the next most-popular brand, followed by a sprinkling of Toyotas and Chevrolets.

The Races

Sherman Balch was hooked up all weekend in his 304-ci V-8 CJ-5 that topped qualifying and the race itself. Balch easily outpaced a pair of Broncos with a great starting launch. The field stretched out quickly, and it was not long before Balch wove his way through lapped traffic.

While the Class 3 race was more of a parade than a race, the Class 4 race more than made up for it. In qualifying, Sandy Cone had his Jeepster with a 401-ci V-8 out front. Cone was out for redemption after his win was protested away from him the previous year. Halfway through qualifying, as he pushed to stay ahead of the pack, the Jeepster broke both front U-joints and damaged the ends of the front axle housing. This dropped Cone to the 24th starting spot. He had to work through the night to repair his front end, just like in 1973. Jerry Colton won the qualifying race in his CJ-3A, which was equipped with a small-block Chevrolet engine.

On race day, the flag fell on a loaded field of modified 4x4s as Colton was quickly overtaken by the Bronco of Bill Rush. In the rear of the field, Sandy Cone had a good start and picked off several trucks before the first turn. Arguably, Rush and Cone had the most advanced trucks in the field. At the end of Lap 1, Cone managed to pass a handful of trucks while Rush held his lead, but Colton started to slip back from the front of the pack.

At the halfway point, Cone passed his way well into the top 10. Before long, he tailed the battle for second, third, and fourth, which included the formidable trucks of Bill Todd's rear-engine CJ-2A and J. M. Bragg and Ray Russell's CJ-5s. Cone, with more wheel travel and horsepower, made some masterful passes and soon caught a glimpse of Rush's Bronco. The laps were winding down and even the crowd could see that Cone was going to battle with Rush's Bronco during the final lap.

They flew down through the famous Riverside esses and over the jumps and hairpins before the big turn up onto Thompson's Ridge for the run home. At the bottom of the lap, Cone made his move on a sharp left turn and got a nose inside the Bronco. The 401-ci AMC plant pulled up on Rush's 351-ci-powered vehicle and got ahead on the ridge. This time, the win was truly Cone's in dramatic fashion. Jeep also took three more positions with Bragg in third, Russell in fourth, and Todd's rear-engine Jeep in fifth.

Oasis 400

Walt Lott was the driving force behind off-road racing in Southern Nevada. For years, he was the man responsible for designing the Mint 400 racecourses and was the president of the Southern Nevada Off-Road Racing Enterprises (SNORE). When the Mint was canceled, Lott put together

two races with some big prize money. One of these was the Oasis 400 out of Jean, Nevada. Pop's Oasis was a popular stop before Las Vegas for fuel, food, and gambling. It was home to the car in which Bonnie and Clyde were killed, which was a big tourist attraction.

It was early December when the race happened on a sunny cool weekend. With no moisture in the area for a while, the course was dusty. Three laps of 130 miles each awaited the racers, but so did some serious prize money out of the $50,000 pot. A class win netted a team $4,000 (more than $25,000 in 2023). To strengthen the prize money, he combined the two- and four-wheel-drive classes for pickups and 4x4s into one class.

The Race

Rod Hall and Jim Fricker used a Stroppe-prepared Ford F series pickup to take a commanding win by nearly half an hour. They outran a pack of Jeeps that included

Bill Todd and George Wallace teamed up to be the fastest 4x4 in the event. (Photo Courtesy tracksidephoto.com)

J. M. Bragg was just over 2 minutes behind the rear-engine-equipped racer of Bill Todd and George Wallace after nearly 400 miles of racing. (Photo Courtesy tracksidephoto.com)

Bill Todd and George Wallace in the aluminum Buick V-8-powered rear-engine CJ-2A that took second place. Just 2.5 minutes later came J. M. Bragg in his CJ-5 just a nose ahead of Phil Incikaya's CJ-5. Ray Russell came in sixth place and gave Jeep four out of the top seven positions in class.

1975

OPEC started the year off by raising crude oil prices by 10 percent. The Watergate scandal came to a close with Haldeman, Ehrlichman, and Mitchell each being sentenced to jail time between 30 months and 8 years. In sports, Muhammed Ali regained his world title from Joe Frazier in a fight labeled the "Thriller from Manila."

Ford announced that the factory Bronco racing program was officially closed. The Stroppe Broncos were either sold off or found other sponsorship. AMC stepped up its contingency and points championship programs to entice teams to switch.

With the oil crisis easing up, the off-road racing world looked forward to getting its beloved Mint and Baja events back.

Parker 400

The Parker 400 quickly became a favorite among the racers. The entry list grew in every class annually from mini trucks to 4x4s to Baja Bugs. The fast, flowing Arizona roads were a contrast to the rougher, rockier California side of the race. It had everything an off-road racer wanted.

Don Adams and Bob Gory switched from a Chevy Blazer to a CJ-5. Adams reasoned that AMC supported the Jeep racers with contingency money and a rich points fund for the end of the year.

Adams and Gory were locked in a battle early with a Bronco, a Ford pickup, and two other CJ-5 Jeeps. Adams started one position ahead of the Bronco and managed to stay ahead for a while on the California side. The Bronco passed them at the pit area on the northern end of the loop. Adams kept the Bronco in sight until the end of the 110-mile lap.

Going into the two Arizona loops, Larry Olsen, driving solo in a CJ-5, chased Adams while Adams chased the Bronco. It was a high-speed chess game that was fought mostly at night. The Bronco held its lead to the end, with Adams and Gory in second about 11 minutes behind. Olsen came home third and 24 minutes behind Adams.

When everything goes right, the modified 4x4s can beat the production-based Class 3 trucks. Sometimes a modified vehicle is less reliable, but in Parker, the win-

Don Adams and Bob Gory tackled one of the many washes that make up the Parker 400 course. (Photo Courtesy tracksidephoto.com)

ning truck was 53 minutes faster around the loops.

Ray Russell drove solo, which meant that he had no ride-along mechanic or co-driver to call out turns. It reduces the vehicle's weight by about 200 pounds, and that sounds great if everything goes right. J. M. Bragg, another Visalia area Jeep driver, did the same thing. Both were strong competitors and extraordinary drivers with exceptional mechanical abilities. Both ran CJ-5s.

Happy to be at the finish, a dusty Don Adams enjoys his first podium finish in a Jeep product. It was the first of many throughout the next two decades. (Photo Courtesy tracksidephoto.com)

Don Adams and Jason Myers teamed up for this race and fought for the win for a while. Second place was still a good reward for the pairing of Adams and Myers, who had many years and wins together. (Photo Courtesy track-sidephoto.com)

J. M. Bragg was hooked up all the way around the Baja countryside, beating the Hightower Jeep by 23 minutes. (Photo Courtesy tracksidephoto.com)

about halfway, the organizers put a mandatory 30-minute stop where they could work on their vehicles, get a sandwich, or switch drivers.

The Class 3 race quickly turned into a two-horse race between equally matched CJ-5s with 304-ci V-8 engines. Don Adams and Jason Myers battled Dick Dahn and Dale Frahm. The two entries started only minutes apart, so the crews gave them accurate split-time information as the race progressed. Halfway through the race, a couple of Broncos were more than an hour behind.

The two leaders were close but could not see each other on the road. Dahn and Frahm had several years more experience in Baja than Adams and Myers, and that was the difference at the finish, as Dahn and Frahm won the class by 90 seconds.

J. M. Bragg ran this race solo. He was a firm believer in reducing the weight of the vehicle by 200 pounds by racing without co-driver. There was another reason to be weight conscience as well. Bragg ran a 225-ci Dauntless V-6 engine in a class that usually ran V-8 engines. He was obviously onto something, as his impressive list of wins and podium finishes with the Buick engine showed that the little engine was competitive.

Bragg whipped around the course in 10 hours and 18 minutes, beating his nearest competitor, the 390-ci CJ-5 of Gene and Allen Hightower, by 23 minutes. Bragg also beat the production-based Class 3 rigs by an hour and a half. A Bronco weaseled its way into third place, while Brian Chuchua in a Jeep Commando took fourth.

Riverside Off-Road World Championships

It was that time of the year to convert the old desert racers into nimble short-course machines and race for the prize money at the annual SCORE event at Riverside Raceway. There was $182,500 up for grabs, which brought out the entries.

Sherman Balch was the hot shot during the hot August weekend. He took both the qualifying race and main event for the production-based 4x4s. He outran four Broncos and a massive field of fellow Jeeps on the 3.5-mile-long course that ran for 10 laps. Sometimes, it is just your weekend.

As Balch had humiliated the Class 3 field, a Bronco earned a repeat win in Class 4. The best of the rest of the

Sherman Balch didn't have a very good year in off-road racing, but if there was one thing that he knew for sure, Riverside could turn that around. Turn it around he did, as he dominated qualifying and then the race itself. (Photo Courtesy track-sidephoto.com)

field was the Jeep of J. M. Bragg with famous motorsports journalist Sam Wilshire riding along. Sandy Cone took a strong fourth place in the Jeepster AMX. Mike and Janet Curran, a husband-and-wife team, took their Jeepster and drove to a fifth-place finish.

Baja 1000

Sal Fish laid out a challenging 801-mile course that reached from coast to coast and as far south as Punta Prieta. However, Fish did not plan for the extreme weather that settled in over the peninsula. It challenged racers with rain, biting cold, and howling winds that produced sand and dust storms. This was in addition to the already-challenging harsh terrain.

In the end, many called it the toughest race since it began in 1967. The intrepid four-wheel-drive entries in the production and modified classes found the conditions abhorrent, as many had open driving compartments and no windshields. A stout jacket, goggles, and a stubborn nature were the best weapons.

Even though the Stroppe Bronco program was officially over, there were some still running out of his stable that were now owned by privateers. The Jeep CJs, Gladiators, Cherokees, Jeepsters, and M-38s were still out there, ready to stick it to Ford.

The race came down to the typical Jeep-versus-Ford affair. Dick Dahn mixed it up with the Bronco of Gale Pike and Willie Stroppe. A Chevy Blazer came up from the pack in the rear. As hard as Dahn drove, he never closed the gap completely to see the Bronco, as it started 7 minutes ahead of his Jeep CJ-5.

Dahn lost an hour for unknown reasons as he came around to the east side of the peninsula and headed over the Three Sisters toward San Felipe. Pike and Stroppe pushed hard to take the win, and Dahn had repairs completed in time to beat the Blazer by 43 minutes.

The story here is a lot like the Class 3 battle, but there were different circumstances in Class 4. Steve Mizel, in a highly modified Bronco, went for the glory of winning.

The 801-mile-long Baja 1000 for 1975 was one of the toughest years for the event. Deep silt, unrelenting rocks, and tricky mountain roads made for a long day and night (and day again) for most teams. (Map Courtesy J. M. Bragg)

Dick Dahn and Dale Frahm fought valiantly in the CJ-5 until repairs needed to be made in San Felipe, Mexico. Quick work in the pit had the pair back on the road to nab second place. (Photo Courtesy tracksidephoto.com)

J. M. Bragg, in his CJ-5, was driving for the money and a second SCORE Class 4 championship, which would garner a significant amount money from SCORE and AMC.

Bragg, a highly competitive driver, had to be patient and keep the long game in mind as the Bronco opened up an hour lead. Another Bronco pushed him from behind, but Bragg was able to keep a 20-minute gap. Bragg earned second place, his championship, and a nice payday.

1976

The United States was in the throes of bicentennial fever. The country was 200 years old, and it was something to celebrate. A Georgia peanut farmer became president and closed the door on 8 years of Nixon-related White House leadership. Two enterprising men named Wozniak and Jobs introduced the Apple computer to the world.

The CJ-7 Arrives

The year 1976 saw big changes to the Jeep line with the much-anticipated CJ-7. A wheelbase that was 10 inches longer wheelbase than the CJ-5 and two parallel longitudinal main C-section rails greatly improved vehicle handling and stability. AMC offered the CJ-7

with every conceivable engine and transmission, including two different 2.5L 4-cylinder engines, two different inline 6-cylinder engines, the 304-ci V-8, and an Isuzu 4-cylinder diesel engine. One automatic 3-speed transmission was available. Over its production life, 3-, 4-, and 5-speed manual transmissions were offered.

Obviously, the extended wheelbase and wider stance was a big draw for off-road racers. The engines offered were close to what was available in the CJ-5. The axles available were a Dana 30 in the front and an AMC 20 in the rear. The AMC 20 two-piece rear axle was excellent for everyday driving and off-roading, but not so much for off-road racing. The work-around was to replace the weak axle tubes with heat-treated 4130 chromoly tubes. It wasn't until 1986 that the Dana 44 was the production rear axle for the CJ-7.

The CJ-7 did not automatically start popping up all over the racecourses. Most people put a lot of time and money into their CJ-5, and starting over would set back most teams. At the first few races of the year, the CJ-5 was still the popular choice.

AMC released the first photos of the CJ-7. This one is in Renegade trim, which was popular with recreational and competition-motivated drivers. A wider wheelbase improved ride and handling, as did the beefy transmission and transfer case in V-8 models. (Photo Courtesy J. M. Bragg)

Parker 400

It was time to start the season along the Colorado River in the welcoming host city of Parker, Arizona. The 110-mile California loop saw Sherman and Jack Balch with a healthy lead on a couple of Broncos in their CJ-5. No one else was close to being in contention.

Somehow, the crew for Balch lost track of the Broncos but were confident in their lead. On the last lap, with information from his crew that he had a huge lead, Balch stopped for a soda and a candy bar. In reality, the Broncos of John Baker and Gale Pike were flying and got information from their crew that they were closing in on the Jeep.

Unaware of the closing speed of his Ford rivals, Balch completed the course and was first back to the finish line in Parker. Quicker than he expected, the Bronco of John Baker came roaring in, followed moments later by Pike. Even though Balch was there first, the elapsed time showed that Baker won by 1 minute, Balch was second, and Pike was a mere 3 seconds behind Balch!

"That was the most expensive candy bar I ever had," Balch said after the race.

The Class 4 race was equally surprising. Bill Todd and his rear-engine Jeep teamed with Glen Emery and led early. He had the CJ-5 of J. M. Bragg and the Bronco of Steve Mizel nipping at his heels. Not many people gave the rear-engine Jeep a chance of finishing—let alone holding its lead on the two 88-mile Arizona loops.

After they cleared the California side lap with a healthy lead, Sherman and Jack Balch head off to tackle the Arizona laps. (Photo Courtesy tracksidephoto.com)

J. M. Bragg repainted the CJ-5 in red, white, and blue to help celebrate the United States' bicentennial and named the CJ the Spirit of 76. Bragg took third place to start 1976 right. (Photo Courtesy J. M. Bragg)

Sherman and Jack Balch look happy to be done with the race. However, moments later, an unexpected John Baker crossed the line in his Bronco and nipped the Balchs by mere seconds. (Photo Courtesy tracksidephoto. com)

Bill Todd and Glen Emery cruised into the California-side finish in a heated battle with a Bronco and J. M. Bragg. After the short break to get to the Arizona side, the pair turned up the wick and brought the homebuilt creation its first win. (Photo Courtesy tracksidephoto.com)

Bill Todd (right, in white hat) and Glen Emery (left) wait at the finish line in Arizona to see if they won the race. They did. (Photo Courtesy tracksidephoto.com)

Emery began the second portion of the race, and after one lap, he reported to the crew that the Jeep felt good. They sent him out with about 10 minutes on Mizel. The Jeep held together and took the win 7 minutes ahead of Mizel. Another half hour behind Mizel was the third-place finisher, the Jeep CJ-5 of J. M. Bragg, for the final podium position.

Mint 400

The winds were continually whipping in the desert north of Las Vegas the weekend of the Mint 400. Dust and sand blew so hard that uncovered skin got sandblasted. The course was not in the best shape, either. Winter rains had carved ruts and cross grain into the desert floor.

This one was so rough that out of 357 starters, only 53 were scored as official finishers. Six of those were 4x4 class entries out of 53 starters in the class. Two brand new CJ-7s were entered in the race. Both barely completed before the start flag flew.

The Race

Ray Russell and Warren Baird drove one of the new CJ-7s, and they came out swinging with a first lap of 2 hours and 50 minutes. The Grant Randall Jeep Honcho had the only other sub-3-hour lap. It is interesting to note that the Jeep CJ-7's odometer had exactly 8 miles on it at the start line. Glen Emery in the rear-engine CJ-2A and J. M. Bragg in the CJ-5 were close in the 3:05 range. Many rigs clocked in around 3:10.

Grant Randall came out swinging with a sub 3-hour first lap to put him into second place. On lap two, the Honcho had a half hour of downtime. Somewhere during lap three, Randall's day of racing ended, but it was a promising run for the Honcho. (Photo Courtesy tracksidephoto.com)

Brakeless Balch

Sherman and Jack Balch had a good first lap with a 3:14 but faded quickly due to brake issues. Balch drove the last 300 miles of the race with no brakes. On the fourth lap, a front wheel came off the Jeep, and the jack broke. His crew was on the spot quickly and managed to only lose about 30 minutes. With all of those problems, he still managed sixth place.

Meanwhile…

The second lap tends to jostle the field at the Mint. Russell and Baird ran the second lap in the second-fastest time after a Bronco that did not finish in the third lap. Bragg ran a steady second lap a minute behind Russell, while Emery had a suspension issue that cost him an hour.

If not for an hour of downtime on the fourth lap, J. M. Bragg would have been in second place. The Nevada desert always has the last word. (Photo Courtesy tracksidephoto.com)

Bill Todd recruited former Jeep driver Rod Hall to drive for him in the Mint 400. Hall was between manufacturer's rides at the moment, but how can you turn down driving such an unusual vehicle? The pair pushed through the Nevada desert and turned consistent laps to take second place. (Photo Courtesy tracksidephoto.com)

At the start of the Mint 400, Ray Russell and Warren Baird were already tired. They had put in weeks of late night prepping into this new CJ-7. Russell looked at the odometer before the green flag fell, and it had 8 miles on it. The two men built it well and won the race to give Jeep its first victory with the CJ-7. (Photo Courtesy tracksidephoto.com)

During the third lap, Russell led his local rival J. M. Bragg with a fastest third-lap time by more than 17 minutes. Later, Bragg had front suspension issues that cost him almost 40 minutes. This allowed the Bill Todd entry to slip into second place, while Bragg held off Glen Emery, who had solid third and fourth laps to climb back into fourth.

Ray Russell and Warren Baird drove as clean of a race as possible at the Mint and gave the CJ-7 its first (of many) off-road racing victory.

Baja Internacional

The Jeeps were ready for another jaunt south of the border around Baja Norte. The course was 423 miles this year, and more than 400 total entries tried their luck against the unforgiving Baja roads.

Sherman and Jack Balch had a rough and rocky road in their CJ-5 to take second place behind a Bronco. In the first 100 miles of the race, things went well. Balch had nearly a 10-minute lead over the Bronco and the CJ-5 of Don Adams and Jason Myers. A stop for fuel was followed by the engine sputtering and a top speed of 30 mph. The crew did a quick fuel-pump change, but nothing changed. The Jeep was wounded.

Returning to his crew after a few hundred yards, further investigation showed that there was water in the fuel. The crew flushed the old fuel, refueled, and sent the CJ-5 on its way. Balch was back at 100 percent and made up for lost time on the Bronco and the other CJ-5.

Balch did not have a chance to pre-run a new section

The ex-Sandy Cone Jeepster AMX was now in the hands of Texas jewelry store owner Paul Holcomb. Despite issues with breaking wheels, the team managed a fourth-place finish. (Photo Courtesy tracksidephoto.com)

If you are going to have a bad day during an off-road race, it helps for others to have a worse day. For Sherman and Jack Balch, fuel issues, getting lost, and a broken driveline attributed to their headaches. However, through persistence, they earned second place. (Photo Courtesy tracksidephoto.com)

Ray Russell and Warren Baird were in the thick of it for 300 miles and pushed hard when a rock punctured the transmission pan of CJ-7. The stops to patch the hole and refill the fluid left them in third place. (Photo Courtesy tracksidephoto.com)

of the racecourse, and it bit him when, while following another Jeep, they both missed a crucial turn. The road was a loop, and they eventually got back to the racecourse but at a cost of about 15 minutes. It was back to playing catch-up and running the Jeep at speeds over 90 mph when he could.

At Valle de Trinidad, Balch had made up 35 minutes and was closing in on the Bronco. The Adams/Myers CJ-5 encountered problems and was now trailing Balch and the Bronco, which had its own issues.

At the sixth checkpoint at El Rodeo, Balch's rear driveline failed and flailed around enough to poke a hole in the transfer case. It took an extra stop to repair the driveshaft and then four more stops to refill the center differential oil. Even with all those issues, Sherman and Jack arrived in Ensenada with a solid second-place finish that was only 9 minutes behind the Bronco. Adams and Myers brought the CJ-5 home about 40 minutes later for third.

This race among the modified 4x4s brought the closest finish in off-road racing's short history, with a 3-second gap between first and second. The protagonists were J. M. Bragg and Allen and Gene Hightower, both in CJ-5s. Other players were Ray Russell, in his new CJ-7, and Paul Holcomb, who bought Sandy Cone's highly modified Jeepster.

Bragg and the Hightowers started 5 minutes apart, so while they weren't exactly in sight of each other, it was easy to get reports on where each other was from the pit crews. Ray Russell started ahead of Hightower by 2 minutes.

Holcomb started ahead of Ray Russell and stayed ahead of him for about 10 miles before the wily veteran passed them. Only a few miles later, Russell pulled over to change a flat, which allowed Holcomb back into the physical lead. Sixty miles later, Holcomb had a wheel break and lost the lead. Holcomb managed to stay in fourth place, as Hightower and Bragg drove past Holcomb as he finished the repair. Hightower was physically first into San Felipe, the halfway point. Bragg and Russell were

tied for second. Holcomb was moments behind them.

On the road up the mountain to Mike's Sky Ranch, the Holcomb Jeep broke another wheel and dropped several positions. By Mike's Sky Ranch, it was nearly impossible to figure out who was leading between Hightower, Bragg, and Russell. The race down the mountain toward Valle de Trinidad shook things out as Russell cracked his transmission oil pan on a rock. He made several stops to repair the pan as well as possible and refill the transmission.

Hightower and Bragg flogged their rides hard as the road snaked its way toward Ensenada. Evening descended on the peninsula, and over long straight stretches, Bragg saw Hightower's taillights in the distance. They started 5 minutes apart, and when Hightower arrived at the finish, Bragg completed the race in what seemed like exactly 5

It is exciting to win the closest finish in off-road racing history (up to that point). However, it is less exciting to be on the short end of that stick by 3 seconds. J. M. Bragg's part in the momentous event was the latter. The 423-mile race came down to only 3 seconds. (Photo Courtesy tracksidephoto.com)

Allen and Gene Hightower spent the day in Baja competing against J. M. Bragg and Ray Russell. It was not a bad way to spend the day, but it was even better to win against that kind of competition. (Photo Courtesy tracksidephoto.com)

minutes later. In the end, timing and scoring gave the win to the Hightowers by a scant 3 seconds.

Russell managed to hang on for a third place and arrived about 35 minutes later with a leaky transmission pan and no spare oil. Holcomb had a third wheel break close to the finish and was out of spare tires. He limped on the broken wheel for about 8 miles before finding a crew with a spare that they could borrow. They came home in fourth place despite the lost time.

Riverside Off-Road World Championships

The annual gathering at Riverside International Raceway was a big hit with the crowds because all the action was laid out in front of them, just like Mickey Thompson intended. It was also a big hit with the racers because there was serious money to be won, but anything that was won would be earned. Riverside was hard on machines and their occupants.

Going into qualifying, Balch was among the quickest, along with a Blazer and several Broncos. Qualifying set the grid for the race. At a track like Riverside, where passing was tough, position was everything. In the end, Lonnie Woods put a Chevrolet Blazer first, followed less than a second by Balch, and then some Broncos. Balch felt good about his chances.

The Race

The start of a Riverside race was staged in a Oklahoma land rush–style with everyone on a single wide start line. The road tapered gradually until it was only wide enough for two trucks. Balch and his 304-ci AMC engine had a slight holeshot on Woods's small-block Chevy and the rest of the field.

Woods, a veteran (like Balch), tried several moves to overtake Balch: inside, outside, out-brake, and

out-accelerate. However, the Jeep driver was on a mission. Kurt Strecker's Viva Bronco kept it close, while Balch held off other Fords. Balch finished a few vehicle lengths ahead of Woods and claimed his share of points and money—just like he planned.

Bill Todd was happy to get Rod Hall to drive his rear-engine Jeep. Glen Emery had the second rear-engine hand-built Jeep, and these two unconventional builds qualified first and second. Hired gun Sandy Cone was third in his former Jeepster, which is now owned by Paul Holcomb.

The Modified Race

At the drop of the green flag, the modified rigs barreled into turn one and swapped paint and bent body panels. The two rear-engine Jeeps took the brunt of the damage and were out early. Cone took the lead on the first lap and started to run away when at the start of the second lap the transmission gave up and left Cone with one gear: neutral.

A Bronco grabbed the lead and took off with a second Bronco on its bumper and Ray Russell's CJ-7 right

Ray Russell bounced, jumped, and slid his way from a slower start than he wanted into a second-place finish. Finishing behind the same Bronco for the second consecutive year was getting old. (Photo Courtesy tracksidephoto.com)

As with the previous year, Sherman Balch was in a must-win situation for points and money to keep going to the end of 1976. He laid out a plan, executed it, and took the win again in the production ranks. (Photo Courtesy tracksidephoto.com)

behind him. It took Russell a few laps to get around the Bronco and allow the leading *Crazy Horse* Bronco to lengthen its lead and eventually win the race. Russell took second place.

Baja 1000

The 1976 Baja 1000 was the shortest one ever, with 532 miles of racing. Mother Nature decided to dump rain starting a few days prior to the race and ending just before the start time. Radio reports came in from all over the course about snow at Checkpoint 1, nearly impassable mud on Laguna Salada, and gigantic washouts and flash floods. SCORE decided to push the start time ahead by 4 hours and move the starting location 20 miles out of Ensenada.

At 10:30 a.m., the new start time, there was no timing and scoring at the new start. There were also very few entries. It was a mess, and radio reports kept coming in about horrendous obstacles. In an unprecedented move, Sal Fish postponed the start of the race 24 hours to give the course a chance to settle down. Luckily, the rain stopped, and winds helped to dry some areas.

Ray Russell and Warren Baird wanted to avenge their loss in the June Baja race. They were confident in their CJ-7 with Cooper tires to get through the mud. In addition, they brought a second driver, Dennis Harris, into the mix. It all worked out for them with a class win. (Photo Courtesy tracksidephoto.com)

In the production ranks, Jeep had only one hero in the top five: the Sherman and Jack Balch entry. Heroes they were, as they powered through the goo and the muck to take a commanding win by almost 2 hours over a Chevy Blazer. After the race, Sherman Balch claimed they only got stuck once for a short time on Laguna Salada.

Balch's victory cemented his driver's championship in Class 3, as well as the overall points title in the Jeep championship. This was also Balch's first victory in Baja California, but it was not his last. It was his last driving a Jeep. In 1977, Balch defected to International Harvester and campaigned the Scout for the next 7 years.

Jeep fared better in the modified class in the tough conditions and swept the podium positions. Ray Russell was dialed into the conditions, and his CJ-7 was way out front by the time he reached Laguna Salada. There were two ways to get past the not-so-dry lake: go across or go around. Going around was quite a few extra miles. Russell decided he had the power, and his Cooper tires performed exceptionally well in the mud. If he could make it across the lakebed surface, he would have an insurmountable lead.

In their farewell to Jeep, Sherman and Jack Balch wanted to go out on top. To ensure that the distance was covered with a fresh driver, Sherman brought in John Deetz to drive for a portion of the race. The plan worked, and the Balchs earned their first win south of the border. (Photo Courtesy tracksidephoto.com)

J. M. Bragg and the Hightowers led a pack of Jeeps and Broncos. It was not worth chasing Russell down. His lead was almost 1.5 hours, and there were not enough miles in the race to catch up, which was an odd thought for a Baja 1000.

The Energizer Bunny?

Meanwhile, Russell charged across the deep mud and felt good about his decision. All of a sudden, the engine quit, the Jeep stopped, and it sank into the mud. He radioed his crew his position and started to diagnose the issue. A damaged battery was the culprit. About 1.5 hours had passed before the crew found Russell and got him moving again.

Amazingly, he still had the lead but by a slim margin at the next checkpoint at El Chinero. J. M. Bragg, with Jeep Motorsport manager Jim Rader riding along, was close after he lost a transmission line before Mexicali and had to stop to crimp the line and beg for oil from spectators. Repairs were quick, but with reports of deep mud on Laguna Salada, Bragg chose to go around but stayed close to the edge of the lake to see if it dried out in the southern end.

The Hitchhiker

Bragg and Rader powered across the desert and edged onto the dry lake, which was still muddy in places. All alone out in the middle of a muddy mess was a single-seater buried up to its belly pan. Bobby Ferro sat on the roof and waved to call the Jeep over. In Baja racing, never leave someone behind if they wave you down. Ferro asked to sit in the back of the stretched

CJ-5 until they got off the lake where Ferro's crew was waiting.

Ferro is a mutliple overall winning single-seater driver with wins in every major race. It was odd to see him back in the field like that. Bragg and Rader had him keep his helmet on as they charged on to chase down Russell. Near the checkpoint at El Chinero, Ferro signaled that he saw his crew. Bragg pulled the Jeep over, and Ferro leapt out and thanked the two men for the lift.

The Second Half of the Race

Russell set about rebuilding a comfortable lead. He charged south toward San Felipe where the course turned west toward the mountains and had some challenging twisty roads. Word filtered through that Bragg was more than 30 minutes behind at San Felipe. The Hightower Jeep lost 1 hour, mired in the mud on the Laguna.

Russell knew Bragg. They were both on the same team for a while. He knew that Bragg would never quit as long as there was a chance of winning. Russell pushed hard all the way back to Ensenada and waited to see when Bragg finished.

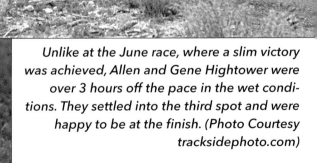

Unlike at the June race, where a slim victory was achieved, Allen and Gene Hightower were over 3 hours off the pace in the wet conditions. They settled into the third spot and were happy to be at the finish. (Photo Courtesy tracksidephoto.com)

A win was not necessary for J. M. Bragg to earn his third consecutive Class 4 championship, but he wanted it anyway. His effort fell 55 minutes short, but his title for the year was secured. (Photo Courtesy tracksidephoto.com)

Russell had cleared the road and made it down the mountain with a slight fog to drive through. By the time Bragg made it to the same area, the fog had rolled in, and it was thick. Bragg and Rader decided that following the barbed wire fence posts on the side of the road was the best way to make their way into Valle de Trinidad. By the next checkpoint at El Rodeo, the fog cleared. Bragg finished the race 55 minutes behind Russell. The Hightower Jeep CJ-5 arrived almost 2.5 hours later for third place.

1977

The year began with Jimmy Carter being sworn in as the 39th president of the United States. The space shuttle program under NASA had its first test flight, as the Enterprise flew, mated to the top of a Boeing 747. A. J. Foyt became the first four-time winner of the Indianapolis 500 in his self-built Coyote chassis.

Parker 400

SCORE brought its high-horsepower circus back to the Colorado River town of Parker, Arizona. It consistently has a huge number of entries for the 4x4s. The new season brought out optimistic teams, and their finish determined if they could continue for the points title.

Rod Hall, now with Chrysler, took the win in Parker by 28 minutes ahead of the Jeep CJ-5 of Don Tobias. The wheelbase of the Dodge pickup was difficult to overcome, but Hall's abilities behind the wheel made him and Jim Fricker formidable. Don Ohnstad managed a fourth-place finish in his Jeepster.

Jeep was shut out on victories at Parker, as a Bronco took the day. Ray Russell took second place in his CJ-7 and was followed 31 minutes later by Glen Emery in his rear-engine CJ-2A.

Mint 400

It was time to get back to Las Vegas for the glitziest race of the year. The course north of Las Vegas was modified slightly to be 89 miles per lap. To keep people from being out in the desert until dawn, the 4x4 races and several other classes were three laps each. This experiment did not continue past 1978.

The good news for the 4x4 racers was that for the first time, the Mint 400 separated the production and modified trucks into their own classes. This made racers happy because there would be two first-place winners, so that meant more prize money.

J. M. Bragg was in a new CJ-7 and a new class. The CJ-7 allowed Bragg to run in Class 3, which meant a quicker and cheaper build than modifying the new platform. The Hightowers were also in a new CJ-7 in Class 3, but that was for this event only. By the following month, they made changes and returned to Class 4.

Bragg came out swinging with a blistering 2:48 lap. The Dodge of Rod Hall was 7 minutes behind, and a Bronco was 2 minutes behind the Dodge. The Hightowers had an hour-long breakdown in the new CJ-7.

Bragg knocked out another quick lap, and the Hightowers were back on track and matched Bragg's lap time. The Dodge had a 2.5-hour breakdown and was out of the running for the win. The Bronco slid down the order

Ray Russell hustles the CJ-7 through a wash on the Arizona side of the course on his way to a strong second-place finish at Parker. (Photo Courtesy Brad Russell)

In a masterful piece of driving, J. M. Bragg earned a commanding victory in his new CJ-7 to win the production class by 49 minutes. (Photo Courtesy tracksidephoto.com)

Kirby Hightower and Dale Frahm overcame a slow first lap and sorted out the new CJ-7. They roared up through the field and managed their fastest laps on the second and third laps to take second place. (Photo Courtesy tracksidephoto.com)

Danny Chandler and Vern Roberts teamed up in a CJ-5 and ran in second place. However, on the last lap, they had an issue that cost them 45 minutes, so they salvaged a third-place finish and were 10 minutes ahead of Dick Dahn. (Photo Courtesy tracksidephoto.com)

Don and Ed Bray, from Tacoma, Washington, earned a third-place trophy and a nice check for their efforts. (Photo Courtesy tracksidephoto.com)

with a 30-minute issue. This allowed the CJ-5 of Danny Chandler and Vern Roberts to move into a heated battle for the second place with several rigs.

The third lap shook up the running order—but not for J. M. Bragg. He turned another quick lap to take a commanding win by 49 minutes. Kirby Hightower and Dale Frahm recovered from their lost hour on Lap 1 and turned a sub-3-hour lap late to take second place. Chandler and Roberts lost a half-hour in the darkness and dropped to third place. Dick Dahn and Tom Barnett drove three consistent laps to nab fourth place ahead of a Bronco.

Jeeps easily swept the top three positions in the modified class. The rear-engine CJ-2 of Glen Emery and Steve

Catlin dispatched the field by a margin of 54 minutes. Robert Minter and his son Robert took their CJ-7 to second place 2.5 hours ahead of Don and Ed Bray. The Brays made the trip from Tacoma, Washington, worth it with the third-place winnings.

Baja Internacional

Rod Hall started from the last-place starting position in the four-wheel-drive class and watched as attrition played a role in the outcome. Only 8 of the 21 starting vehicles finished the race.

Class 3		
Place	**Driver**	**Vehicle**
1	Rod Hall/Jim Fricker	Dodge Pickup
2	J. M. Bragg	Jeep CJ-7
3	Lonnie Woods	Chevrolet Blazer

J. M. Bragg and Jim Rader flew the Jeep to second place in Class 3. (Photo Courtesy tracksidephoto.com)

Class 4		
Place	**Driver**	**Vehicle**
1	Don Barlow/Coco Corral	Ford Bronco
2	Allen Hightower	Jeep CJ-7
3	Ray Russell	Jeep CJ-7

Allen Hightower and that unmistakable long-nose CJ scooted around the course to a second-place finish in Class 4. (Photo Courtesy tracksidephoto.com)

Riverside Off-Road World Championships

August means a trip to the historic Riverside International Raceway to drive in front of big crowds on hallowed ground usually reserved for names such as Richard Petty, A. J. Foyt, Mark Donohue, Carroll Shelby, and Ken Miles. The pavement was not the star this weekend. It was the dirt in the areas where those above-mentioned names do not dare tread.

Rod Hall's Dodge started out in front with the Balch Scout in second and J. M. Bragg in third. Late in the second lap, the Dodge had a front-end failure but continued onward at a reduced speed. This allowed Balch to get around the Dodge and look for his fourth consecutive Riverside win. J. M. Bragg easily dispatched the Dodge and chased the Scout to stay ahead of Hall and a gaggle of three other Internationals.

Balch checked out and left Bragg alone in second place while Hall made the Dodge go wide to hold on to third place. This was the parade that led these three to the finish in that order.

Don Barlow was untouchable for a second year in a row in his *Crazy Horse* Bronco, much to the Jeep contingent's dismay. Behind the leader was a great battle between Ray Russell and Allen Hightower in a CJ-5. Lap after lap, the two were either nose to tail or side by side. In the penultimate lap, Hightower got the edge in traffic and passed a slower car and Russell in one move. Russell took third place.

J. M. Bragg stretched out the legs on his CJ-7 and was rewarded with a second-place finish in his class. (Photo Courtesy J. M. Bragg)

Baja 1000

This year was much drier than 1976 and considered to be a more typical Baja 1000. There was still damage from the rains a year ago, and that brought up new exposed rock. This year, a 220-mile loop comprised of the dreaded Summit, Diablo Dry Lake, Mike's Sky Ranch, and the San Matias Pass would be run two times before heading back toward Ensenada.

"The drivers say this Baja 1000 will separate the flat trackers from the drivers who can keep their right foot hooked up with their brain," SCORE president Sal Fish said about the course.

Twenty-one 4x4s started the Class 3 race, but only 6 officially finished the grueling course. All of the manufacturers were represented, and each of their marketing departments wanted to run an advertisement that its brand won the race.

Early in the race, it became obvious that this was a race of attrition. Almost from the moment that racers left Ensenada, broken motorcycles, cars, and trucks littered the sides of the trail. By the time that Class 3 left the start line, sections of the course looked like a junkyard.

There is no easy way to say this, but Jerry Boone, an International Harvester dealer from Parker, Arizona, had the field covered. Boone ran hard early to build a

lead as the course took care of the rest of his competition. J. M. Bragg and Jim Rader finished the race 2 hours behind the Scout. The third-place finisher, a Bronco, was almost another hour behind.

Alfonso Barbosa, in a Bronco, jumped out to a lead early in the race, with Ray Russell and Warren Baird as

Allen and Gene Hightower avoided any major issues in the reliable CJ-5 and took second place in Class 4. (Photo Courtesy tracksidephoto.com)

well as Allen and Gene Hightower not far behind. At Tres Posos (Checkpoint 3), Ray Russell jumped out of his CJ-7 unannounced to his co-driver Warren Baird, who slid over to the driver's seat to solo the next 220 miles until the course looped back to Tres Posos.

Baird knew that he had to make a charge to catch the Bronco and pressed onward alone. Allen Hightower also pressed hard to catch who they thought was Russell driving. Baird was no slouch behind the wheel. Because he built the CJ-7 alongside Russell, he knew what it was capable of.

Somewhere in that 220-mile loop, the Bronco pulled off with a mechanical issue, but neither Baird nor Hightower saw him on the side of the road. They were chasing a ghost. When they arrived back in Tres Posos, Russell slipped back behind the steering wheel, and Baird moved to the passenger seat. This is when Baird found out he was ahead of the Bronco and the Jeep CJ-5 of the Hightowers. No one else was even close, as entry after entry fell by the side of the road.

Russell and Baird did not set a foot wrong all race and arrived back in Ensenada 19 hours and 20 minutes after they left. They won by 24 minutes over the Hightower Jeep. In third place, which was almost 26 hours later, was a Bronco.

1978

In this new year, the primetime soap opera was born when the television show *Dallas* debuted. Reinhold Messner and Peter Habeler became the first humans to summit Mount Everest without the use of supplemental oxygen. Al Unser Sr. collected his third Indianapolis 500 win driving for Jim Hall. Most importantly, the first use of insulin to help patients manage diabetes began in 1978.

Al Unser had a nice resume of driving and riding in some off-road races. Here, competing for Chaparral Racing in a backup car, he celebrates winning the 1978 Indianapolis 500. It was his third time winning the event. In 1987, he won the Indianapolis 500 for a fourth time. (Photo Courtesy Unser Museum)

The highly modified CJ-5 of Kirby Hightower and Dale Frahm withstood hits like this over and over in the tough, dependable Jeep. (Jere Alhadeff Photo courtesy The Lions Drag Strip Museum)

Off-road racing was becoming very popular. Entry lists were larger than ever, and the competition was tough as always, but now everyone was going faster. The manufacturers of off-road aftermarket parts learned their lessons and produced better tires, wheels, shocks, lights, engines, and transmissions.

The Mexicali 300

The Parker 400 looked to be epic with 450 entries total, and 70,000 spectators were expected the weekend of February 10. With just one week until the event, SCORE was told by its insurance carrier that it would not provide liability insurance for the event. Without time to secure new insurance, a cagey Sal Fish implemented an alternate race in Mexicali, Baja California. Not many knew that Fish, who was not one to be caught off guard, always had something else laid out for situations like this.

With very little warning, the majority of the entries headed south to the border town. The new course was a 330-mile adventure from Mexicali to San Felipe and back. The day before the race started, the entire Mexicali area was inundated with rain that soaked the roads. Fish set out the night before the race to recon

Ray Russell drove solo for the entire 330 miles and earned the Class 4 victory. (Photo Courtesy Brad Russell)

J. M. Bragg chases after an International Scout. If not for a late flat tire, he could have won instead of taking second place. (Photo Courtesy J. M. Bragg)

the roads to make sure they were passable. Fish radioed to hold the start for an extra 2 hours while he checked one vital area. With everything clear, the delayed race began due to Herculean efforts by Sal Fish.

Several Jeep teams declined to make the trip to Mexicali. Many who did compete were met with mechanical issues. The only highlight for the Jeep contingent was the Class 4 victory by Ray Russell in his CJ-7.

Return to Mexicali

Five weeks after the Parker race was hastily moved, SCORE, its volunteers, and the race teams returned to Mexicali for the regularly scheduled race of the Mexicali 250. With the racecourse identical to the February event, teams felt very confident, especially with drier conditions.

It was a hard-fought day between J. M. Bragg and the Scout of Sherman Balch. Both came out strong with another Scout trailing them. From checkpoint to checkpoint, it was a cat-and-mouse game, as the lead was swapped a couple of times.

Heading back north toward Mexicali, Bragg dropped some time with a flat tire, providing Balch the breathing time that he needed to win the race. Bragg beat another

Ray Russell and Dennis Harris ran away with the Class 4 win in Mexicali. They distanced themselves from the Hightowers and a Bronco. (Photo Courtesy Brad Russell)

Bob Townsend took his CJ-7 to a third-place finish with a solo effort behind the wheel. (Photo Courtesy trackside-photo.com)

John Deetz and Neil Cameron fought hard all day and into the night. Their Archer Brothers–sponsored CJ-5 performed well to take one of the narrowest winning margins ever seen at a Mint 400, which was just 42 seconds. (Photo Courtesy trackside photo.com)

Scout for second place by an hour.

Ray Russell and Dennis Harris teamed up for this one and took first place by 15 minutes. The CJ-5 of Allen Hightower ran after the CJ-7 all day but to no avail. A Bronco nabbed the third spot.

Mint 400

The area north of the Las Vegas Speedrome was familiar ground after three years of Mint 400s in the vicinity. Some favorites went down early in both classes, including Ray Russell, J. M. Bragg, and Allen Hightower.

The fight among the production rigs never really included a Jeep. That darn Dodge and a Bronco had a battle for first and second. Third place was claimed with a determined drive by Bob Townsend, who did the whole race solo in his CJ-7. The Dodge won and was followed by the Bronco 10 minutes later and Townsend 50 minutes later.

It was a titanic fight in Class 4 after early leader Ray Russell was sidelined. John Deetz and Neil Cameron in an Archer Brothers–sponsored CJ-5 battled with the Rice Brothers Bronco. The two started far back in the field just 4.5 minutes apart. That meant they were physically very close all day.

In the final lap, Deetz and Cameron checked on their position with their crew on the radio at every opportunity. The usual answer from the crew was, "It's close! Go!" The Jeep was first to the finish line, and watches were scrutinized as they could hear the Ford V-8 coming in the distance. Deetz and Cameron won by a narrow margin of 42 seconds. The final podium spot went to Nick Coupe and Dan Tobias in a narrowed, single-seat CJ-2A 90 minutes after the leaders finished.

Nick Coupe and Dan Tobias took turns behind the wheel of a customized Jeep CJ-2A that featured a narrowed body and the driver was mounted in the center of the vehicle. It was a popular modification in the Pacific Northwest events run by the Valley Off-Road Racing Association (VORRA). (Photo Courtesy trackside photo.com)

Glen Emery's Day

The rear-engine Jeep of Glen Emery was well suited to the conditions at the Mint 400. Therefore, he was confident that he could finish well. In the first

Glen Emery had a tough day in the Nevada desert. He was rear-ended, parts were bent and broken, and axles and tires were lost. However, Emery never quit and was rewarded with sixth place and a bit of cash. (Photo Courtesy tracksidephoto.com)

lap, Emery was rear-ended by a single seater hard enough to bend a tie rod. At the next pit, the crew straightened the part instead of replacing it. Several miles down the road, the tie rod failed completely. More time was lost.

In the final lap, the rear axle failed. Emery's crew caught up to the stricken racer, and in the ensuing frenzy, a rear tire was not tightened properly. The tire came off the racer twice in that final lap. Emery eventually got to the finish and had the crew pack everything up and head back to the hotel. What Emery did not know until later that week was that he finished in sixth place and earned $600. That was enough to cover the entry fee with an additional $200. It pays to press forward regardless.

Baja Internacional

Baja California is mostly desert, and that means heat, especially in June. The topography of the peninsula typically has milder temperatures along the Pacific Ocean side, which has high elevations, and a cooler Pacific breeze than the Gulf of California side, which is low desert. Even for Baja, the temperatures soared, with some areas predicting highs of up to 118°F. The heat spelled the end for a lot of racer's machines.

The Jeep teams lined up to do battle against all comers. Fifteen entries started in the production 4x4 class. Sherman Balch and Russ Kirkpatrick in an International Scout led the field by 10 minutes at race mile 90 as he wheeled toward the dreaded Summit. A tight field followed with the Jeeps of J. M. Bragg, Dale Frahm, and Vern Roberts. Once over the Summit, the Jeep CJ-7 of Bragg had caught Balch and had a 1-minute lead by San Felipe. Dale Frahm was 4 minutes behind in his CJ-7. Only four more rigs made it as far as San Felipe, which is considered the halfway point.

By the next checkpoint, Balch was missing. Word came in that his lug nuts failed, possibly crystalized by

Things were going J. M. Bragg's way until the CJ-7 rolled and the steering box was torn away from the frame rail. This happened not far from the finish line, and it cost Bragg 2 hours and the race. However, he salvaged second place. (Photo Courtesy tracksidephoto.com)

Losing almost 4 hours in the late stages of the race cost Don Adams and Jason Myers a possible second-place finish. They fell to fourth place, and they were the final finisher in their class. (Photo Courtesy tracksidephoto.com)

the desert heat, and the rear wheels went flying and destroyed the brakes. Balch parked it to fight another day.

Heading into the final 100 miles, Bragg and Frahm were just minutes apart. Bragg rolled his CJ and the steering gear box broke away from the frame. He lost more than 2 hours chaining the gear to the frame and nursing his way back to Ensenada for a third-place finish. This left Dale Frahm and Bobby Grimes to motor into Ensenada as the winners. Out of 15 starters only 3 finished.

In the modified class, 1 Jeep started the race. By the first checkpoint, Ray Russell, who was running solo, had 5 minutes in hand over the Bronco of Steve Mizel. Ivan Stewart took over driving the *Crazy Horse* Bronco and was close with the lead pack through two checkpoints until the engine overheated and the distributor failed. The Randall Cherokee also stopped at this point.

It was obviously a two-horse race, as Russell's Jeep CJ-7 and the "funny" Bronco of Mizel turned north for the final half. By San Matias Pass, the two were nearly within sight of each other as they started up the mountain to Mike's Sky Ranch. Allen Hightower was nearly an hour behind at this point and was followed by Don Adams. They were both in CJs.

Down the mountain and into Valle de Trinidad, the two swapped the lead at fuel stops. Within a few miles of Ensenada, both expected a photo finish when Russell had a fuel pump pack it in, which left him stranded.

Mizel flew past and was a few miles from the finish when his motor quit in a sand wash. It took a few panic-stricken minutes, but Mizel willed the engine back to life and roared into town as the eventual winner. Russell arrived 46 minutes later for second place 15 minutes ahead of Hightower. It was 3.5 more hours before Don Adams and Jason Myers rolled in as the final finisher in class.

Riverside Off-Road World Championships

For the fifth annual visit to the Riverside Raceway, the crowd was the largest to date. Word got around that it was an exciting weekend to watch some action-packed off-road racing. The celebrities raced again in their Jeeps, which did not hurt the crowd count.

It was Dodge's day under the hot Riverside sun, as Rod Hall fended off a hard-charging J. M. Bragg, who was rarely more than 2 seconds off his tailgate at any time. The CJ-5 of Dick Montague was in third place after a tight battle with the CJ-5 of Dale Frahm.

It was a loaded field in the modified class, as some wild machinery took to the course for the race. Eyes were on the veteran Ray Russell, Don Adams, and a host of Ford and International entries. What they should have looked out for was the wild-looking Jeep of Dan Randall.

Alan Hightower grabbed the lead off the start with Ray Russell on his tail, followed by a Bronco and a Toyota. The Bronco began to pressure Russell as the Toyota

Dick Montague had a good day in the race after a stellar start put him in the top five. The CJ-5 clawed its way up to third place at the finish line, right behind the second-place finisher. (Photo Courtesy tracksidephoto.com)

pulled off the course. Dan Randall carved through the field like a hot knife through butter. He advanced from seventh place to fifth and then to fourth within a few laps.

Hightower had troubles and pulled off the track, which allowed Russell, the Bronco, and Randall to fight it out. On the next lap, the Randall Jeep dispatched the Bronco and set his sights on Russell. The battle raged lap after lap as Randall tried everything to pass the CJ-7 as the Bronco closed in.

On the last lap, the three looked like they were chained together nose to tail. The Bronco made a move to the inside of Russell, they made contact, and both trucks bobbled. This allowed Dan Randall to slide past to take the win. The Bronco took second and Russell was third.

J. M. Bragg had to watch a Dodge's bumper for 12 laps. Bragg was close throughout the race but wasn't able to execute a pass. Keeping an eye behind him, Bragg drove a clean race and held off all challengers. (Photo Courtesy tracksidephoto.com)

Ray Russell had a tenuous grip on first place, as he was harassed by the Bronco of Steve Mizel. Late in the race, the Bronco tripped up Russell. Third place was a disappointing end to Russell's race weekend. (Photo Courtesy tracksidephoto.com)

Dan Randall brought the first major win to the Randall family as he carved his way up the field to finally make the winning pass on the 11th lap out of 12. (Photo Courtesy tracksidephoto.com)

Baja 1000

This year's version of the Baja 1000 was like a grand tour of Baja Norte. Starting in Mexicali, the course went west and paralleled the border for a few miles before it turned south toward Morelia Junction, where the course did a 120-mile loop south of San Felipe. From there, the course took its usual path back to Ensenada. In total, it was 580 miles. It was a rough one, where 219 vehicles started and only 56 finished.

For the Jeep contingent, this was a forgettable race weekend because not one Jeep finished in a position of note. Russell hit a rock and took out his front end. The Hightowers were out early. Not one Jeep finished the race in Class 4. If you can call it a high point, J. M. Bragg had several issues and nabbed an inconsequential fourth place in the production class.

J. M. Bragg drove one of the only Jeep vehicles to make it to the finish in Class 3 or Class 4. After many issues and a significant amount of downtime, Bragg finished the race in a forgettable fourth place. (Photo Courtesy tracksidephoto.com)

1979

The Voyager 1 spacecraft made its closest approach to Jupiter and revealed that it also had rings like Saturn. Rick Mears, who cut his teeth in off-road racing, won his first of four Indianapolis 500s. In England, a writer for Monty Python named Douglas Adams wrote his first novel, which was called *The Hitchhiker's Guide to the Galaxy*.

This year witnessed a truly iconic moment in the Jeep ranks, when Texas oil millionaire Mike Moore decided to go off-road racing in a Jeep Honcho (see the Mears, Moore, and the *Budweiser Honcho* sidebar). The celebrity series continued to draw attention to the sport and helped spike sales of CJ-7 Golden Eagles.

Where Have the Honchos Been Before Now?

The Gladiator/Honcho/J Series trucks were a part of the off-road racing history from the beginning. There were not many of them, and until now, their performance did not merit much mention. The Arizona-based Randall Racing team dialed in its Honcho about the time

The Jeep Honcho took some time to come to prominence in off-road racing. Several competitors attempted to run them from 1968 to 1978 with limited success. The breakout year was 1979, thanks to teams such as Mike Moore and the Randall Family. (Photo Courtesy tracksidephoto.com)

that Mike Moore decided to build his team. The Chuchua team tried running one previously but did not have much success. From this point in time to today, the Jeep J Series has shaped 4x4 class racing from Baja to Canada, whether in cross country–style races or closed-course racing.

Parker 400

The new year began in grand style with more than 400 entries for the lead-off event of the season. After the tumult around the 1978 event, it was nice to get things back to normal.

The course was deceptive and brutal in some areas, which led to numerous rollovers in all classes.

For Jeep fans, this one stung, as a Dodge and a Scout ran away with the race. Dale Frahm managed to get the last podium spot in his CJ-5, 2 minutes and 20 seconds behind the former Jeep driver Sherman Balch.

It did not help that frontrunner J. M. Bragg rolled his CJ-7 early which took him out of contention. Roger Mears ran in an under-powered, under-suspended Jeep Celebrity Challenge CJ-7 to get some points in class. Walker Evans was still finishing his new Honcho. He had a slow day but managed to get sixth place in class.

Things were much better for the Jeep drivers in the modified class. Don Adams debuted his new CJ-7 that was built by Warren Baird. David Bryan was in Brian Chuchua's Jeep CJ-6, which tipped the scales at just over 5,000 pounds. The usual suspects were all there, including Ray Russell, Glen Emery, Allen Hightower, etc.

Don Adams started strong and jumped into a sizeable lead on the California side. Hightower was next but was almost 20 minutes behind. Ray Russell cracked a

David Bryan followed a great start to the season in Parker with another strong second-place finish in Mexicali. Even though his CJ-6 is heavier than most others in his class, Bryan found ways to use it to his advantage. (Photo Courtesy tracksidephoto.com)

Big-Time Entertainers Turned Loose on Racetrack

Jeep went into the race knowing that its CJ-7s would get beat up. How could they not, with celebrities driving and overzealous coaches pushing them from the passenger's seat. Richard Roundtree and Dick Montague wrinkled the sheet metal during practice with a rollover. (Photo Courtesy Judy Smith Collection/Off-Road Motorsports Hall of Fame)

Jim Rader, the head of AMC Motorsports, saw the positive effect that the Toyota celebrity races at the Long Beach Grand Prix had on sales. He decided to put a Jeep/off-road spin on the concept and came up with the Jeep Celebrity Challenge. In early 1977, Rader approached Mickey Thompson and Sal Fish, the heads of SCORE International, and they hammered out a plan of action.

All of the races were on a closed course, first in Las Vegas, then at Riverside, and the finale was at the Los Angeles Coliseum. Rader, Fish, and Thompson agreed that tracking the celebrities over the course of a wide-open desert race led to many logistical issues. The closed course races provided easier access for television cameras.

Sal had a long-standing relationship with AMC since his days at Petersen Publishing. This included an ill-fated AMC Javelin project at the Bonneville Salt Flats, where rain turned the dry lake into a quagmire. The key players from that project seamlessly filled important roles in the Jeep project. Walker Evans, the legendary off-road racer who prepped the Javelins, built the Jeeps. Fish, now the head of the premier off-road racing organization, gave AMC a place to race.

Mickey Thompson offered his services to contact celebrity candidates to race the inaugural event. It kicked off in Las Vegas at the Silverbird/SCORE Race of Champions during the third weekend of June 1978.

Walker Evans Racing Modifications

AMC delivered nine brand-new Jeep CJ-7s with the Renegade package to Walker's Riverside shop. The stock seats, windshield, gas tank, exhaust, tires, and wheels were all removed from the CJs. The plan was to build each

Jim Rader (left) was the head of Jeep Motorsport when the idea of a celebrity race was approved by the powers that be at AMC. He tasked Walker Evans with building the CJ-7 racers, Mickey Thompson with rounding up celebrities, and Sal Fish with administering the rules and regulations of the races. J. M. Bragg (right) was Rader's teammate at the time. (Photo Courtesy J. M. Bragg)

Jeep to SCORE's safety regulations and Class 3 (the short-wheelbase production class) rules.

Roll cages went in first; 75 linear feet of 2-inch chromoly tubing was used to create them in each Jeep. Thirteen more feet of tubing went into the front and rear bumpers. Further safety upgrades included a 24-gallon fuel cell. Mastercraft seats with seven-point harnesses and window nets held the occupants in place. A fire suppression system was installed in case things went really bad. Luckily, they were never needed.

Evans purchased special motor mounts built by Ray Russell's Four-Wheel-Drive Shop and added a second transmission mount in the rear for additional support. The differential housings were removed, welded, and trussed for extra durability, and larger axles were installed. Rough Country Suspension supplied its leaf spring packs and the shock absorbers, two at each wheel.

The engine was largely stock except for some bolt-on help from a Holley 500-cfm 2-barrel carburetor with a K&N air filter and air vents. Cragar supplied the headers and a Hot Pipe exhaust system to maximize exhaust flow. The transmissions each had a B&M Shift Kit, B&M Quick Click ratchet shifter, and an extra transmission cooler.

All of this rode on experimental (at the time) 11.5 x 15 Goodyear Wrangler RT tires wrapped around Cragar wheels. In total, with the suspension upgrades, the celebrity Jeeps had 7.5 inches of wheel travel. Each Jeep was painted in an available color from AMC. One was painted red, white, and blue to represent the racing colors. Celebrities often fought for that Jeep, and in the end, it was driven by the likes of James Garner and Ted Nugent.

Famous People Love Racing

Singers, movie stars, and television personalities have always been drawn to racing. Broadcast journalist Walter Cronkite raced a Volvo at road courses all over the Northeastern United States. Jackie Cooper held a land speed record at Bonneville and raced in the Sports Car Club of America (SCCA) for many years. Paul Newman, perhaps the greatest of all the celebrity racers, ushered in a new generation of racing celebrities, including Eric Bana, Patrick Dempsey, Jason Priestley, etc.

Off-road racing drew adventuresome racers from the start. At any given NORRA Mexican 1000 or Mint 400, you could bump into James Garner, Steve McQueen, orchestra leader Ray Conniff, or singer Michael Nesmith. Paul Newman took a stab at the 2004 Baja 1000 and performed very well.

1978 Silverbird/SCORE Race of Champions

Sal Fish had an idea to run an invitational short-course event for all previous class winners. Teaming with the Silverbird Casino and putting up an impressive $76,000 prize fund ($376,000 in 2024), the best of the best racers traveled to Las Vegas to compete on a 1.24-mile course at the Speedrome north of town. This was the starting point for many Mint 400 races.

This was also the premiere of the Jeep Celebrity Challenge with a cavalcade of stars wheeling specially modified CJ-7s. Among the entries were Arnold Schwarzenegger, James Brolin, Elke Sommer, Redd Fox, Dan Hagerty, Dick Smothers, Paul Williams, and Richard Roundtree. The special race traversed the same course as the seasoned off-road racers and lasted for 10 laps. Robert Conrad intended to race but was a no-show due to work commitments on the television mini-series *Centennial*.

Each celebrity was paired with an experienced off-road racer to help with the steep learning curve of racing a tall short-wheelbase vehicle on a bumpy, manmade course. AMC took every step possible to keep the drivers safe. Of those entered, Dick Smothers and James Brolin had racing experience on pavement. Some took the race very seriously, and others were less serious.

J. M. Bragg, who was assigned to Redd Foxx, could not get the *Sanford & Son* star out to practice or qualify. Finally, just before the race, Bragg lassoed him and took him outside the Speedrome and into the desert for some practice on Mint 400 roads that he knew well.

There was a qualifying session to set the grid for the race the following day. James Brolin and Grant Randall took the first spot by 1.12 seconds over Arnold Schwarzenegger and Ray Russell. Dick Smothers and Jim Hightower were third, 1 second behind Schwarzenegger and Russell. The rest of the field included Dan Haggerty and Don Adams, Richard Roundtree and Dick Montague, Elke Sommer and Dick Dahn, and then the missing Redd Foxx.

On race day, a strong wind swept over the Las Vegas Speedrome and added an extra challenge to the largely inexperienced field. At the drop of the green flag, the 8 Jeeps roared off for 10 laps.

Brolin jumped into the lead from the pole position, and Dick Smothers immediately pressured Schwarzenegger. Roundtree moved around Haggerty quickly as he got out of shape and recovered. Foxx's inexperience with the Jeep showed, as Sommer easily moved past him. Going into the second lap, the pressure from Smothers caused Schwarzenegger to make a driving error, and he rolled the

Big-Time Entertainers Turned Loose on Racetrack
continued

Lauded as a natural by his driving coach, Grant Randall, James Brolin took to the Jeep like a duck to water. Brolin swept the pole position in qualifying and won the race convincingly. (Photo Courtesy Judy Smith Collection/Off-Road Motorsports Hall of Fame)

This board shows how each team did and the money won. It was low-tech (even by 1978 standards), but it worked. (Photo Courtesy J. M. Bragg)

"Jeep Celebrity Challenge"

Car #	Driver/Co-Driver	Qual. Time	Starting Pos.	Finish Pos.	Race Time
1					
2	Richard Roundtree / Dick Montague	1:25:06	5th	3rd	$2,000
3	Redd Foxx / J.M. Bragg	—	7th	4th	Roll Over!
4	Dan Haggerty / Don Adams	1:22:76	4th		Twice Roll Over! D.N.F.
5	Dick Smothers / Gene Hightower	1:21:71	3rd	2nd	$3,000
6	Robert Conrad / Steve Mizel		DID NOT SHOW		
7	Arnold Schwarzenegger / Ray Russell	1:20:74	2nd		D.N.F. Roll Over!
8	James Brolin / Grant Randall	1:19:62	1st	1st	$20,000
9	Elke Sommer / Dick Dahn	1:29:66	6th		Mechanical D.N.F.

All drivers will be awarded a new Jeep CJ-7

Jeep and was unable to continue. Smothers hunted down Brolin as the field behind them began to self-destruct. Haggerty was righted and continued forward, and Elke Sommer had a mechanical issue and was forced to park the Jeep. Richard Roundtree moved into third place.

Halfway through the race, Foxx's inexperience caught up to him, and he rolled the Jeep but went far enough to be credited with fourth place. Brolin kept the pace and took a 9-second margin of victory over Smothers.

While it was an expensive day for the American Motors Corporation and Walker Evans, it provided job security, as the celebrities made lots of repair work for his team. The upside was that after the race was televised, AMC saw great dividends from sponsoring the race. The experiment worked.

1978 SCORE Off-Road World Championships

The SCORE Off-Road World Championships brought big spectator numbers every year. It was the perfect venue for tens of thousands of spectators and millions more on television to see their favorite entertainers battle it out over Mickey Thompson's chunk of Baja.

The lineup was slightly different than in Las Vegas two months prior. Actor Clint Walker was known mostly for Westerns. Comedienne Ruth Buzzi was known for her work on the television show *Laugh In*. Ken Norton was a professional boxer. Dick Smothers was a race driver of note on pavement (and one half of the Smothers Brothers). James Garner had solid off-road racing experience. Kent McCord was in the television show *Adam-12*. Basketball star Wilt Chamberlain and singer Ricky Nelson were signed up but had to be replaced at the last minute, so Kent McCord's

Troy Donahue (left) was lucky to draw J. M. Bragg (right) as his driving coach when Donahue was a last-minute substitute for Robert Conrad. (Photo Courtesy J. M. Bragg)

co-star Martin Milner and actor Troy Donahue gladly filled in.

The Jeep Celebrity Challenge was the finale to the weekend of racing at Riverside. The green flag flew, and Kent McCord stormed off into the lead and was chased by James Garner. Martin Milner and Clint Walker fell in behind with a hard-charging Dick Smothers, who was moving upward quickly through the field.

Toward the end of the second lap, Smothers had masterfully maneuvered from the sixth starting spot to second place, and he pressured McCord for the lead. Meanwhile, toward the rear, Ken Norton showed a driving style that defied description. He left no part of the racecourse untouched. Buzzi, who was leery of mixing it up in the fight, stayed toward the back of the pack. Clint Walker looked steady and drove a smart race and eventually took fourth place.

Dick Smothers was on a mission. He passed Kent McCord before the end of the second lap and started to run away. Garner, not being one to back down from a fight, moved up to challenge him. McCord, perhaps from trying to stay in the lead or chasing down Smothers, damaged his suspension and had to pull off. Garner pushed onward.

Some time in those early laps, Martin Milner hooked a rut and flipped the Jeep. Luckily, he landed back on his wheels, was able to continue, and looked every bit like an off-road racing veteran. Norton kept finding new lines around and off the track, as he chased some officials around the infield and almost hit a water truck. It was not long before the inevitable happened, and he plowed a front bumper into the dirt and went end over end. After the race, Garner, being ever the gentleman, spoke about Norton's race.

"I'll say one thing, he sure is brave," Garner said. "I was afraid to pass him. I didn't want to be part of his accident. I

The second 1978 Jeep Celebrity Challenge at Riverside International Raceway featured the following participants (from left to right): Clint Walker, Troy Donahue, Ken Norton, Ruth Buzzi, Martin Milner, Kent McCord, Dick Smothers, and James Garner. (Photo Courtesy tracksidephoto.com)

The race did not last long for Donahue and Bragg, as the Quadratrac transfer case failed during the opening laps. (Photo Courtesy tracksidephoto.com)

knew it was coming."

Garner noticed that his steering began getting loose and his transmission was slipping. With Smothers pulling farther ahead, looking forward to a $20,000 prize money payday, Garner backed off to preserve a second-place

Big-Time Entertainers Turned Loose on Racetrack
continued

finish and $3,000 in prize money. Milner recovered from his rollover and nabbed third place and $2,000 in prize money. Clint Walker was steady and finished in fourth place. He was followed by Buzzi— or maybe not! Buzzi tooled around at the back of the pack and was in way over her head. Her driving coach, Ray Russell, saw what was happening and had Ruth pull off at the bottom end of the course. He switched seats with her and drove the last few laps. Troy Donahue never had a chance to fight, as his transfer case failed early in the race.

The aftermath of the Ken Norton wreck made two things apparent. First, the Walker Evans crew built a safe racer. Second, they had a lot of work to do after the race. (Photo Courtesy tracksidephoto.com)

James Garner leads a group down a short paved section around the famous Turn 6 at Riverside Raceway in pursuit of Dick Smothers (not pictured). (Photo Courtesy track-sidephoto.com)

Dick Smothers drove an impressive race and passed most of the field to win at the famed Riverside Raceway. Smothers receives his trophy while still seated in the CJ-7 Renegade. (Photo Courtesy tracksidephoto.com)

radiator early on in the race and was never a factor. The Emery entry was plagued with issues and never posed a threat. David Bryan had a clean run on the California side and slogged the 2.5-ton, long-nose Jeep CJ-6 through the desert.

Heading into Arizona, it was Adams who had the hot setup. He lengthened his lead each lap to win by almost an hour. Second place was a determined David Bryan, who utilized the Jeep for what it was originally built for: rally. The Arizona side of the race is completely different than the California desert with smoother, winding roads and fewer rocks.

Bryan knew he had to drive hard to catch up to the Hightowers. So, he cinched up his seat belts, enjoyed the rally seats, and turned it loose. On the first Arizona lap, he closed the gap to almost nothing. On the second lap, he clawed his way to a 3-minute cushion to take second place.

"Ten years later, I was pre-running the Baja 1000 with Gene Hightower," Bryan said in a recent interview. "It was his final race. We were on the road for 6 days going over the course from Ensenada to La Paz. Every day, he asked me how I made up all that time and beat his team at Parker that year."

Mexicali 250

The springtime visit to Baja quickly became a favorite among teams. It broke up the long break between the Parker and Mint races. Nicer still, the racecourse was not very rough, so you wouldn't tax your machine too much before the Mint, which had a rough racecourse. That darn Dodge was on a tear again and quite easily dispatched the competition. Its longer wheelbase, better suspension, and driver were formidable for years to come.

Dick Montague and J. M. Bragg had a battle for second in their CJ-7s

After a disappointing Parker 400, Bragg bounced back with a strong second-place finish behind the Dodge. (Photo Courtesy tracksidephoto.com)

Dick Montague and Don Campbell ran fourth at the Parker 400 the month before and found themselves in third place at Mexicali. Things were looking up for Montague. (Photo Courtesy tracksidephoto.com)

It was a steady drive and easy win by over an hour for the wily veteran. Ray Russell enjoyed this new team, as each Jeep had won so far this season. (Photo Courtesy tracksidephoto.com)

with Dale Frahm, Roger Mears, and the Randall Jeep Honcho not far behind. Mears faded in his not fully desert race–prepped CJ-7. Frahm had a flat that cost him time, and the Honcho reportedly lost brakes and faded back.

Montague chased Bragg down a bit heading into Cohabuzo Junction (within 5 minutes). Heading north toward Laguna Salada, J. M. Bragg opened up a lead of 15 minutes and held it all the way back to Mexicali for a second-place finish.

Ray Russell ripped around the Mexicali racecourse like it was a Sunday drive. He won the class by 1 hour and 10 minutes. David Bryan, in a CJ-6, took second place and beat Don Adams's CJ-7 by 17 minutes.

Mint 400

This Mint 400 was the debut of the Walker Evans–built Jeep Honcho for Roger Mears and Mike Moore in Class 3. The pair drove a CJ-7 loaned to them by Evans to accrue some class points for the first two events of the SCORE season. Now, it was time to unleash the Firecracker Red Budweiser-liveried Honcho and go after that darn Dodge.

There were over 30 entries in the class, as the Mint always brought out the big numbers. Many were there because the Mint is a bucket list item. Still, over half the field was considered a threat for a good finish.

The anticipated fight between Mears and the Dodge

Competitors at the start of the 1979 Mint 400 were full of hope and determination. However, most did not complete the first lap. (Photo Courtesy Brad Russell)

Hampered with teething problems on the new build, the team used the race as a test session for the Budweiser Honcho. *It took 14 hours for Mears and Moore to finish.* (Photo Courtesy tracksidephoto.com)

Second place was the best that Dale Frahm and Bob Grimes could do against the Dodge. They finished exactly 1 hour behind, which meant that the Dodge picked up 15 minutes on every lap over the CJ. (Photo Courtesy tracksidephoto.com)

Starting in 389th place at the Mint 400 makes for miserable conditions to drive through, even if you are as talented as Ray Russell, who had Clairmont Hamm riding along. The long day was filled with traffic to pass, dust to ingest, and quickly deteriorating road conditions. Russell ate it up, and so did his CJ-7 for the win. (Photo Courtesy Brad Russell)

never really materialized, as teething issues hit the newly built Honcho. The debut became a testing session that accrued far less glory, but the lessons learned about the new build were valuable. As the Dodge sailed off into the desert, it was a battle for scraps among the Jeep- and International-mounted crews.

J. M. Bragg was in the hunt early, but his rear axle housing started to succumb to the pounding. Bragg's crew welded on it to keep the CJ-7 moving at several pit stops. Bragg kept fighting to get to the finish and was rewarded with fourth place almost 3 hours behind.

Dale Frahm and Bob Grimes had a battle with Sherman Balch in his Scout on the time sheets. The two entries started almost 2 hours apart because the Mint still launched vehicles by drawn number, not by class. Even though Balch started 60th off the line and the Jeep 221st, it was Frahm who came away with second place by 15 minutes. Mears and Moore nursed the Honcho home fifth after 14 long hours.

Ray Russell and Clairmont Hamm drew a horrible starting position: 389th out of 471 entries. That meant several things: First, there would be a lot of dust. Second, there would be a lot of passing in that dust. Third, the course would be much rougher than those earlier in his class. Russell and

Hamm's teammates Don Adams and Jason Myers, in an identical CJ-7, drew the 98th starting position and were able to drive in better conditions.

The field thinned out quickly, as it does at the Mint. The teammates of Russell and Adams were clearly in the lead and battled by the end of the second lap. The rear engine Jeep CJ-2A of Glen Emery and Steve Catlin was a distant third, with Don and Ed Bray lurking in another Jeep.

Adams kept up his pace and tried to stay ahead of his teammate who was a multiple time winner of the Mint. At the final pit on the last lap, Adams's engine quit and would not crank. Warren Baird, one of the builders of the two Jeeps, was at the pit and looked for jumper cables, but they were missing. He pulled the battery from the pit truck, and in a dangerous maneuver, he turned the battery upside down and did a post-to-post jump. Luckily, it worked—instead of blowing up in his face. Baird made sure that the alternator was charging, which it was, and sent them on to the finish.

The downtime at the Valley of Fire pit was enough to allow Russell and Hamm to sail into the Speedrome with the win by 9 minutes. Emery finished in third place, and the Brays took fourth place. Jeeps took all of the top five positions in the class.

Baja Internacional

A week after one of their own won the Indianapolis 500, racers gathered in Ensenada for the annual loop around Baja Norte. Rick Mears was talked about just as

Dale Frahm and Bob Grimes could not catch the Dodge, but they were able to get within 30 minutes for second place. (Photo Courtesy tracksidephoto.com)

Mears, Moore, and the *Budweiser Honcho*

The sight of the big red Honcho bounding across the desert thrilled spectators and quickened the pulse of competitors in front of them when the "This Bud's for You" text on the front push bar appeared in their rearview mirrors. (Photo Courtesy tracksidephoto.com)

For many off-road racing fans in the late 1970s and early 1980s, no sight that was more thrilling than seeing a certain Firecracker Red Jeep Honcho thundering across the desert. Clad in Budweiser decals, shod with Goodyear Tires, driven by Roger Mears, and owned and co-driven by Mike Moore, the *Budweiser Honcho* was the most popular Jeep.

The Budweiser Honcho

In reality, three Jeep J-10 Honcho pickups were built for and by Mike Moore's racing team from 1979 through 1983. Truck 1, as it was known, was the original, and it was used for desert and short-course events. Truck 2 was built prior to 1981 and was strictly for short-course, off-road racing events, such as Riverside. Truck 3 was a new replacement for Truck 1 with upgraded suspension.

For now, let's review the original *Budweiser Honcho*. Truck 1 was built by Walker Evans Racing in Riverside, California. The primary builders were Tom Strong and Chris Robinson, who were two of the best at their craft.

Before the short-course truck was built, the Mike Moore team modified the desert truck, as most other teams did. The spare tires and 5-gallon water container were removed, and everything was lightened as much as possible. (Photo Courtesy tracksidephoto.com)

Drivetrain

Under the hood was an AMC 401-ci V-8 built by Traco Engineering. It featured a set of Hooker Headers, a Mallory Ignition, a Holley double-pumper carburetor, a custom crank and camshafts, and trick heads. The beast of an engine was fed from a 53-gallon fuel cell that was mounted in the bed of the truck and connected with Earl's best aircraft-style AN fittings at the time.

The engine was mated to a Chrysler 727 automatic transmission that was built by B&M Transmissions. At the tail end of the unit was a Quadratrac transfer case.

Dana differentials resided under each end of the truck. A Dana 44 was featured on the front and rear. The truck was originally built with a Dana 60 rear end, but to save and balance some weight, they eventually went with a Dana 44 in the rear. Both housings were heavily reinforced and strengthened by Summers Brothers Axles.

Suspension

The suspension featured four Rough Country Shocks per corner and specially arched leaf springs. There were laterally mounted kicker shocks that attached to the differential housing and the forward mount of the leaf spring pack. This shock stopped axle wrap, or, as some call it, "axle tramp." Essentially, it helps to keep the tires planted more firmly on a loose surface under heavy acceleration.

Interior

There were no frills. It had two seats, three gauges, and lots of chromoly tubing.

The Pre-Runner

At the same time that Truck 1 was being built, a second truck was constructed in much the same way as the race truck. As far as performance, the suspension was the same as the race version. The engine was de-tuned a little for pump gas, and the exhaust was quieter.

The big differences were in the interior of the cab. The pre-runner still had its side windows, door panels, carpet, and air conditioning. The stock seats were removed, and race seats were mounted along with five-point harnesses.

The pre-runner was painted identically to the race truck. It was so identical at a casual glance that the pre-runner was used in some of the commercials featuring the race truck.

Roger Mears

Roger Mears was born on April 24, 1947, in Wichita, Kansas, to Bill and Mae Louise (affectionately known as "Skip") Mears. He was the first of two sons. His little brother Rick came along four years later. The Mears family was a racing family. Bill could be found on dirt tracks around Wichita and as far away as Oklahoma accumulating wins and championships. His sons followed in his footsteps.

In unforgiving terrain, such as the terrain at the 1980 Mint 400, the suspension is key to the truck surviving the Nevada desert. Tom Strong designed this Honcho's suspension for a hard-charging Roger Mears. (Photo Courtesy tracksidephoto.com)

Mears, Moore, and the *Budweiser Honcho*
continued

By 1955, Bill and Skip bought an excavator and made the move from mechanic to excavation business owner. The Kansas winters limited his opportunities to get work, so they packed up and moved the family west to Bakersfield, California. The family worked together in the business and on the race cars.

Roger grew up racing go-karts, motorcycles, and eventually a dune buggy at the Ascot off-road events in Los Angeles. Before long, he took offers to drive Midgets, Stock Cars, Modifieds, open-wheel cars at Pikes Peak, and whatever he could find. Then came the SCORE Off-Road World Championships at Riverside International Raceway in 1973. Roger built a reputation as a winner there. Most years, he raced in multiple classes. Roger is the winningest driver in the history of the Riverside off-road races.

By 1979, Roger received a call from AMC Motorsports manager Jim Rader and was hired to drive the Mike Moore Jeep Honcho in the Southern California Off Road Enthusiasts (SCORE) and High Desert Racing Association (HDRA) series. The team was an instant favorite with the fans, and the rivalry with Dodge factory driver Rod Hall fueled both impassioned fanbases.

Roger and Mike Moore won 12 of their 22 events together. Roger and the *Budweiser Honcho* were featured in print advertisements, television commercials, and television shows. They also made in-person appearances.

Roger moved on to race Indy Cars and recorded 15 top-10 finishes, with three fourth-place finishes being his best result (at Riverside, Mid-Ohio, and Atlanta). In 1983, he was voted the most improved driver despite competing without the latest technology available. Roger returned to off-road racing in 1985 with Nissan and ran short-course and desert programs.

Roger and his wife, Carol, who have been married for 43 years (at the time of this writing), retired to the Baja Peninsula. Skip Mears passed away in 2015, and Bill Mears followed in 2022 at the age of 93.

Mike Moore

Mike Moore is a wealthy Texas oil man who one day decided to enjoy himself and race off-road. He knew he wanted a Jeep Honcho, for Walker Evans to build it, and for a high-profile driver to drive it. Moore contacted Jim Rader at American Motors to see who might be available to drive for his new team. Rader suggested Roger Mears, who he knew was looking for a factory ride.

Moore could not believe that a quality driver like Mears was on the open market. The two met in Riverside at Walker Evans's shop and hammered out a deal.

Truck 2 and Truck 3

The short-course racing scene had Moore thinking that since it seemed to be the way off-road racing was going, he needed a short course-only truck. That idea became Truck 2. Before this, most teams converted their desert machines for the occasional short-course event. Spare tires and parts were removed, a smaller fuel cell might be used to save weight, and custom grooved tires were installed.

Where extra weight was required for a desert machine to live after 1,000 miles of Baja or 400 miles through Nevada, weight is the enemy in short-course racing. Truck 2 was built with emphasis on saving every ounce wherever they could. The engine needed more power, as reliability was not the focus for 12 or so laps around a 1- or 2-mile course.

This truck was built in house by Tom Strong, who built Truck 1 while working for Walker Evans. They were the first of two in-house built Jeep Honchos.

Truck 2 saw duty in 1981 and 1982 at Pikes Peak, Riverside, Phoenix, and Colorado. Truck 3 was built in response to radical rule changes in the four-wheel-drive class that allowed for more innovative modifications to the suspension. This suspension setup was based on torsion bars.

The team planned to debut the truck at the 1982 Mint 400, but Roger was stuck in Michigan due to a rain-delayed Indy Car race. To garner points, Mike Moore took the start but immediately pulled into his pit before the truck got dirty. The last time the *Budweiser Honcho* attended a desert race was at the Frontier 250 in December 1982. Mears and Moore broke Truck 1 early.

ROGER MEARS OFF-ROAD RACING CAREER

• Four Baja 1000 class wins
• Two season points championships in SCORE and HDRA
• One Mickey Thompson sport truck championship
• Twenty wins at the Riverside Off-Road World Championships
• Five Pikes Peak International Hill Climb class wins
• 1986 enshrinement in the Bob Elias Kern County Motorsports Hall of Fame
• 2020 enshrinement in the Off-Road Motorsports Hall of Fame

Mears versus Hall

It took only a few races for the fans to acknowledge the rivalry that formed for wins and championships between Jeep and Dodge. This was years before Chrysler absorbed Jeep, so it was more like AMC versus Dodge.

Dodge had three cagey veterans heading its team. Bill Stroppe built the truck, Rodney Hall drove, and Jim Fricker occupied the passenger's seat as the mechanic, navigator, and caretaker of Rodney.

The Jeep had a well-funded ballsy owner, who liked to ride along, as well as a young but supremely talented driver. The truck was built at a shop owned by a man who learned from Bill Stroppe. The two teams were so different.

What the fans believed was a rivalry was anything but. Mears and Hall had a lot of respect for each other. No matter what happened out in the desert, it did not affect the friendship. That is not to say there were not some heated moments behind the wheel. There were, but things always got straightened out quickly after the dust settled over the desert.

Urine Trouble

Roger Mears recently recalled a situation during a race in Barstow, California, in 1980. Roger started one position in front of Rod Hall and was determined to stay there. Late in the second of four 60-mile laps, Roger was still out front when he started to feel a front tire going down.

Moore said that a pit was not far and to keep driving on it. Roger knew he was losing time, but where was Hall? The thick Barstow dust made it hard to see anything behind you. Suddenly, Hall slammed into the back of the Jeep Honcho with such force that it drove Roger's and Moore's heads back into the plastic rear window.

"It was a heck of a hit—maybe the worst I ever got," Roger said.

Roger was mad. He and Hall usually raced each other clean. Why did he hit him so hard? Roger punished the truck to try and keep Hall in range. Suddenly, the pit was in view. Who was pitted right ahead of the Budweiser crew? Rod Hall.

Roger saw that Hall was not in the truck as it was getting serviced. Roger jumped out of his Jeep and ran into Hall's pit to look for him. He was told that Hall was behind the pit truck. Roger came around the truck, and there was Hall with his back to him. Roger, who was very angry, spun Hall around and yelled at him. However, Roger felt that something was not right. He glanced down to see that Hall was peeing on his driving suit and shoes. What Roger didn't realize when he grabbed Rod Hall to spin him around was that he was relieving himself.

"It was one of Rod's favorite stories to tell people, and he cracked up every time," Roger said.

The End

By 1982, Roger Mears had his eyes set on a switch to Indy Cars. It was something that Mike Moore supported. Since 1978, Roger had sporadic rides in less-than-competitive equipment. By 1982, he had a full-time ride with the Machinists Union Indy Car Team. Without Roger behind the wheel, Mike Moore shuttered the team.

Moore sold off his entire team to Larry Casey and his sons Tim and Chris. The livery was changed from AMC Firecracker Red to the colors of Casey's company, La Paz Drink Mixes. The trucks competed for the next several years with some success, including a Mint 400 victory.

In 1983, the Budweiser Honchos *received new life when Larry Casey, owner of La Paz Drink Mixes, bought the entire Mike Moore team.*

Some competitors ran in both the Class 3 and Class 4 races with the same truck. There was only about 20 minutes between races to wipe down the truck, change numbers, change tires, and clean the windshield. Roger Mears, with the Budweiser Honcho, has the Class 4 number displayed on the truck. (Photo Courtesy tracksidephoto.com)

Coming off the off-camber Thompson's Ridge, the course featured a tricky transition going opposite camber in a right-hand corner. Track designers added a bump to upset the racers and give the crowds in the stands a show. Ray Russell knew the fast way through that section. (Photo Courtesy tracksidephoto.com)

After qualifying, Grant Randall, in the roofless Honcho, found himself with the pole position followed by Mears, Hall (also running the same truck in both classes), and Ray Russell. It shaped up to be a great race. The challenge for the teams running in both Class 3 and Class 4 was that there was only 15 minutes between the races.

This made for a mad scramble to wipe the trucks off, apply the class-appropriate numbers, and change tires.

At the start, Allen Hightower and Roger Mears had a slight advantage at the first turn, with Randall and the *Crazy Horse* Bronco glued to their tails. Ray Russell and that Dodge were within a truck length, followed by the

In the second turn of the Class 4 race, Allen Hightower leads the pack and is followed by Roger Mears, the Crazy Horse *Bronco, and Grant Randall's Honcho. The white Jeep front end that is barely in the right side of the frame was driven by Ray Russell. (Photo Courtesy tracksidephoto.com)*

To the victor goes the big trophy and a micro-phone in your face. From left to right are Miss BFGoodrich, Roger Mears, the announcer, Mike Moore, and Skip Mears at Riverside. (Photo Courtesy tracksidephoto.com)

Balch Scout. Mears pressured Hightower in the tight hairpin section and was impatient to get past.

At the far end of the course (Thompson's Ridge), Hightower bobbled just enough to allow Mears to get his nose under the leader. Hightower, who was sideways, could not get the power to the ground as well as Mears, who was pointed straight. Mears motored into the lead and into the distance.

With little momentum to stay up on the ridge, Randall, Russell, and the Dodge slipped past. Russell had good momentum and moved into second place. He was followed by the Dodge and Grant Randall all the way to the finish.

Baja 1000

For the first time since 1973, and the first time in the short history of SCORE, the Baja 1000 returned to La Paz. It was an excellent way to close out the 1970s and return to where it all started in 1967. Sal Fish promised the race would return to La Paz about every 4 years going forward.

This was notable because it was as close (987 miles) to a true 1,000-mile race that Sal Fish could make it. At the start, there were 247 hopeful teams, and 123 finished within the official time limit.

Everything came together for the Mike Moore team—and not a moment

It is a long way to La Paz, as is evidenced by this official course map. (Map Courtesy J. M. Bragg)

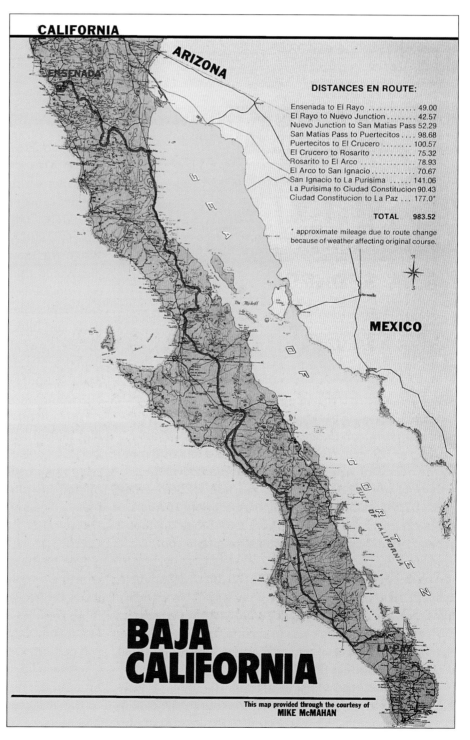

CALIFORNIA

ARIZONA

ENSENADA

DISTANCES EN ROUTE:

Ensenada to El Rayo 49.00
El Rayo to Nuevo Junction 42.57
Nuevo Junction to San Matias Pass 52.29
San Matias Pass to Puertecitos 98.68
Puertecitos to El Crucero 100.57
El Crucero to Rosarito 75.32
Rosarito to El Arco 78.93
El Arco to San Ignacio 70.67
San Ignacio to La Purisima 141.06
La Purisima to Ciudad Constitucion 90.43
Ciudad Constitucion to La Paz . . . 177.0*

TOTAL   983.52

* approximate mileage due to route change because of weather affecting original course.

MEXICO

GULF OF CALIFORNIA

BAJA CALIFORNIA

This map provided through the courtesy of
MIKE McMAHAN

Roger Mears drove every inch of the course from Ensenada to La Paz. He and Mike Moore did it faster (by 4 hours) than any other 4x4 vehicle that was entered in the race. (Photo Courtesy tracksidephoto.com)

Jason Myers started the race and had a great 12 miles until the top end of the engine broke. His chase crew did an amazing job finding the parts and completing the engine repair in about 3 hours. Limited to 3,000 rpm by the boss, Don Adams, the team trundled down the peninsula and just barely cleared checkpoints before they closed. They finished after 32.5 hours (roughly 10 hours slower than they hoped). Mindbogglingly, they still took second place! (Photo Courtesy tracksidephoto.com)

too soon. Mechanic Tom Strong did an amazing job prepping the Honcho for the long race. Roger Mears drove flawlessly for almost 23 hours, and Moore navigated a perfect race. The Dodge was in second, but 4 hours after the Honcho, and he was barely ahead of a Bronco that was only 10 minutes behind.

Sometimes, the worst things in the longest races happen very close to the start. This is true in the case of Don Adams and Jason Myers in their CJ-7. Instead of running their usual hot motor, Adams opted to run a Mouse motor. This means the compression was lowered and a smaller carburetor was installed along with a slightly smaller camshaft and valvetrain.

Twelve miles off the start line, the engine lost oil pressure, and Myers parked the Jeep and called for help. When the crew arrived and looked into the issue, they discovered that the pushrods were too short. The crew drove back to Ensenada and found the correct pushrods and new gaskets. They headed back to install the new parts and hoped that more damage would not occur. As the Jeep was almost ready, Adams contacted Myers and issued a mandate to keep the engine under 3,000 rpm. Now, 3 hours down to the field, it was a race to beat checkpoint closing times.

Meanwhile, up the road a ways, perennial favorite Ray Russell had an issue with broken wheels and flats. He lost gobs of time when a friend drove by with his own brake issues. Russell begged for their spare tire and offered his pit crew at the next checkpoint to fix their brakes. You can probably guess that the truck got a flat shortly after Russell left and limped a long way to the checkpoint. No good deed goes unpunished.

Problems struck the entire modified class. Instead of winning by driving fast, it was a race dictated by mechanics. A Bronco managed to get a bit of a lead. Russell had more troubles and parked it. Myers and Adams plodded along at 3,000 rpm, and a Scout went from one mechanical malady to the next, and those were the lucky ones!

After 31.5 hours, the Bronco made it to La Paz. Adams brought the Jeep home 1 hour later, a solid 3 hours ahead of the stricken Scout. Someone had to win, and others had to lose, but Baja always wins in the end.

1979 Mickey Thompson Off-Road Grand Prix

When Mickey Thompson formed SCORE, it was an acronym for Short Course Off-Road Enterprises. When he came up with the idea to do spectator friendly events on his own, he had not yet been approached by the Mexican government to take over the Baja races. He later renamed it SCORE International to reflect organizing races in two countries. He had the Riverside race, which he started in 1973, but he envisioned more. As SCORE (now under the guidance of Sal Fish) was the leader in desert-racing promotion, Thompson formed his own team to bring off-road racing even deeper into the metro area of Los Angeles.

Mickey Thompson Entertainment Group (MTEG) approached the impressive open-air stadium in Los Angeles (the Memorial Coliseum), which was the home of the Los Angeles Rams of the National Football League and the 1932 and 1984 Summer Olympics. It sounded crazy to truck in tons of dirt and cover the floor of the stadium (but not the football field) and build a chunk of Baja. Even crazier was building a race track up the steps to the peristyles to race around them. If you ever knew Mickey Thompson, nothing was ever entirely impossible.

On the third weekend of June 1979, Mickey Thompson and track builder Dick Dahn, who was an accomplished off-road racer himself, converted a football stadium into a racetrack. As it turns out, the Coliseum was no stranger to it.

A Quick History Lesson

In 1903, when the area was known as Agriculture Park, there were some auto exhibitions for prizes. In 1945, as WWII wound down, race promoter Bill White decided that it would be easy to pave the Coliseum and make a quarter-mile track. Midget races were popular in California at the time, and they were invited to race inside the Coliseum. Two races happened in 1945 that drew more than 36,000 spectators for each one. By 1946, they ran 15 races. Racing politics killed the events in 1947 after just five races. A short resurgence happened in 1948, when a banked board track was constructed in the Coliseum, but the crowds didn't show up by then. The stadium was without the sweet smell of racing gas until 1979.

A Show for Everyone

Thompson put on a thunderous event—complete with full-size trucks in two- and four-wheel drive, mini trucks, Baja Bugs, VW-powered race cars, and stunt driving. The Jeep Celebrity Challenge joined in the show and added the

One of the unique aspects of racing in the Los Angeles Memorial Coliseum is driving the 80 feet down from the peristyle to the floor. Celebrity racers took to it quickly. (Photo Courtesy trackidephoto.com)

touch of Hollywood that Southern California events desire. Celebrities who joined the race included Judy Norton Taylor from television's *The Waltons*, *CHiPs* cast member Robert Pine, actor Chad Everett, country singer Charley Pride, Los Angeles Rams defensive end Fred Dryer, and Olympic gold medal winner Bruce Jenner. Singer Vikki Carr was back for another try, as was the "Motor City Madman" Ted Nugent.

The evening featured two heats for the celebrities. In Heat 1, Vikki Carr rocketed off into the lead followed closely by Bruce Jenner, Ted Nugent, and Fred Dryer. In an action-packed first lap, singer Lou Rawls found himself on his roof. Rawls comes by racing honestly, as his father was a notorious street racer. Several others got sideways and

1979 Mickey Thompson Off-Road Grand Prix
continued

and his driving coach Grant Randall ended their weekend prematurely by tumbling off the hair-raising Thompson's Ridge at 75 mph and going end over end before coming to rest.

Heading into the first race, James Brolin was considered the favorite due to his practice times and a pole position in qualifying. The real surprise in qualifying was the greasy fast times of country singer Tanya Tucker, who was second. John Schneider, Larry Wilcox, and Patrick Duffy were very quick in the second and third rows.

Tucker outdueled Brolin down the Oklahoma land rush start and stayed ahead going into the first corner. Brolin was glued to her bumper as they started around the racecourse with Schneider, Wilcox, and Duffy right behind. Brolin tried everything he could, but Tucker stayed staunchly in the lead. John Schneider had a mechanical issue and pulled off the course. Larry Wilcox edged past Patrick Duffy in the closing laps, but Tucker and Brolin were checked out, and that was the finishing order.

In Heat 2, Schneider's Jeep was repaired, and he returned to the track as the Jeeps were ready for another six laps to determine the big money winners. James Brolin was a natural in a Jeep. He was certainly dialed in to Riverside in the second race, as he ran away with the win, another $20,000 check, and another new Jeep. Schneider redeemed himself, kept the Jeep together, and took a commanding second place to record a third-place finish for the weekend and a $2,000 check. Patrick Duffy was third in

James Brolin accepts his first-place trophy after an epic battle with country singer Tanya Tucker. Brolin was two for two in Jeep celebrity racing. No one else could say that in its short history. Note Walker Evans's ever-present cowboy hat over the trophy. (Courtesy Judy Smith Collection/Off-Road Motorsports Hall of Fame)

the race but second for the weekend and took $3,000 from AMC in the process. Vikki Carr and Tanya Tucker finished fourth and fifth after some rough racing. Denver Pyle and Larry Wilcox both had mechanical issues and did not finish the second race.

Into the 1980s

Jeep rode a wave into the new decade. Roger Mears and Don Adams carried the Jeep colors forward with the Randall family and Doug Robinson on their heels. Two stalwart competitors, J. M. Bragg and Ray Russell, stepped aside for a time and shuttered their teams to concentrate on other opportunities. Bragg returned in 1984, but Russell, aside from one race in 1981 in a two-wheel-drive Ford, didn't race again.

Ray Russell passed away on May 2, 2007, in a vehicle accident near Las Vegas, Nevada. Russell left an indelible mark on off-road racing and Jeep history. (Photo Courtesy tracksidephoto.com)

CHAPTER 5

THE 1980s

The United States hosted the world for the 1980 Winter Olympics in Lake Placid, New York, and the 1984 Summer Olympics in Los Angeles, California. The US abandoned the 1980 Summer Olympics in Moscow, Russia, due to political and humanitarian reasons. In addition, Mount St. Helens, an active volcano, had a massive eruption that caused a deadly landslide, resulting in 57 deaths and $3 billion in damage.

1980

The new decade started with more manufacturer involvement in off-road racing than before. Jeep, Dodge, Ford, Datsun, and General Motors were all in to show the toughness of their products. Involvement from aftermarket performance products also stepped up with associate sponsorships from suspension, lighting, and exhaust companies. More predominant were the tire wars between Goodyear, BFGoodrich, Sandblaster, Formula Desert Dog, and Bridgestone.

Parker 400

There were 467 entries that came to Parker, Arizona. After an incredibly hard Baja 1000 closed out the 1970s, teams welcomed the three month break to lick their wounds and repair their Jeeps. This year, the race started with an Arizona lap, the California lap, and a second lap through Arizona.

The production class was chock full of heavy hitters. Mears had a driveline issue that cost him half an hour right off the start.

Mike Randall and Bob Bower were flying, but in the Cunningham Wash, Mike went too fast into a corner and rolled the Honcho. Luckily, it landed back on its wheels—albeit one of them was flat. Bower changed the tire, which put them back on the road. An International passed the Honcho during the tire change, so it was paramount to catch and pass it.

John Randall drove the California side so quickly that he was in second place. On the final Arizona lap, Mike was back behind the wheel. The International was about 10 minutes behind, followed by the CJ-7 of Doug Robinson and Charlie Mason, which had a damaged rear fender due to the driver of a Ford pickup who lacked passing skills.

Doug Robinson, shown on the California side of the border, set a good pace for the CJ-7s maiden voyage and netted second place. (Photo Courtesy tracksidephoto.com)

TOP: Jeeps, such as this Scrambler in the Osborne Wash on the Arizona side of the Parker 400, soared in the early 1980s.

Mike and John Randall finished the first Arizona lap in the Honcho. At this point, they were still chasing the Dodge to make up time from an early rollover. (Photo Courtesy tracksidephoto.com)

Glenn Emery started three positions ahead of Don Adams and stayed there despite the fact that Adams held the lead for a time on corrected time. In the end, Emery had the advantage by 1 minute and 22 seconds. (Photo Courtesy tracksidephoto.com)

Mike Randall pushed hard to chase that darn Dodge and tried to stay ahead of the International and Robinson. Randall was content with second place because Hall's vehicle rarely broke. When Mike came around a corner, a Dodge sat along the road with a broken transfer case. A second identically painted Dodge was entered in Class 4, so Mike assumed that it was not Hall.

"Everyone was going crazy and cheering at the finish," Mike said. "Bob and I looked at each other and mentioned people were going awfully nuts for a second place. When we came to a stop, our crew said that it was Hall back there. That was how we found out we won.

Since the rollover, we broke the radio antenna off, so we had no radio for most of the race."

The International came in second about 23 minutes later, followed by Robinson for third, and then Mears.

Some people and race cars just do well in certain races. This seems to be the case with Glen Emery's rear-engine Jeep CJ-2A. Emery had a race on his hands with the CJ-7 of Don Adams. The modified race quickly boiled down to these two very different Jeeps. Adams led at the end of the first lap. Emery took the lead in California but by a slim margin. In the final loop, Adams pressed hard but fell 1 minute and 22 seconds short.

Mexicali 250

The opening Baja race of the new decade did not disappoint the 4x4 class fans, as action abounded between Mexicali and San Felipe.

Sometimes the smaller and seemingly easier events are the hardest on the field. One reason for that is in off-road racing, a 250-mile race is considered a sprint. Pit stops need to be quicker, and the driving has to be faster (rather than saving a vehicle as you would in a 1,000-mile endurance race).

Mears and Hall streaked away from the field early. By El Chinero, about one-third of the way into the race, Mears came through first with the Rod Hall/Jim Fricker Dodge 2 minutes behind. The Randall Honcho came through 14 minutes later. After pit stops, they headed off into a sandy portion of the course. At the next checkpoint, Mears was 18 minutes ahead of Hall, who had a flat tire. Randall followed, and Robinson quickly moved up.

Everything changed in the last 40 miles of the race. Mears was behind a single seater in heavy dust. He caught some air and landed on the single seater, which rolled both of them. Moore radioed for help from the crew, who was nearby. Hall went by the scene, and even though he saw Mears out of the truck with his helmet off, he stayed on the gas. On a rolling dirt road, Hall moved left to pass a buggy and hit a washout that sent the Dodge flying.

"I think I lost count of rollovers at seven," Hall said.

Simultaneously, Mike and John Randall gained the lead but then also rolled their Honcho. Along came Doug Robinson (in his second race) in his Ray Russell–built CJ-7, and he roared into Mexicali with the win.

This post-rollover shot of the wounded Budweiser Honcho *shows the truck headed to the finish line to take second place. (Photo Courtesy tracksidephoto.com)*

After a second rollover in two races, the Randalls joined the synchronized rolling team with Roger Mears and Rod Hall but were able to get back on their wheels for third place. (Photo Courtesy tracksidephoto.com)

Joining the trio of rollovers in the last quarter of the race was Rod Hall and Jim Fricker in a Dodge. It was a heck of a race until that point. (Photo Courtesy tracksidephoto.com)

Meanwhile, Mears and Moore were able to right the Honcho and repaired a wheel with the help of their crew. They came in 12 minutes later for second place. Mike and John Randall, also able to get going after their second rollover in two races, nabbed third place just 3 minutes behind Mears.

The modified rigs had their own battle early, with Grant Randall, Don Adams, two Broncos, and Mike Giurbino in a new Walker Evans–built Honcho all covered by a blanket at El Chinero. Between there and San Felipe, one Bronco and Giurbino had issues and dropped back.

The remaining Bronco had a good day and pulled ahead of Randall and Adams, who both reported flats. The Bronco motored into Mexicali 30 minutes ahead of Adams and Randall, who finished second and third, respectively.

Taking advantage of the misfortune of others in the last quarter of the race, Doug Robinson earned a win in the CJ-7's second outing. (Photo Courtesy tracksidephoto.com)

For a while, the race was going well for Mike Guirbino and Russ Derby in the Walker Evans–built Honcho before they lost time with transmission issues. (Photo Courtesy tracksidephoto.com)

Mint 400

For the first time in Mint 400 history, the 474 entries started bunched by class. This move made it easier for teams to keep track of their competition, but more importantly it made things safer. Of those 474 starters, only 139 saw the checkered flag.

Usually, a rookie stands little to no chance to do anything but get beat up by the Nevada desert. On this day, a rookie toppled the factory boys.

For three laps, Roger Mears and Rod Hall were out front. In the fourth lap, the front differential housing broke on Hall's Dodge. Then, Mears's engine expired soon thereafter.

Lowell Arnold built his J-10 Honcho at his auto center in Apache Junction, Arizona. He put in almost three consistent laps when his right front leaf spring broke, which slowed his pace considerably. In the pits, Arnold thought the broken spring would most likely hold for the last lap, albeit a slow one. His crew let him know that Mears had left for his final lap 90 minutes earlier, with Hall not far behind. Arnold steeled himself for one slow tour of the roughest lap in off-road racing.

Attrition dealt Arnold a strong hand, as he passed the Dodge and then Mears. He kept plugging away at a patience-testing pace through the rock garden and the soft silt, and then down the rocky two tracks as the lights of Las Vegas became visible. In what Arnold described as "the longest lap for a class-winning vehicle in Mint 400 history," he arrived back at the finish the winner. It pays to be persistent.

It was a good day for Jeep in the modified ranks, as Don Adams and Jason Myers took a commanding win in their CJ-7. Louie Toste, also in a CJ-7, managed to nab third place after fighting with some Broncos.

Driving a strong race and trading the driver's seat with Jason Myers every other lap to reduce driver fatigue, Don Adams and the tidy CJ-7 took a commanding lead in the class and never looked back. (Photo Courtesy tracksidephoto.com)

In his first major race with the Honcho built in his auto center, Lowell Arnold struck pay dirt. He won the off-road race with the biggest purse of the year and beat the best of the best. (Photo Courtesy tracksidephoto.com)

Baja Internacional

Springtime rains pummeled the Baja Peninsula and caused the 482-mile-long 1980 edition of the race to be labeled as the most treacherous to date.

It was a humdinger of a race when Roger Mears and Hall in the Dodge broke away from the field early and left everyone else to race for third. Mears was hard on the gas, got around Hall early, and was first into Ojos Negros. Mike Randall's Honcho and Doug Robinson's CJ-7 were not far behind in third and fourth place, respectively.

At each checkpoint, Mears stretched his lead until near Checkpoint 5, the Honcho was beached in a silt bed. It took about a half hour of furious digging to get moving again. By that time, Hall was 12 minutes ahead. Farther back, Randall had a scant 2 minutes on Robinson.

Mears knew that he had half the race to make up a lot of time on a rough course. The Honcho made it through more silt beds without stopping. Up in the mountains near Mike's Sky Ranch, Mears spotted and passed Hall and Fricker. Mears kept the pace up and motored into the finish first. After the race, a reporter asked Rod Hall what happened.

"Maybe Roger had a heavier foot this race," Hall replied.

The Randall Honcho disappeared and left Robinson to gather important points for third place, which tied him with Mears for the championship with two races left.

Don Adams and Jason Myers were something of an unbeatable combination with their Goodyear-shod CJ-7. The duo reported no downtime and no flats on their way to a convincing win over the Honcho of Paul Price and Dick Dahn by 47 minutes.

Involved in a four-way battle for the win, Doug Robinson took third place. (Photo Courtesy tracksidephoto.com)

Despite some time being stuck in a silt bed, Roger Mears and Mike Moore worked hard to pass the leader just after Mike's Sky Ranch and take the win. (Photo Courtesy tracksidephoto.com)

Paul Price and Dick Dahn fought hard all day but could not reel in the CJ-7 of Don Adams. (Photo Courtesy tracksidephoto.com)

Riverside Off-Road World Championships

It was time to go bake in the Southern California heat in August at the Riverside Raceway. It was a packed field of talent throughout the two 4x4 classes, and the battles were fiercely fought.

When it comes to off-road racing at Riverside, it would be foolish to bet against anyone on the entry list named Mears. This has been true since 1973, and it continued until the Riverside Raceway closed for good in 1988.

The flag dropped and 20 4x4s thundered down the ever-narrowing start to turn one. As expected, Mears edged Hall going into turn one with another Dodge and Honcho right behind. Behind the top four were a bevy of Jeeps and Broncos, but never bet against a Mears at Riverside. Hall followed closely for second and fought off another Dodge of Lee Wheeler in third. Dick Dahn was fourth in Paul Price's Honcho.

The old dirt track driver Grant Randall was right at home on the Riverside track in his modified Honcho. When the race started, it was all Jeep at the front, as a mix of Honchos and CJs tied up the top five places. Randall and Don Adams were out front and fought for the lead. Behind them were Allen Hightower and John Deetz.

Bill Mears, substituting for his son Roger since race mile 200, lights up the Baja night as he brings the Budweiser *Honcho home in second place to secure the season championship for his son and team owner Mike Moore. (Photo Courtesy tracksidephoto.com)*

It was not much of a fight, as Don Adams and Jason Myers dominated the modified rigs in Class 4. (Photo Courtesy tracksidephoto.com)

Randall managed to out-distance Adams by a football field early and held that lead to the end. Deetz managed to get around Hightower for third and fourth respectively.

Baja 1000

After the 1979 edition that ran the entire peninsula, the loop race format returned in 1980.

How bad do you want to win?

Six weeks before the Baja 1000, Roger Mears raced a midget at Ascot Raceway. Roger's car flipped at the famed track and he had two broken wrists and a broken left arm. Thirteen metal screws and two steel plates later, he hoped he would heal enough to make the Baja 1000.

At the time, the SCORE rule book required the driver must complete a minimum of 30 percent of the total race distance to earn points. The race was 660 miles long, which meant that Roger just had to make it 199 miles and hand off the Honcho to someone else. It was decided that Roger's dad, Bill, would drive the Honcho. Bill was an accomplished racer on Midwest and West Coast dirt tracks and had off-road experience.

Everyone knew that Roger was busted up and would only drive 30 percent of the race. The Bud Crew was all about keeping the Honcho running. Doug Robinson was all about staying ahead of the Bud Crew. There were other entries, but all eyes were on this battle.

Rod Hall in his Dodge took advantage of being second on the road and quickly dispatched a Land Cruiser ahead of him and set the pace. Robinson was behind Hall and tried to keep ahead of Mears, as everyone watched the race between these two for the championship.

Roger made it to race mile 200 and handed the *Budweiser Honcho* over to his dad. Robinson passed the Honcho during a fuel stop earlier, so Bill Mears had his work cut out to catch up. Bill had to be at least 30 seconds or less behind Robinson to win the championship for his son. A few hundred miles down the road, Robinson pulled off with a bad transmission. Mears and Moore thundered onward to finish the race in second place.

It was a high-attrition race for the modified rigs, as entry after entry succumbed to the desert with broken axles, blown engines, and broken suspensions. One of the few who managed to make it to the end relatively unscathed was the CJ-7 of Don Adams and Jason Myers, who won handily.

1981

The year began with the inauguration of Ronald Reagan as the 40th president of the United States. Moments after he was sworn into office, Iran released the American Embassy hostages after 444 days in captivity. The very next day, John DeLorean introduced his long-awaited sports car, the DeLorean DMC-12, to the world. It was an auspicious start to 1981.

Parker 400

The Jeep contingent came out in force for the annual Parker 400. New vehicles often debuted at Parker. It was at this event that spectators received their first glimpse of Doug Robinson's new Honcho for Class 3.

In what was a master course in driving, vehicle preparation, and race planning, Roger Mears and Mike Moore decimated the field. Not only did they win the class by 26 minutes over Rod Hall but they also beat the

Ken Correia and Charles Morrison ran a good consistent race and were rewarded with a third-place finish in Class 3. (Photo Courtesy tracksidephoto.com)

With a commanding performance, the Mike Moore team gave Roger Mears what he needed to not only win his class but also to beat the typically faster Class 8 trucks. (Photo Courtesy tracksidephoto.com)

Paul Price is going so fast that he can barely be seen in this photo. A field of Broncos and CJs saw the same view, as Price and Dick Dahn shared the driving and the win. (Photo Courtesy tracksidephoto.com)

1980 Mickey Thompson Off-Road Grand Prix

Even though Mickey Thompson lost a considerable amount of money on his 1979 race at the Los Angeles Memorial Coliseum, he had faith that word had spread and that the people would come. Advertising was increased across Southern California, and Jeep once again provided its CJ-7 fleet for the celebrities to thrash.

By 1980, hot new celebrities were incorporated into the lineup to attract younger fans. Willie Aames and Laurie Walters from the hit TV show *Eight Is Enough* were invited. Keeping up the *Dukes of Hazzard* theme, Catherine Bach agreed to drive. Country singer Charly McClain signed on, as did out of this world actor Dirk Benedict from *Battlestar Galactica*. Those returning to the Jeep wars included Ted Nugent, Larry Wilcox, and Patrick Duffy.

In the first heat, many of the experienced and favored drivers were tangled up in a jam, when Catherine Bach caught the inside of a turn and rolled 2.5 times after coming down from the peristyle. This allowed newcomers Aames and Benedict to squirt out into the lead. They were followed by veterans Larry Wilcox and Patrick Duffy. Ted Nugent got tangled and was too far behind to catch the racers who were in the first through fourth positions, and they became a parade and finished in that order.

Bach's Jeep was too damaged to be fixed in time for the second heat, so only seven participated. Ted Nugent was determined to stay clear of trouble and get the win. With a good start, he was in the lead within a few corners. Hot on his bumper was singer Charly McClain and Larry Wilcox, who knew if he stayed put, he would win the night due to the strength of his finish in the first heat.

Catherine Bach takes a severe cut inside of Charly McClain during practice for that evening's race. The celebrity drivers took this race very seriously. (Photo Courtesy tracksidephoto.com)

Eventual winner Ted Nugent stays out in front of Laurie Walters and Willie Aames. Nugent drove the sought-after red, white, and blue Jeep. (Photo Courtesy tracksidephoto.com)

Aames and Benedict, possibly a little overconfident with their successes in the previous heat, had troubles with the tighter corners on the floor of the Coliseum, which set them back. Laurie Walters moved up and started to push Wilcox for third. As Duffy, Aames, and Benedict languished at the rear of the field, McClain tried everything but could not get around Nugent, who took the win. Wilcox drove smart and took the $20,000 for the overall win and a new Jeep.

The End

After the Coliseum event, Jeep reassessed the series. It was a massive success in terms of advertising and sales bumps after the televised race. Jeep went to extreme lengths to protect the celebrities and their coach/ co-drivers. It even went as far as pre-admitting them into local hospitals and had air ambulances at each event. Ruth Buzzi recalled how unnerving it was to wear a hospital bracelet before even getting in the Jeep.

The downside was the liability of turning loose some of America's most beloved entertainers. The series was full of lots of near misses and small dings on various celebrities. As the series went on, a win was considered a badge of honor, and the celebrities were willing to lay their safety on the line to attain it.

Jim Rader realized that AMC had squeezed excellent value out of the series, but it was time to stop while they were ahead. AMC instructed Walker Evans to find homes for each of the Jeeps. Several were raced after more modifications, and some were stored. To date, the author has located two of the former Jeep Celebrity Challenge Jeeps. One is in Arizona being renovated. The other is owned by J. M. Bragg, who coached many celebrities and used the black Jeep Celebrity Challenge Jeep to win a Mint 400.

It was the driving coaches who benefitted from interacting with the celebrities. They coached them in a day to do what had taken years to learn. Where can a guy, such as Ray Russell, get to stand under the Los Angeles Memorial Coliseum peristyle with Vikki Carr and Judy Norton Taylor on either side of him? Several coaches stayed in contact with their pupils long after the series ended. (Photo Courtesy Brad Russell)

two-wheel-drive trucks in Class 8 by an hour. Ken Correia and Charles Morrison in a CJ-7 took third place an hour later.

In what was a Jeep sweep of the 4x4 classes, Paul Price and Dick Dahn took their Honcho to the class win. They beat a handful of Broncos and CJs handily.

Barstow Classic

SCORE International had long promoted the bulk of its schedule in Baja, with the exception of the Parker 400 and Riverside. Jim Moses, the Bureau of Land Management director at the time, was able to expand available race dates for the area, which allowed SCORE to get a date.

The date was not optimal. It was three weeks after the Mexicali race and three weeks before the Mint 400. Sal Fish grabbed the date anyway to establish SCORE in the area. Only 98 entries showed up.

The technicality of the Barstow course was an issue for many of the frontrunners. A strong drive by Doug and Ken Robinson brought the Honcho its first win. It was a sizeable margin of victory over a Chevy Blazer in second place.

Carl Johnson was a late entry in his CJ-7, and he intended to drive all four laps. Coming into the pit after the first lap, Johnson told his standby co-driver Allan Sheldon to take over driving due to a back problem. Sheldon jumped in the CJ-7 and took off. He covered the remaining laps in quick time and took the win.

Mint 400

The 1981 version of the Mint 400 went down in history as the highest entry for the event ever, with 500 entries. As the last starters waited to start the race, the lead open-wheel cars were already coming around to start Lap 2.

The Mike Moore–owned Honcho driven by Roger Mears and navigated by Mike Moore had a strong showing at the Mint and easily outdistanced the competition around the four laps. The day after his Mint 400 victory, Mears flew to Indianapolis for his rookie ride at the Indianapolis 500. The story that leaked into the garage area was that he could barely sit down for his seat fitting because of how sore he was.

It was a Bronco day in Class 4, but Jeep honor was upheld by Adams and Myers, who took second place, and Marshall Mahr in third place.

Marshall Mahr battled all day and most of the night to get his third-place finish. The Jeep suffered some downtime along the way, but he finished in the money. (Photo Courtesy tracksidephoto.com)

Baja Internacional

A month later, teams were still licking their wounds from the beating the Mint 400 handed out. But when Baja calls, you must answer.

Out front early, Roger Mears and Mike Moore led the way having started one position ahead of the Dodge that was piloted by Rod Hall and Jim Fricker. Mears held the position through the first couple of checkpoints and over the Summit. In the deep sand washes leading away from the Summit and toward the east side, the transmission failed in the Honcho. The Dodge motored around unchallenged over John Chillinsky and Don Magley in a CJ-7 for second place.

The modified 4x4s put on a better show. A trio of Jeeps filled out the podium covered by just 24 minutes. Paul Price and Michael Giurbino had two of the best-prepared Honchos out there, and it was these two that had a battle for the win, with the CJ-7 of Don Adams and Jason Myers just minutes behind.

Price and Dick Dahn were out front getting split times between them and Giurbino and Adams. As the Jeeps pressed on, Price and Dahn picked up a small advantage, while Adams slightly gained on Giurbino. At the finish, Price and Dahn won by 21 minutes. Giurbino charged hard and took second place. The Adams CJ-7 was 3 minutes behind for third place.

John Chillinsky and Don Magley took on the big boys and beat most of them with a fine second-place finish in Class 3. (Photo Courtesy tracksidephoto.com)

Price and Dahn flew down a hill to hit the water crossing that had already flooded a Volkswagen Beetle. The pair kept up the pace despite pressure from two other trucks in the class and took a big win. (Photo Courtesy tracksidephoto.com)

Carving up the corners in the hills east of Ensenada, the Honcho of Mike Guirbino chased the competition all day and took second place. (Photo Courtesy tracksidephoto.com)

Riverside Off-Road World Championships

Short-course racing really took off, not just in Riverside, but all over the United States and Canada, just as Mickey Thompson hoped that it would.

In what turned out to be an unremarkable race, Mears squirted off the start and thundered ahead of the Dodge to take the lead. He was never seriously challenged, but the Honcho of Rick Grumbein bookended the podium with Jeeps.

Jeep absolutely ruled the modified 4x4 class. They swept the top five places, and like the Class 3 race, it was a runaway, as Don Adams took his CJ-7 to the win over another CJ-7 driven by Kevin O'Connell and the Honcho of Mike Giurbino.

Baja 1000

For 1981, SCORE laid out a devious 805-mile route that extended as far south as Punta Prieta, where bottomless silt beds awaited the field. This area of the course saw 30 percent of the 270 entries end their race.

It was total domination by Rod Hall and Jim Fricker, as the Dodge held the lead from start to finish. Only two finished in the class. A CJ driven by Donald Bagley was a full 8 hours behind the Dodge.

Don Adams and Jason Myers had a rough start to the race when they fell behind the Paul Price Honcho with brake and power steering hose issues before Santa Inez. Myers then got stuck in the silt beds at the south end of the course. The Jeep was not equipped with a shovel, so Myers and his co-rider dug by hand, shoved cacti under the tires for traction, and eventually freed the Jeep.

The CJ was handed over to Adams, and he headed north toward San Felipe, where he noticed the power steering occasionally locked up without warning. Adams figured that there was an air pocket from the earlier power-steering fix. Coming into San Felipe, there was a noticeable drop in horsepower, which is not something you want heading into the mountains, so he stopped to pit. The air filter was completely packed with

Returning to Baja after a successful Baja Internacional, Don Magley powered the CJ to another second-place finish a few hours behind a Dodge. (Photo Courtesy tracksidephoto.com)

Jason Myers piloted the potent CJ-7 in the early going and set a wicked pace despite getting stuck in the infamous silt beds of Punta Prieta. Don Adams continued the race and brought it home solidly in the lead. (Photo Courtesy tracksidephoto.com)

silt and nearly sucked inside out. It was replaced, and Adams felt lucky that they did not lose the engine completely. The CJ was the lone official finisher in its class.

1982

The Falklands War topped the headlines for much of 1982 as Argentine forces declared war on British forces. Argentina failed to complete the liberation of those islands. Former off-road racer Rick Mears came up 0.16 seconds short in his bid for a second Indy 500 win

after an epic duel with Gordon Johncock. The year 1982 was the first year that Richard Petty went winless in his remarkable career.

The 4x4 classes saw a big change to the rules in SCORE, as the sanctioning body separated the production class by wheelbase. The CJ and Bronco competitors were at a huge disadvantage to the pickup trucks. So, to address this, Class 3 was divided into short-wheelbase (Class 3S) and long-wheelbase (Class 3L) categories.

In the High Desert Racing Association (HDRA) camp, a new race was introduced as the longest off-road race in

America. The Frontier 500 ran from Las Vegas to Reno, Nevada. All of it was off-road, and none of it was easy. The HDRA also divided the 4x4s by wheelbase; Class 3 for short wheelbase and Class 4 for long wheelbase.

Parker 400

The annual dual-state visit to the Parker area yielded some success for the Jeep teams. SCORE had its annual issues with environmentalists who wanted to shut down the race on the California side where desert tortoises were known to be. It would be a battle for years to come.

For Roger Mears and Mike Moore, the new suspension on the third *Budweiser Honcho* gave them a nice lead on Rod Hall and Jim Fricker Dodge headed into Arizona.

On the first Arizona lap, things remained static between the Jeep and Dodge. Mears held about a 10-minute lead into the final 89 miles. In the northern end of the course near Swansea, in a remote section of the lap, the Honcho stopped running. The ignition issue was resolved in time for Mears to salvage a second-place finish.

Don Tobias and Judy Wilson in a CJ-7 from Washington state took the win in Class 4. The duo had a clean run and took the only notable finish for a Jeep in the class.

Don Tobias towed his Jeep down from Washington state and made the trip pay by winning Class 4. (Photo Courtesy tracksidephoto.com)

Michael Giurbino and Henry Escalera ruled the field of Honchos by placing second behind Rod Hall and Jim Fricker's Dodge. (Photo Courtesy tracksidephoto.com)

Mint 400

Roger Mears started to chase his dream of Indy Car success, so team owner Mike Moore scheduled the *Budweiser Honcho* around Roger's schedule in CART. A rain delay for the Stroh's 200 at Atlanta Motor Speedway meant that he would miss the Mint 400. Mike Moore took the start and drove straight to his pit where he parked the Honcho just to get some starting points. Mears posted an impressive fourth place finish on the high-banked oval in a Penske PC-7.

Allen and Gene Hightower drove a great race in Class 3. Their CJ-7 finished hours ahead of second and third place. The CJ-5 of Marshall Mahr outran George Barnett and Dick Dahn by 24 minutes to sew up second.

In Class 4, when Mears is away, the Dodge will play. Michael Giurbino and Henry Escalera brought the Honcho in for a second-place finish an hour ahead of the rear-engine CJ-2A of Glenn Emery.

Baja Internacional

Baja was waiting for the 12 four-wheel drive rigs in three classes. It was a low turnout with three trucks each in production short and long wheelbase, and another six in modified.

The Jeeps did not reach the official finish in either wheelbase class. However, Jeep products took second place based on how far they went.

They made winning look easy, but a lot more went into their wins besides driving. The preparation by Warren Baird was a big part of the team's success. (Photo Courtesy tracksidephoto.com)

It was a tight race with the top three covered by 28 minutes. Don Yosten took third place in his Honcho after chasing the Adams and Tobias CJs. (Photo Courtesy tracksidephoto.com)

Don Coffland and Rick Peacock made it to Checkpoint 7 in their CJ-7.

Jeep had better results in the modified class and took the top three positions in a close battle. Jason Myers and Don Adams battled for hundreds of miles with Don Tobias and Judy Wilson, both in CJ-7s. Myers started at the rear of the six-truck field. A rear start is a calculated and often-requested move in off-road competition.

Myers and Adams passed Tobias at some point in the race, but they were often within sight of each other's dust cloud. About 15 minutes behind were Don Yosten and Bill Donahoe in a Honcho.

In the end, Myers and Adams's experience in Baja prevailed over Tobias when they took a win by 6 minutes. Yosten rolled in 22 minutes later to complete the Jeep sweep.

Riverside Off-Road Championships

Mike Randall did all he could to uphold Jeep's honor as he battled with a Scout and a Bronco for all 12 laps. Former Jeep ace Sherman Balch had his Scout dialed in and ran off and hid from the field. Mike Randall settled into a solid second place ahead of a Bronco and staved off his attack.

The boys at Mike Moore Racing built a special Honcho for short-course events, as they were becoming more frequent. The build was radical enough that SCORE put it in the modified class. That did not matter to Roger Mears. He wins in any class at Riverside, and he did by easily outdistancing John Randall in another Honcho and Don Adams CJ-7 who took second and third.

Mike Randall battled but could not catch the Dodge in his Honcho. He was able to hold off the other competition to take second place. (Photo Courtesy Randall Family)

The new short course build from the creative mind of Tom Strong was just the thing that Roger Mears needed to notch another Riverside win. (Photo Courtesy Mears Family)

Frontier 500

Las Vegas to Reno is a long drive under any circumstances, mostly because it is a two-lane highway. Imagine how it would feel if you ran it all off-road. Walt Lott spent years putting the route together and drove tens of thousands of miles off-road.

The short-wheelbase trucks were in for a rough ride over some of Nevada's worst terrain. The early silt beds and hills scattered the field, as Don Adams and Jason Myers were uncharacteristic early casualties. Not far from the start line, Myers went to make a pass on the Honcho of Mike Randall and hit a rock that shoved the axle back and broke the transfer case off the transmission.

Coming into Pahrump, Nevada, it was close, as the Jeep CJ-7 of Marshall Mahr, Bronco of Gale Pike, and CJ-7 of John Deetz filed through close together. A few Broncos and a rear-engine Jeep trickled through later. Coming into Beatty, Mahr, Pike, and Deetz were still close together. By Tonopah, Deetz had fallen behind about a half hour as Pike and Mahr battled onward within 5 minutes of each other.

After 452 miles, the Bronco nudged its way to victory by a mere 6 minutes over Mahr. Deetz came in 42 minutes later for third place and was the final finisher in the class.

One of the early favorites to take it to the Dodge was the Randall Hon-

John Randall headed the best of the rest, as he took second place for the weekend in the modified 4x4 class.

cho. John Randall started the race, and the plan was to hand it off to Mike Randall for the second half. Things went well early as John kept the pressure on the Dodge through Beatty.

It was a tight race all the way north to Reno, Nevada. Marshall Mahr was in a good position to win the Short-Wheelbase class until the final miles, when a Bronco nipped him for the win.

In third place, Jim Bell splashes through the riverbed and into Beatty, Nevada, as he chases Rod Hall and Mike Randall. He eventually passed a broken Randall and claimed the runner-up position.

A lone Scout was driven by Sherman Balch in Class 3S, four were in Class 3L, and four were in modified. Conspicuous in its absence was the Mike Moore team. Rumors swirled that the team was for sale, as Roger Mears tried to make it in Indy Cars. Without him behind the wheel, Moore was not interested in going forward.

Three of the four starters saw La Paz. The lone exception was the team of Brian Chuchua and David Bryan, who lost a transmission 9 miles from the start in their Jeep Grand Cherokee. With Chuchua out, there were no other Jeeps running.

All eyes were on the Jeeps of Jason Myers (paired with and Don Adams) as well as Don Tobias (paired with Ed Bray), who were fighting for the season championship in Class 4. Myers needed to win, and Tobias had to "DNF" the race to lose the championship. Myers and Adams led the whole race from start to finish doing what they had to do.

Tobias and Bray ran their own race—which was to not race but to finish. Things went well until the dreaded Three Sisters south of San Felipe. During the drivers' meeting before the race, SCORE president Sal Fish called it the "17 worst miles in the race." Tobias was behind the

Just after Beatty, the course turned to the northwest and was very silty and rough in places. There was little access for pit crews if things went wrong. Guess what? The front hub broke and the wheel and tire went sailing into the desert. The crew could not access the broken Honcho until it was impossible to finish the race within the time limit.

Jim Bell and Walt Laycock were second. Russ and Kathy Kirkpatrick were third. Vernon Roberts and Bill Donahoe overcame many issues to take the last finishing position 2 hours later.

Baja 1000

It was always a big deal when the Baja 1000 returned to its roots and ran the length of the peninsula from Ensenada to La Paz.

Short Field of 4x4s

Mark Thatcher, the son of British Prime Minister Margaret Thatcher, was entered in a Dodge pickup in Class 3L. It was an older Rod Hall truck, and the driver received coaching from perennial Jeep racer John Randall. The English media was out in force to see what would happen.

The 4x4 classes were hit pretty hard, as only nine rigs took the start.

Don Tobias had 15 minutes of fame for punting Margaret Thatcher's son off the road in the movie **Three Sisters** *while being filmed by the British press. He finished in second place and tied up the season championship. (Photo Courtesy tracksidephoto.com)*

Don Adams Racing Enterprises fielded two vehicles for 1982: the venerable Jeep CJ-7 and the ex–Parnelli Jones Blazer that he codrove with motorcycle legend Malcolm Smith. It all came together at the Baja 1000, where both vehicles won their class. Adams started in the Blazer and drove halfway. Then, he handed it over to Smith. Adams rested until the CJ-7 arrived, and Jason Myers gave the wheel to Adams to bring it home. (Photo Courtesy tracksidephoto.com)

wheel when he came up on the Dodge of Mark Thatcher, who was running at a reduced pace due to broken motor mounts. The Englishman was unaware of Tobias closing in and held up the CJ for a few miles before Tobias felt he had to give him a nudge from behind, which sent the Dodge sideways and allowed an avenue for him to pass. The British press saw the whole thing from a helicopter, and it made headlines in England.

Myers and Adams finished the race in just over 26 hours and waited to see if Tobias and Bray would finish in the CJ. Just short of 2 hours later, Tobias and Bray crossed the finish line and took second place in the race and won the championship. For Adams, it was a bumper day. His two-seater Blazer won the two-seat unlimited class by an hour, which made him a two-class winner. Don shared driving duties in the ex–Parnelli Jones Blazer with motorcycle legend Malcolm Smith.

1983

The year started with a motorsports headline, as A. J. Foyt won the 24 Hours of Daytona in a Porsche 935 with drivers Bob Wollek, Preston Henn, and Claude Ballot-Léna. In March, the legendary television series *M*A*S*H* signed off for the final time in a 2.5-hour finale watched by nearly 122 million viewers. NASA's Pioneer 10 passed the orbit of Neptune, which made it the first manmade object to view the outer solar system.

The year started with a slight change to the 4x4 class rules. SCORE kept the Class 3 and Class 4 production classes divided by wheelbase. The new Class 14 was for modified rigs regardless of wheelbase. The HDRA decided to keep the wheelbase classes and lumped modified and production trucks together.

The rumors were verified at the beginning of 1983. Mike Moore sold the entire team of *Budweiser Honchos* to Larry Casey, owner of La Paz Drink Mixes. He and his sons, Tim and Chris, fielded a few trucks starting with the HDRA Nissan Classic.

Parker 400

The season-long grind starts in Parker for every team.

Five short-wheelbase rigs started the race and three saw the finish. Early on, Don Adams and Jason Myers kept a Bronco behind them, as Tuba City, Arizona, truck-stop owner Don Coffland was in the mix in his CJ-7.

At the top of the California loop where it crossed Highway 95, Adams stormed past 2 minutes ahead of the Bronco and Coffland, who were very close together.

In His Own Words...

Don Coffland remembered the following details during a recent interview:

"We did not think we were going to make the race," he said. "Out testing a few days before the race, we lost the whole Quadratrac system. Jeep promised they were going to have a new one at the race and we could install it there. So, we headed to Parker and installed everything the day before the race.

"We did okay on the California side and the first Arizona loop. We pitted before going out on the final loop, and there was Adams right across the road from us also pitting. Adams left first, and we followed a few minutes later. About 5 miles out in the sand wash, we caught him.

"Adams started first in class, so catching him meant that Don, who started fourth, was in the lead by 2 minutes. The Bronco had some downtime and was no longer a threat.

"My co-driver, Tom Wood, told me to pass him, but I thought better of it, knowing we had him on time. So, with the lack of dust due to the snow and rain, it was easier to just follow him. Coming into Bouse, I was surprised to see him pull into his pits, so now I was in the lead. Not too far after that, Don passed me, so I just followed his taillights all the way to the finish. I won the race by a minute and a half and even got a big congratulations from Rod Hall."

It was quite an ordeal to get the CJ-7 to the start line when the transfer case broke in testing before the race. The Randalls saved Don Coffland's race with a replacement that they hauled to the race for him. (Photo Courtesy tracksidephoto.com)

Closing in on the finish line, Don Coffland was right behind Don Adams (who started ahead of him), which meant that Coffland won on corrected time. (Photo Courtesy tracksidephoto.com)

More Results

Rod Hall and Jim Fricker had a nearly flawless race in their Dodge except for some blown shocks at the end of the California side. It was such a dominant run that the Honcho of Russ Kirkpatrick and V. L. Hutchins was 1 hour and 9 minutes behind in second place.

Kirkpatrick reported that he and Hutchins lost the windshield wipers early on the California side. As the weather brought some light rain to the course, the Honcho had vision issues, as mud obscured the windshield. On the Arizona side, where it was dark and raining harder, Kirkpatrick had to be careful and not get mud on the driving lights. This forced the drivers to exit the rig and clean off the lights and windshield. Still, after pressing onward, they were rewarded with second place.

Just 5 minutes back was Vern Roberts and Bill Donahoe who had the same issues. They finished in third place.

Jim Bell and Walt Laycock drove their immaculate Honcho to a commanding win in the new modified class. Bell put 1 hour and 39 minutes on the wildly stretched CJ-7 of Richard Stumpfhauser and Bob Ripley.

Russ Kirkpatrick and V. L. Hutchins had to deal with the mud and rain without wipers, and they stopped occasionally to clean off the driving lights and windshield. Still, they were fast enough to take second in Class 4. (Photo Courtesy tracksidephoto.com)

HDRA Nissan Classic
Short-Course Races

A few weeks after the Parker 400, many of the 4x4s that ran at Parker were back in action for a short-course event that was organized by Walt Lott. Datsun had recently became Nissan, and it threw a lot of money into HDRA because Toyota had already established a relationship with SCORE. The mini truck wars were about to heat up between manufacturers, but that's a topic for another book.

Firebird Raceway, as it was known when it opened in 1983, was brand new when the off-roaders came to race. Walt Lott and his crew carved

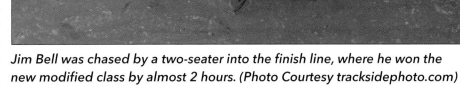

Jim Bell was chased by a two-seater into the finish line, where he won the new modified class by almost 2 hours. (Photo Courtesy tracksidephoto.com)

The trucks once piloted by Roger Mears were now in the hands of the Casey family. Repainted in the colors of the family company La Paz Party Mixes, they were in good hands. (Photo Courtesy La Paz Racing)

With two heat-race wins for Don Adams, he earned the overall win for the Class 3 field. (Photo Courtesy tracksidephoto.com)

Don Coffland, the Parker 400 winner a few weeks earlier, piloted his Jeep to third- and second-place finishes. (Photo Courtesy tracksidephoto.com)

Mike Randall goes hard into a turn to stay ahead of the pack. After a transmission change the previous day, he was hungry for a win in the borrowed truck, and he did just that. (Photo Courtesy tracksidephoto.com)

a 1.2-mile racetrack around the road racecourse. Most of the top teams came out to race, and it was here that the Mike Moore Honchos made their debut in La Paz colors with Larry and Tim driving. Competition was divided into two "motos," and the overall average between the two motos determined the overall winner.

Don Adams was back in form at the short-course race and led everything from practice times to race starts. Others were determined to knock him off, but none made it happen. Adams easily took both moto wins. Don Coffland eased into second place overall with a third and second place finish in the motos. Jeep swept the overall standings.

The long-wheelbase ranks were stacked with potent Honchos, including two La Paz trucks, three Randalls, Mark Acuna, Rick Grumbein, and Jim Bell.

The Randall Racing team had more talented drivers than race trucks. It made sense to let Grant, John, and Mike all enter, so they borrowed a Honcho from Charlie Nelson for Mike to drive. In the first moto, the borrowed Honcho suffered a transmission failure.

John Randall was able to uphold family honor and take the win in Moto 1, followed by Larry Casey and then Rick Grumbein.

In the second moto, the repaired Honcho of Mike Randall got a good jump at the start and bolted into the lead. Grumbein was right between the Randall brothers as John fell in behind Grumbein. No one caught Mike this day, as they finished in that same order.

Due to his first- and third-place finish, John Randall took the overall win in class, followed by Grumbein in second place.

Rick Grumbein was steady all weekend and kept the truck out of danger to take second place overall for the weekend. (Photo Courtesy tracksidephoto.com)

Mint 400

It was a huge short-wheelbase class with 23 entries, and there was carnage, as more than half of the field failed to complete a single lap. Don Adams and Jason Myers had a clean run and took the class win with several Broncos behind them.

Rod Hall and Jim Fricker in their Dodge ran away with the win—but not without a challenge from 19-year-old Tim Casey and his brother Chris.

Tim and Chris stayed close to Hall, who started three positions ahead of them for two laps.

"We had a clean race until halfway through the third lap," Tim said. "We heard a banging noise as we were coming to one of our pits. One of the

It was a runaway from the start, as the Don Adams CJ-7 led the 1983 Mint 400 from flag to flag.

Tim and Chris Casey gave it all they had and almost came away with the win until suspension issues cost them the win. Second place was still quite an accomplishment for the brothers.

front upper shock mounts had ripped out a section of the down bar. A major structural component still had to support the one remaining shock.

"We didn't have any tubing at the pit, so our guys welded a tire wrench into the missing part of the down bar. We ran the last lap and a half on one shock. Classic off-road racing field repair."

The field repair and slowed pace cost them a chance to challenge for the win, but it did net them second place.

Riverside Off-Road World Championships

The 4x4 classes ran in one big heat on Saturday with delayed starts between Class 3, Class 4, and Class 14, so the land-rush start was by class, and a new class launched every 30 seconds. This way, a Honcho could not affect the race between some CJs or a wildly modified rig from Class 14.

Don Adams drove the CJ-7 to an impressive wire-to-wire win for Jeep and easily outdistanced the Bronco of Midwestern driver Chuck Johnson. Dan Randall borrowed a CJ-7 for the race and brought it home in third place. Doug Robinson and Kevin O'Connell, each on CJ-7s, rounded out the top five.

The Randalls brought two of their Honchos and hoped to take down the Hall/Fricker Dodge and host of other Honchos that were entered in the class. The Dodge streaked ahead into the lead, with a determined John Randall within an arm's length. Mike Randall fended off the Minnesota-based Honcho of John Witt for third while Rick Grumbein held down the fifth spot.

The Dodge could not shake John Randall, who charged hard and looked for a way around. Mike Randall gained slightly on his brother and put some distance on the Witt Honcho. Down at the west end of the

John Randall was a show for the spectators all by himself. Running down and passing Rod Hall was not an easy feat. (Photo Courtesy tracksidephoto.com)

Mike Randall took the third podium spot after battling hard for second place and fending off the attack of John Witt in his Minnesota-based Honcho. (Photo Courtesy tracksidephoto.com)

Curt LeDuc is a terror on the East Coast and Midwest off-road tracks. Out West, he battled and came away with a big win at Riverside. (Photo Courtesy tracksidephoto.com)

Wes Banks is one of the group a single-seater Jeep CJ drivers who are popular in the Central California and Pacific Northwest off-road races. He drove well and took second place. (Photo Courtesy tracksidephoto.com)

track in Turn 6, John Randall got alongside the Dodge, and a drag race ensued down Thompson's Ridge until the Honcho was able to nudge into the lead. With a clear track ahead, John Randall inched away from the Dodge, who now had Mike Randall on his bumper.

In the end, they finished in the same order. Three Randalls raced in the combined race, and all went home with trophies.

The modified rigs were mostly from the East Coast and the Midwest where off-road racing is mostly short-course based on manmade tracks. This makes for some wildly modified rigs and some ingenuity on a level that has trouble surviving the desert but is amazing on a short course.

Curt LeDuc drove a wild race and led wire to wire in his Jeep Honcho. He had some early challenges from a Blazer and a vehicle that was labeled as a "special," but they faded. Joe Janis settled into second in another Honcho that, like Le Duc's, was more akin to a Funny Car than a stock Honcho. Wes Banks, a California driver in his single-seater Jeep CJ, ran just behind the leaders in third place, followed by a Bronco and then another West Coast single-seat CJ driven by Don German.

Frontier 500

The second annual run from Las Vegas to Reno had 22 4x4s entered in the two classes.

It did not look good for the super team of Don Adams and Jason Myers as the CJ-7 transmission packed it in not far from the start line. His crew doubled back from the first pit in Pahrump and made the repair in just under 3 hours.

The two Broncos and the CJ-7 of David Bryan and Jack Towne battled for the lead unknowingly as Adams and Myers opted for a rear start. This meant it wouldn't be until teams reached Beatty (168 miles into the race) before they found out about Adams. It was at Beatty where a modified Bronco jumped into the lead and distanced itself from Bryan and the other Bronco.

By this time, Adams was repaired and headed north with a head of steam. Myers, who drove first, had two problems. The first issue was catching the competition. The second issue was making it to the checkpoints before the set closing times, and he was dangerously close to not making it in time. In the end, he made two checkpoints by minutes and then built a cushion so that he did not have to worry about it anymore.

Battling for the early lead, David Bryan was in the lead pack most of the way before his motor mounts broke and he could not continue. However, he was awarded fourth place, which was based on the number of miles driven. (Photo Courtesy tracksidephoto.com)

Flying the Honcho in the early miles, Tim and Chris Casey overcame major issues to reach Reno in second place. (Photo Courtesy La Paz Racing)

Jason Myers catches air while trying to catch the pack that passed him while his transmission was being replaced near the start line. In an epic comeback, he and Don Adams caught and passed every truck to earn the win. (Photo Courtesy tracksidephoto.com)

The modified Bronco had a big lead as he closed in on Virginia City, and then it was a short run to the finish. However, disaster struck as the Ford ran out of fuel in a difficult area to access for the chase crew. It took several hours for the crew to find them, during which time Adams closed in. Bryan and Towne were between Tonopah and Gabbs when they suffered broken motor mounts and had to retire, but they were awarded fourth place on distance traveled.

After Adams heard the news about the Bronco, he was on it even harder and passed it as he did earlier to the other Bronco. Adams stormed into the finish 16 minutes ahead of the Bronco. The second Bronco was only 15 minutes behind in third place. It was an epic win for Jeep against the odds.

Aside from a single flat tire, the Rod Hall and Jim Fricker team had a near flawless drive and won by 3 hours

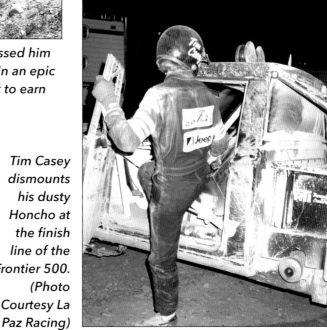

Tim Casey dismounts his dusty Honcho at the finish line of the Frontier 500. (Photo Courtesy La Paz Racing)

and took 11th place overall. The Jeep contingent could only shake their heads and wonder how to stop the veteran driver.

It was the duty of the Randall family and Casey family to find a way to do that, but issues sidelined both

A lot of mechanical work and perseverance paid off for Vern Roberts and Bill Donahoe with a third-place finish. (Photo Courtesy tracksidephoto.com)

Randalls early in the race. The Honcho of Tim and Chris Casey, who started second off the line, hoped to take it to the Dodge, since he started 11th off the line.

Casey knew something was wrong with his drivetrain almost immediately. It felt like it was binding or fighting itself. He thought that if the transfer case was bad, it might be a short day for the La Paz team. While they tried to get to the pits in Pahrump to see if it could be repaired, the Dodge caught them on a narrow road. Tim tried to find a place to pull over, but there was nothing available. Hall, being a cagey veteran, nudged him a few times, but the third time he rammed them harder than Tim had ever been hit before. Finally, a place opened up and they pulled off to let Hall past. After they got going again, they felt a flat tire, which added insult to injury since they had to stop to change it.

At the pit stop, the team diagnosed the issue as different gears were installed in the front and rear axles. If they continued, the drivetrain would eat itself. Their only hope was to remove the front driveshaft and run in two-wheel-drive. As the repair took place, upon inspection of the rear axle, it was a short-course gear, which meant that it would limit top speed. The front axle was a desert gear.

Now in two-wheel-drive, the road just out of Pahrump was where some of Nevada's nastiest silt beds were located. Thanks to power from their 401-ci engine, Goodyear traction, and

the shorter gear that was mistakenly installed, they made it through the silt with little downtime. Hall was now gone, so the plan was to run it until they either saw Reno or broke it. They saw Reno and took second place. It was another 15 minutes before the Honcho of Vern Roberts and Bill Donahoe arrived in third place. Russ Kirkpatrick and Shane Hutchins were another hour back in their Honcho for fourth place.

Baja 1000

The granddaddy of them all, the Baja 1000, featured a new twist with a mandatory overnight layover in San Felipe on a multiple-lap course around the area between Ensenada and San Felipe.

The short-wheelbase rigs did not turn out in force, as only three took the start: two Jeeps and a Bronco. The Jeep teams were the Don Adams and Jason Myers CJ-7 and the Doug and Ken Robinson CJ-7. In an unusual turn of events, late in the first day, Myers was driving and was distracted by his co-driver falling asleep. While he tried to reach over and shake him awake, he veered into a large rock that catastrophically broke the front end.

The Robinsons had a large lead in their CJ-7 and were headed for the overnight when word filtered through that the Bronco had retired as well. Doug and Ken took their Bridgestone-sponsored Jeep around the next day in good time to win the race.

The lightly attended Class 3 was ripe for the picking by Doug and Ken Robinson, who drove smart and quick and were victorious. (Photo Courtesy tracksidephoto.com)

In Class 4, it was survival of the fittest. Lowell Arnold took second place. (Photo Courtesy tracksidephoto.com)

Six long-wheelbase rigs started the race, five made it to the overnight halt, and the Hall and Fricker Dodge sat with a half hour lead. In the end, only the Dodge made it back to Ensenada for an uncontested win. The Jeep Honcho of Lowell Arnold was awarded second place by distance traveled.

Barstow Classic

SCORE decided to move the Barstow event from March to December and make it the season finale. Sal Fish and Jim Moses strung together an amazing 65-mile course that managed to take anything resembling a straightaway or smooth piece of ground away from the racers. Yet, as rough as it was, a hefty 72 out of 127 participants finished.

It was an easy day for Adams and Myers. The pair circulated the four laps in just a tick over 7 hours. The next to finish was a Bronco (90 minutes later). Ken Correia and Chuck Morrison took third place in a CJ-7.

The well-known Dodge was not a factor in the long-wheelbase class, as the transfer case broke right off the start line. The team did a quick swap and sent it out again, but that transfer case failed after 30 miles, so they parked it.

This opened the door for a trio of Honchos. John Randall took the family Honcho and jumped into the lead. On the third lap, the Honcho had a terminal problem that ended its day. This launched Vern Roberts and Bill Donahoe into the lead with only a Chevy an hour behind them. The Roberts and Donahoe team stormed off into the last rainy lap only to have 4 hours worth of mechanical problems, which allowed the Chevy to take the win. The stricken Honcho managed to limp home as the last official finisher with only 11 minutes left before the time limit.

Four quick laps were no contest for the competition, as Don Adams and Jason Myers whipped around and won handily. (Photo Courtesy tracksidephoto.com)

Ken Correia and Chuck Morrison took third place at Barstow. Racing short-wheelbase 4x4s in Barstow is a test of the driver, rider, and machine as the ever-undulating terrain tests kidneys as well. (Photo Courtesy tracksidephoto.com)

In his debut in the desert, Roger Mears Jr. showed excellent speed and agility. It was unfortunate that some downtime spoiled what would have been a podium finish, but fifth place is better than not finishing. (Photo Courtesy tracksidephoto.com)

Jim Bell and Walt Laycock beat up on a homebuilt 4x4 and won the modified class easily.

Don Adams won two major championships (Class 3 and the Overall Truck championship) for himself and Jeep with his win.

What is Class 7S? It is a production-based, mini-truck class that up until now had seen very few Jeep entries and fewer impressive finishes. Today, however, the Country Off-Road Racing team fielded a Jeep Scrambler for Roger Mears Jr. Yes, Junior. Did you think all Roger Sr. ever did was race cars?

Mears Jr. put in two very impressive laps and ran in the top 50 percent of the field, but it was followed by two very difficult laps with mechanical issues. Still, he pressed on for fifth place and gave Jeep a finish in a new class.

Two entries, a Jeep and a Datsun, started in the modified class and both finished. Jim Bell and Walt Laycock took the Jeep Honcho to a commanding lead over the homebuilt 4x4-conversion Datsun and never looked back.

Frontier 250

Just two weeks after SCORE closed out its season in Barstow, many teams did a quick prep on their vehicles and headed for Las Vegas for the 250-mile race. While SCORE threw some rough stuff at the entries, Walt Lott and his HDRA team gave teams the best of the best roads around Jean Dry Lake for a fun race.

Everyone wanted to run the Frontier 250, as eight rigs entered. Four of those finished the race. Adams and Myers wanted to make sure that they won the race and clinched not only the class points championship but also the combined truck championship between Class 3, Class 4, and Class 8. It would be a big feather in Jeep's cap.

Adams and Myers did just that and took a commanding lead on the first lap, never looked back, and won the day. Don Coffland took third in his CJ-7 and narrowly edged David Bryan in his CJ-7.

Tim and Chris Casey tried to take advantage of that darn Dodge's issues, but they had a few issues of their own and settled into second place.

It was not as easy as usual for the Dodge of Hall and Fricker. Tim and Chris Casey were the next finishers in their Honcho. Twenty-five minutes later, Vern Roberts and Bill Donahoe claimed the third spot in their Honcho.

Epilogue

The year 1983 ended on a high note for Jeep when it claimed the championships in Class 3 for SCORE and HDRA and the overall truck title in HDRA.

1984

SCORE threw the short-wheelbase rigs a curve ball when it announced that Class 3 was now for short-wheelbase 4x4 vehicles with a maximum engine displacement of 2,850 cc. This meant that SCORE was betting on manufacturers entering the smaller SUV vehicles, such as the Jeep Cherokee. Class 4 was now the place for anyone with V-8 power regardless of wheelbase.

Mint 400

Heading into the Mint 400, uncertainty surrounded the racecourse. The Moapa Band of Native Americans

It was not a typical Don Adams/Jason Myers wire-to-wire win. There were things to overcome, such as an uncharacteristic rollover and driver changes every lap. The team was able to regain the lead in Lap 3 and held it to the end.

For a brief time, John Deetz had the lead and looked good, but Nevada decided otherwise. He did not finish.

who had always graciously let the race happen on 30 miles of roads at the north end of the racecourse dramatically increased their fee. This led to the racecourse being modified to cut north to south twice, which utilized an infamous dry lake that had deep silt.

There were 19 short-wheelbase rigs at the start of the race, and almost half of them never saw the start of the second lap. This indicates how rough that piece of Nevada was.

At this Mint race, Don Adams and Jason Myers decided to change drivers every lap due to the roughness of the desert. Myers drove first and stepped out to a good lead, with one Bronco and a gaggle of CJs behind them.

On Lap 2, Adams wrinkled the CJ-7 during an uncharacteristic rollover. Luckily, the damage was cosmetic, so his time lost was not too damaging. This moved John Deetz into the lead by 11 minutes over Adams, with a Bronco in third another 11 minutes back.

Lap 3 shook things up when the Deetz CJ-7 lost an hour, which allowed Myers to regain his lead. Adams brought the wrinkled Jeep home in 13.5 hours, a full half hour ahead of the Bronco.

In his return to off-road racing, J. M. Bragg (with his sons Mike and Greg, each riding two laps) was third (and the final finisher in the class). Deetz failed to finish.

One fewer 4x4 entered the long-wheelbase class for a total of 18. Out of that number of starters, only two completed all four laps and both of them were Jeep Honchos.

Making a great return to off-road racing after a break to establish his walnut farm, J. M. Bragg and his sons were able to shake off the rust and take third place.

Tim and Chris Casey put it all together and earned a major win. It was a magical day, as they never had to get out of the Honcho during the race. (Photo Courtesy tracksidephoto.com)

It was one of those magical days that you dream about in off-road racing, where you climb in the race truck at the start, and four laps later, you get out and are crowned a Mint 400 class winner. Tim and Chris Casey experienced such a day. Starting 16th off the line in their class, by race mile 50, they were physically in the lead. The vehicle of their father, Larry Casey, broke during the second lap, but the joy of seeing his sons' win made his day better.

Vern Roberts and Bill Donahoe had a three-lap battle for second place with Lowell Arnold until Arnold was stopped with mechanical issues and did not finish. Roberts and Donahoe took the second spot almost 2 hours after Casey finished.

When compared to the winner, it took two extra hours to cover the four laps of the Mint. However, Vern Roberts and Bill Donahoe kept the Honcho moving and garnered a nice finish.

Lowell Arnold was in the mix for second place for much of the first three laps and most of the fourth lap. When the Honcho stopped, he saw the lights of Las Vegas ahead.

Using his new Scrambler for short-course racing, Don Adams swept the all-Jeep field in both heats.

The start of the Class 3 race resembled a Jeep pinball machine, with short-wheelbase rigs ricocheting off bumps and jumps.

Mears Gang Rumble

The HDRA was on a tear with promoting short-course off-road racing and created a separate championship for it. The explosion caused by the Mickey Thompson Off-Road Championship Grand Prix put scores of short-course racers looking for places to compete.

The Mears gang owed a lot to the city of Bakersfield, California. Even before Rick Mears won an Indianapolis 500, the city embraced the brothers and their father for their racing exploits. Their way of giving back to Bakersfield was hosting a race in their hometown. The event was held at Sprocketts Park Raceway, and fans came out in force. Rick Mears, who had just won his second Indianapolis 500 a month earlier, drove a Nissan desert truck and thrilled the crowd.

The short-wheelbase class was nearly an all Jeep CJ-7 affair, except for the wildly modified Bronco of Steve Mizel, who had a transmission fail in the qualifying heat. He packed it in and left the Jeeps to play among themselves.

Doug Robinson battled other Jeeps and came away with third place for his weekend effort.

John Randall always seemed to come from behind to win his heat races. At the end, he was in the right place: first.

In each heat race, Larry Casey started well and looked to be on his way to victory lane. In the first heat race, his brakes faded, and so did Casey. In the second heat race, he dealt with a power-steering failure. Still, Casey was a crowd favorite in Bakersfield for his driving style and ex–Roger Mears Honcho.

Rick Grumbein stayed out of trouble (but not the dust) with consistent finishes in both heats to net a third-place finish for the weekend.

The course was challenging with sharp jumps and nasty whoops. The heavy hitters were all there, including John Randall, who borrowed the DirTrix CJ-7. Don Adams, Doug Robinson, and David Bryan were also among the entries. The action was amazing as the solid-axle CJs bounced over the course, but the competition was less exciting, as Don Adams easily won the heat races and took the win for the weekend. John Randall was second in both heats and took that spot. It was the same for Doug Robinson in third.

In the first heat, the Hall/Fricker Dodge succumbed to the rough course with a broken front axle after two laps. Larry Casey, who got the jump on John Randall, inher-

ited the lead, but shortly after, it was Randall in the lead with Casey, Mike Randall, and Rick Grumbein following. John Randall was challenged at every opportunity by Larry Casey for several laps until the La Paz Honcho lost brakes and faded. After 12 grueling laps, it was John Randall, Mike Randall in second, and Grumbein in third.

The Dodge returned for the second heat. It got the jump at the start with Larry Casey in second, and John Randall fell in exactly where he wanted to be. John simply stayed behind the La Paz Honcho because he knew he would win the weekend on points. Casey lost his power steering at the halfway point and faded, which allowed Randall into second place, followed by his brother Mike.

The Randalls took first and second place for the weekend and were followed by Rick Grumbein to make an all-Honcho podium. Sadly, the race was never repeated.

Barstow Fireworks 250

The annual Fourth of July bash in Barstow was always a big favorite with the drivers. Multiple lap races result in easier pre-running and reduced costs for running the race (unlike a Baja race or Frontier 500).

Don Adams's absence was notable. He had other obligations at the Pikes Peak Hill Climb. There were still 13 entries that started the race and the bulk of them were Jeeps. Doug and Ken Robinson came out swinging in the first lap with a new suspension from Warren Baird and led by 1 minute over a Blazer, which didn't finish, and 2 minutes ahead of J. M. Bragg and his sons. The Marshall Mahr Jeepster was in fourth but lost an hour on the second lap.

On Lap 2 of four, J. M. Bragg made a sub-2-hour lap and took the lead. Robinson nursed some engine troubles, which eventually was the reason that he stopped for good on the final lap. A Bronco worked its way into second place but could not match Bragg's pace. No one could.

Bragg, with sons Mike and Greg riding along, won handily by half an hour. The Mahrs repaired their issues and earned third place. Don Coffland and Buck Griffin ran a new CJ-8 (Scrambler) and finished in fourth place.

Of the eight starters in Class 4, five of them were Jeeps. One Jeep in particular, John Randall's Honcho, came around the first lap with a solid 4 minutes in hand over Rod Hall/Jim Fricker in the Dodge. Tim and Chris Casey were fourth and looked to move up into third, which was occupied by a Chevy.

On the second lap, the Dodge cut the lead to 1 minute over Randall. The Chevy broke the steering box, and

Nursing a new-build Scrambler to the finish, Don Coffland and Buck Griffin were happy to get four solid test laps and take fourth place.

Many issues plagued the Honcho, but the driver and pit crew brought it to the finish in fourth place.

the younger Caseys found themselves just 12 minutes out of the battle for the win.

Randall turned up the wick and burned off two 1 hour and 38 minute laps, which kept him ahead of the Dodge by 6 minutes. The Caseys had an hour of downtime but managed to stay in third place. The fourth and final finisher was Vern Roberts and Bill Donahoe in their Honcho.

Frontier 500

The third annual trek from Las Vegas to Reno was all about getting through the first 150 miles. The move from September to mid-October made for cooler weather, but much less wind, which made for a dusty haze over much of the desert.

It was a scant field of four in the short-wheelbase class. At the 50-mile mark, only two rigs made it there in good time. The rear-engine Jeep of Glenn Emery and Carl Cook was first and followed by Marshall and Michael Mahr in their modified Jeepster. The rear-engine machine suffered a mechanical issue not much farther down the road, and the Mahr team continued unchallenged and was the only finisher.

Rod Hall brought the Dodge home to Reno in grand style, while the Jeep contingent put in some mechanical work to fill out the podium. John Randall moved down the course well to Checkpoint 2, but the Honcho needed a new radiator while he was there, and he lost more than 30 minutes. Not much farther down the road, a cracked transmission case damaged the Quadratrac unit and forced them to continue in two-wheel drive.

Meanwhile, Vern Roberts and Bill Donahoe, in their Honcho, needed to make some repairs on the way up

Vern Roberts did not have a clean run, but his crew helped the Honcho move into second place late in the race. (Photo Courtesy tracksidephoto.com)

Marshall and Michael Mahr were the lone survivors in the trek northward across Nevada. (Photo Courtesy tracksidephoto.com)

The Randall team's mechanics allowed the Honcho to take third place after they replaced and patched every major system on the race truck. (Photo Courtesy tracksidephoto.com)

north, but not as many as the Randalls. Roberts was able to scoot past the Randall Honcho and finish in second place. The Randalls patched the poor Honcho up at every pit and finished in third place.

The Jeepless Baja 1000

There were no Jeep entries in the Baja 1000 for the first time ever.

1985

The year started with Ronald Reagan privately getting sworn in for his second term as president of the United States. In April, the Coca-Cola Company committed the bungle of the century when it introduced New Coke. In July, the largest rock and roll event since its inception occurred, as Live Aid raised more than $50 million for famine relief in Ethiopia. In September, the *Titanic* was found after 73 years at the bottom of the Atlantic Ocean.

Parker 400

The weather played a part in the race this year. Friday was wet and cold, and it was colder and snowy on race day. Layering every piece of clothing you brought for the weekend was the call of race day. However, off-road racers are a hardy group of people, and they take whatever comes their way and adapt to it.

Don Adams started California in a new Class 3 Cherokee with the 4.0L straight-six engine. The debut was short-lived, as the rear driveshaft failed at Checkpoint 1.

The Hightowers showed no rust, as they finished California with 10 minutes to spare over a Bronco. Pre-race favorite Don Coffland and

Vern Roberts and Bill Donahoe dealt with the cold and slippery conditions better than most in their class and were rewarded with a third-place finish.

In 1972, the Hightowers won the very first Parker race in a CJ-5. Then, they were back in a CJ-7 and continued the tour by winning the 1985 Parker 400 in the cold and snow. (Photo Courtesy tracksidephoto.com)

John Randall kept it close through California and half of Arizona before he lost 30 minutes to the Dodge. The Honcho took second place.

Buck Griffin were close in fifth place here but never registered a time in Arizona.

Everyone had some downtime in the first Arizona loop, but the Hightower CJ-7 had less of it. With the big lead earned in California, they were comfortable going for their last 90-mile Arizona loop. The Hightowers returned to off-road racing in a big way and had a dominating win.

In the battle between John Randall and Hall/Fricker, Randall only trailed by 4 minutes at the end of the California loop. Several other Honchos lurked behind but were not close enough to make a race of it.

The Dodge ripped a hot loop in the first Arizona go around and led Randall by 30 minutes. In the final loop, Randall matched the Dodge for the second loop, but it was not enough. They settled into second place. Vern Roberts and Bill Donahoe filled out the podium in their Honcho.

Laughlin Desert Challenge

The High Desert Racing Association (HDRA) began its season in Laughlin, Nevada, where the desert winds blew hard. It was a joy for the drivers but not so great for the pit crews and checkpoint workers.

It was a two Cherokee duel in Class 12, as Jason Myers took on Tom Peltier. Peltier had mechanical trouble and was an hour behind after the first lap. At the end of the second lap, Peltier's issues were terminal, and he parked. Myers set four consistent lap times and won the class.

At the end of the first lap, Don Adams and Larry Olsen trailed a Scout by 11 seconds with the Hightowers 5 minutes back. A struggling Don Coffland stopped often to fix gremlins. On Lap 2, Adams picked up 8 minutes over the Scout but slowed a little on Lap 3, when he saw the Scout was close to within 1 minute. In the last lap, the Scout broke.

The Country Off-Road Racing team from Bakersfield, California, jumped into the Class 12 fray with a Jeep Cherokee to challenge the mighty Don Adams team. It took some time to sort out the Cherokee, but it was competitive later in the season.

Early in the race, Larry Olsen's Cherokee battled an International truck from Oregon. They were so close that it was difficult to know who was in the lead. Don Adams jumped in for the last half of the race and brought it home victorious.

Struggling from the start, the Hightowers could only get within 5 minutes of the lead battle. They eventually took second and trailed the leader by 16 minutes.

The Hightowers turned up the volume in the last lap but could only close to within 16 minutes of Adams who notched his first win in the Class 3 Cherokee and gave the team a twofer. Coffland arrived at the finish 80 minutes later in third place.

Great Mojave 250

SCORE had an opportunity to open a new area to off-road racing in Lucerne Valley, California. After an emergency event in 1984 to replace the Baja Internacional, SCORE returned to the joy of merchants in Lucerne Valley.

Once again, it was a two-horse race among the Cherokees. This time, both Jeeps completed all laps. Tom Peltier had an hour downtime in the first lap, and Myers had some in both laps but won anyway.

By the halfway point in the first lap, about 66 miles from the start, Rod Hall and Jim Fricker had a 40-minute lead. The hope for a battle with the John and Dan Randall failed to materialize when John got stuck in the silt early in the lap. Still, John and Dan held on for second place. Vern Roberts and Bill Donahoe almost took second, as the two Honchos got to racing for the position all the way through the second lap. In the end, the Randalls

With the Dodge leading, it was a battle between the Randall Honcho and Vern Roberts Honcho for the runner-up spot. The Randalls won the spot by 4 minutes, despite getting stuck in the soft stuff for a bit. (Photo Courtesy tracksidephoto.com)

They were so close they could almost taste it, but Vern Roberts had to settle for third when the Randalls just had too much speed for the terrain.

had 4 minutes in hand and kept the position.

Mint 400

The promise of a course change for 1985 to avoid the dry lakebed and its silt beds was not relayed to the big horn sheep population in the mountains to the west of the racecourse. The sheep came down much earlier than expected and forced the organizers to reuse the dry lake twice in a 20-mile stretch.

Myers versus Peltier moved to the Nevada desert. Both covered some serious mileage and were close for quite some time, but Peltier was not able to complete the third lap. Myers finished the third lap, and after 14 hours out there and Peltier not continuing, they parked the Cherokee and took the win.

The roughness of the course due to the sheep made some say that it was too rough for the short-wheelbase rigs. Twenty-three of them disagreed and threw their hats in the ring.

At the end of the first lap, only six were in contention for the win. By the end of the race, only two finished all four laps. Maybe there was something to that "too rough" statement. Going into Lap 2, the Hightowers were leading Eric and Mark Heiden in a Scrambler by a few minutes, and they were followed by J. M. Bragg and his sons.

The legendary J. M. Bragg enjoyed his second stretch in off-road racing with another Mint 400 win. He drove all four laps without stopping for anything but fuel.

Jim Bell and Walt Laycock are consistent drivers with a tough Honcho. That combination results in Mint 400 finishes, and this one time, they took second place.

Even though Coffland and Griffin made it to Ensenada, it was past the official finish time. They took second place for their time to the last timed checkpoint.

Marshall and Mike Mahr were also in the hunt.

After Lap 2, the Hightower CJ-7 was still in the lead, followed by J. M. Bragg (6 minutes behind), the Heidens (40 minutes behind Bragg), and the Mahrs (8 minutes behind the Heidens). Lap 3 claimed the Hightower CJ-7 and the Heiden Scrambler, which left the Braggs out front with the Mahrs far back. Due to the Heidens clearing more checkpoints in the third lap, they were credited with third place. J. M. Bragg won by 3 hours.

Sixteen entrants started the race, but only eight saw the end of the first lap. The dominant Dodge of Hall/Fricker led the first and all consecutive laps. The battle for second place came down to the potent Chevy pickup of Tom Strong (who built the Mike Moore Honchos) and Tim Casey (whose truck Strong built seven years previous). Strong went out in the second lap, and in the third lap, the Caseys coughed up a transmission and called it a day.

Jim Bell and Walt Laycock, in their Honcho, were consistent and rewarded with a second-place finish. Vern Roberts and Bill Donahoe were in third place a few hours behind Bell and Laycock.

Baja Internacional

It was going to be a hot one on the east side of the peninsula with temperatures hitting 116°F along the beach and even higher inland. Baja temperatures in June are no joke at lower elevations.

Three entries showed up—all of them CJs. Ken Correia and Chuck Morrison had the lead at checkpoint two but disappeared shortly thereafter. Gene and Kirby Hightower were now in the lead with Don Coffland and Buck Griffin an hour back. By Mike's Sky Ranch, the Hightower lead was narrowed to 30 minutes. The Hightowers axles broke and Coffland had some issues as well.

Both rigs made it to Nuevo Junction, which was Checkpoint 8. Hightower arriving 24 minutes sooner than Coffland and Griffin. Both rigs reached the finish line but after the official time limit had expired. The race was timed through Nuevo, and the Hightowers were awarded first place.

Big V-8 engines generate a lot of heat, and so does Baja. The pairing of these made for an extra-long day for everyone. Only five rigs entered and one of them blew an engine about two miles out of Ensenada. The Dodge of Hall/Fricker was out front by seven minutes early

Broken axles aside, Gene and Kirby Hightower squeaked out a win with the fastest time to Checkpoint 8 when they overran the official time limit. (Photo Courtesy tracksidephoto.com)

John Randall overcame broken drive-line pieces to earn a second-place finish thanks to his dedicated pit crew.

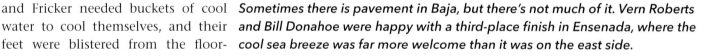

Sometimes there is pavement in Baja, but there's not much of it. Vern Roberts and Bill Donahoe were happy with a third-place finish in Ensenada, where the cool sea breeze was far more welcome than it was on the east side.

with a determined John Randall in tow. The gap was the same at Checkpoint 2 until shortly after, in a deep sand wash, Randall broke a U-joint and tried to carry on. The vibration cracked the transfer case and his crew went out to change all the broken parts, which took about 2 hours.

At El Chinero, on the hot eastern side, the Dodge pulled into the pits with a broken front axle truss. Hall and Fricker needed buckets of cool water to cool themselves, and their feet were blistered from the floorboard heat.

In the end, Randall rolled into Ensenada in second. With the win, the Dodge had already sewn up the season championship. Vern Roberts and Bill Donahoe finished 50 minutes after that for third.

Barstow Fireworks 250

Twenty-four rigs came out to the summer sizzler. While it was still over 105°F, it was better than the Baja Internacional four weeks prior. At least Barstow had some intermittent clouds to help shade the desert from time to time.

The next installment of the Myers versus Peltier battle was spoiled for Peltier by some alternator and battery issues in Lap 2 that brought the silver Cherokee to a stop in a part of the course that was difficult to access by the chase crew. Both rigs finished, and Myers notched another win.

An even dozen rigs came out to play in the Mojave. Don Coffland came out strong and set the fast lap for the class doing 60 miles in 1:45:16. Unfortunately, his next lap was over 4 hours.

The race quickly came down to J. M. Bragg versus Eric Heiden and Peter Colaci in his Scrambler. At the midway point, Bragg had 13 minutes on Heiden. In the third lap, Heiden cut the gap to 9 minutes. Bragg picked up 3 minutes in the final lap and won by 13 minutes.

Despite changing the front driveshaft at the end of Lap 1, that darn Dodge stayed undefeated in the desert once again. John Randall and Josh Bruner had some small issues on their way to second place, 40 minutes ahead of Vern Roberts and Bill Donahoe.

Riverside Off-Road World Championships

Jeep had an up and down Riverside weekend. The course was revamped to be a little longer so that the desert bred rigs had fairer conditions against purpose-built short-course machines.

It was a talented field of drivers taking on the challenging Riverside racecourse. Don Adams brought his Scrambler out of retirement. Geoff Dorr from Illinois made the long trip to try his luck. Doug Robinson came back out to race his CJ-7. The Scramblers had a wheelbase

Midwest racer Geoff Dorr went from second at the starting line to pass Don Adams and take the checkered flag at the famed Riverside racetrack.

advantage, so Adams, Coffland, and Dorr looked to use that advantage.

At the land-rush start, Adams had the horsepower and traction to take the lead and had Coffland and Dorr right on his tail. Doug Robinson headed a pack of trucks who looked to take his fourth position. At the halfway point, Dorr had dispatched Coffland and looked for a way around Adams. Two laps later, Dorr made a daring pass and edged Adams out of the lead. At the same time, Doug Robinson got around Coffland for the final podium spot.

Jeep's only other highlight for the weekend was John Randall, who heroically chased down that darn Dodge but could not get it and settled for second place in Class 4.

Don Adams streaks down Thompson Ridge and chases down eventual Class 3 winner Goeff Dorr, who is also driving a Jeep Scrambler.

and decided to end the race upon the return to Beatty.

The Jason Myers and Don Adams Cherokee suffered terminal ills early in the race. Tom Peltier and Dave

Frontier 500

The fourth annual Frontier 500 didn't run from Las Vegas to Reno. Walt Lott had trouble securing road permissions at the north end of the course. He redesigned the race into a single loop race that left from south of Vegas as usual and went north to Gabbs, Nevada, before it looped west and headed south back to Beatty before retracing the route to the start.

Many teams groaned at the idea of having to retrace the path through some of the worst silt beds in Nevada. Shortly before the race weekend, HDRA saw the folly in that decision

Tom Peltier and the Country Off-Road Team finally nailed down a win in the Cherokee during an ultra-rough tour of Nevada.

Gene and Kirby Hightower were crowned as the sole survivors in Class 3. They were the only team to make it to the finish line in the durable CJ-7.

high for the class). Myers and Adams rolled along and clicked off the miles, finishing 2 hours ahead of the small field.

Just three rigs competed in Class 3: two Jeeps and a Bronco. Don Coffland and Buck Griffin took the CJ-8 into the lead through four checkpoints, with 20 minutes in hand over the Hightower CJ-7. Between Checkpoint 4 and Checkpoint 5, Coffland rolled the CJ-8 hard and lost a door in the process. Repairs were attempted along the way, but there was too much damage. Coffland and Griffin packed it in at Checkpoint 7.

Mendrin kept going until the crew told them that they had secured the win and could stop.

In an odd coincidence, both the CJ-7 of Ken Correia and the CJ-8 of Don Coffland coasted to a stop with engine issues less than 5 miles off the start line. This thinned the already-thin field to three rigs.

A Scout ran in the lead to Beatty, but cooling troubles sidelined them there. Gene and Kirby Hightower assumed the lead at that point and were hours ahead of the nearest competitor in second place, which was a Bronco. The Hightower CJ-7 was the only entry to complete the course.

If not for the Honcho of Vern Roberts and Bill Donahoe, Jeep would have had a really bad day. The Randalls scattered an engine early in the race, and Tim Casey broke a leaf spring and had transmission issues early and stopped. Through tremendous grit and determination, Roberts and Donahoe were able to take second place.

Baja 1000

SCORE laid out a very long loop that totaled 800 miles for this year's granddaddy of all off-road races. In all, 12 4x4s entered the race and half were Jeeps.

Jason Myers and Don Adams were the lone Jeep entry in Class 12, which featured three entries (an an all-time

It was an easy Baja 1000 (if there is such a thing) for Don Adams and Jason Myers. They reported no issues on the 800-mile course. (Photo Courtesy tracksidephoto.com)

The Hightowers had their battles along the way with various competitors. They vanquished each one and emerged victorious in their return to Ensenada. (Photo Courtesy tracksidephoto.com)

Vern Roberts and Bill Donahoe were on the ball all race long and were precise in strategy and driving to take second place. (Photo Courtesy tracksidephoto.com)

Gene and Kirby Hightower inherited the lead and left the Bronco in their dust as they arrived in Ensenada 26.5 hours after they started for the win.

The fight for second place was evident early on, as the usual suspects ran off into the distance. One potent Chevy and several Honchos fought for the runner-up position, with the Randalls in front through Checkpoint 5 when the suspension broke. Vern Roberts and Bill Donahoe put in a great consistent drive in the Honcho and easily outpaced the Chevy by 3 hours at the finish.

1985 Wrap Up

At the end of the season, the La Paz Drink Mix team liquidated the Jeeps and equipment to other teams. The last season saw the Honchos get faster, but the price was that the transmissions failed at a high rate before any wins were secured. With no answer to fix the weakness in sight, it was decided to sell the team. La Paz came back later and ran a vehicles of a different manufacturer in a different class.

1986

The year started sadly with the space shuttle Challenger disaster in late January. Things did not get much better in April, when a terrorist bomb was set off in a Berlin disco that was frequented by US soldiers. Later in the year, long-suffering New York

Mets fans were rewarded for their patience with a World Series win over the Boston Red Sox.

In off-road racing news, SCORE and HDRA announced that they would combine forces and have one championship. In response to sponsors and racers requests, the schedule was trimmed down and the San Felipe and Laughlin races were eliminated.

Parker 400

The new combined championship kicked off at everyone's favorite race in Parker, Arizona.

With the Cherokee far from ready, Don Adams made the call to repair the often-raced CJ-7 and bring it to Parker. At the start, there were only five entries in Class 3. Four of those were Jeeps.

At the top of the California loop, Buck Griffin and Don Coffland led the Jeep CJs of Adams and the Hightowers by a few minutes, while David Bryan and Darren York were close behind in fourth place in Bryan's CJ-6.

Across the river on the Arizona side, the Hightower Jeep put in a heck of a lap and built a 12-minute lead over Adams. Griffin and Coffland had some gremlins pop up and lost time to the leaders.

At the finish, Kirby Hightower and Gary Currier were 23 minutes ahead of Adams. Griffin and Coffland were an hour behind in third place, and Bryan and York finished fourth for a Jeep sweep.

Rod Hall and Jim Fricker were back again in the

The Hightowers made a great return to off-road racing by winning the Parker 400 by a 23-minute margin. (Photo Courtesy tracksidephoto.com)

John Dyck drove the Honcho to a convincing second-place finish and sandwiched himself between two Dodge competitors. (Photo Courtesy tracksidephoto.com)

Dodge. Of course, they picked right back up where they left off by winning Class 4 convincingly in the season opener. Honestly, it didn't get any better for Jeep teams for a while. John Dyck and Al Baker took second place in their Honcho (21 minutes behind Hall and Fricker and 1 hour and 20 minutes ahead of another Dodge). Rodney Inch and Jim Roebuck were fourth, which gave Jeep Honchos two in the top five.

Great Mojave 250

Teams followed SCORE from Parker to Lucerne Valley. Heavy rains all winter made the already-rough 132-mile racecourse even rougher than before. For that reason, SCORE increased the official time limit from 9 to 10 hours.

Five of the six entries were Jeep products. Don Adams and Jason Myers had the Cherokee back in action, but many little issues kept them an hour down at the end of the first lap. Kirby Hightower was out in the first lap with a broken frame. Mike Schwellinger took 7 hours to complete just one lap, and David Bryan went missing on Lap 1.

It probably did not matter because Don Coffland and Buck Griffin had a perfect race and ripped around two laps in an identical time of 4:11.

Buck Griffin and Don Coffland had one of those perfect days with no downtime and two laps completed. (Photo Courtesy tracksidephoto.com)

Don Yosten and Bill Donahoe lead a train of three Honchos (not pictured) into the finish to nab the third spot at the 1986 Great Mojave 250. (Photo Courtesy tracksidephoto.com)

Adams and Myers came in 1 hour and 10 minutes later for third place. They were followed very closely by J. M. Bragg for fourth place.

Two Dodges laid waste to the field this time around and left a group of Honchos to battle for the last podium spot. Don Yosten and Bill Donahoe were able to keep their rig together and outlasted two other Honchos to the finish. Jim Bell and Walt Laycock were next followed by Shane and Vic Hutchings.

Mint 400

There were big changes to the Mint 400. The desert north of the Las Vegas Speedrome, the Mint's home for 10 years, was unavailable to racers. Gone for now were the rock garden and the nasty silt beds at the north end of the course.

All the usual festivities were still in place around the Mint hotel and casino downtown, and the race had good entry numbers, as 367 took the green flag. Eighteen hours later, only 113 finished.

A hearty 17 short-wheelbase rigs came out to play. There is an old saying that "old age and treachery will overcome youth and skill every time." Quite often in off-road racing, this tends to be the case. Last year's champion, J. M. Bragg, did not lead wire to wire, but he kept his nose clean as faster rigs fell by the wayside on the rough course. J. M. and his sons did not move into the physical lead until the third lap.

It took them 13.5 hours of scrambling over the desert, but they arrived at the end of the fourth lap with a half

John Dyck and Al Baker moved quickly throughout the day and stayed ahead of the Don Yosten Honcho. Sadly, they were overtaken by a brakeless Dodge. They finished second in class. (Photo Courtesy tracksidephoto.com)

It took until the third of four laps for J. M. Bragg to take the lead, but once he had it, he didn't let go. This was Bragg's third of four Mint 400 class wins. (Photo Courtesy tracksidephoto.com)

Eric Heiden had a tough 14.5-hour day battling the Nevada Desert, and it netted him a third place. (Photo Courtesy tracksidephoto.com)

Lowell Arnold has a knack for the Mint 400. This was his second win in the fabled race. It took almost the entire time limit, but a win is a win.

hour lead over the second-place Dodge Ramcharger. Eric and Mark Heiden were in third place (another 32 minutes behind in their CJ-8). Buck Griffin and Don Coffland were in fourth place in another Scrambler.

The long-wheelbase trucks had only eight starters, and half of them did not finish the first lap. It is not always easy to get back to first place, and the Dodge had brake issues all race long after Hall clobbered a rocky bank on Lap 1. John Dyck and Al Baker were the first around, followed by Don Yosten and Bill Donahoe both in Honchos, and the Dodge came around for third.

The Honchos stayed in place, with Jim Bell and Walt Laycock occasionally getting close in their Honcho, but they broke on the third lap. The Dodge worked its way back into the lead, as small issues plagued both Honchos to allow the Dodge to pull away by 40 minutes without brakes.

Class 14 was for heavily modified 4x4s and had been around for almost two seasons. Up until now, only a few Broncos and a Chevy Blazer regularly entered the class. Five started, and Jeep took the top two places in the end.

Lowell Arnold and Tom Kepler were first around with the fastest lap in the class: 3:57:05. A Bronco was in second place (20 minutes behind) headed into Lap 2,

Dale Lenig and Robert Hughes brought their highly modified CJ-2A with great hopes of completing the roughest event in America. It took them nearly the entire 18-hour time limit to finish, and they did so in second place.

JASON MYERS 1946–1986

Prior to the Baja Internacional, Jason Myers did his second favorite thing besides desert racing. He was piloting an aircraft at an air show in his hometown of Buena Vista, Colorado, and it crashed, killing him at the age of 40.

Jason Myers (left) poses with Don Adams in their early days with the CJ-7. Myers was a talented off-road driver and pilot who was well liked and is still missed today. (Photo Courtesy Brad Russell)

where it stopped with terminal ills. Dale Lenig and Robert Hughes brought their CJ-2A all the way from Pennsylvania. At the halfway point, they were in second place and just 7 minutes behind.

The third lap was a bit longer for the Honcho due to deterioration of the roads, but the CJ-2A slowed a little more. At the finish, Arnold and Kepler used 17 hours of the 18-hour time limit to make the finish. Lenig and Hughes cut it even closer and arrived at the finish with just 10 minutes left before the cutoff. For Arnold, it was his second class win at the Mint.

Baja Internacional

The huge entry trend continued south of the border, as many teams came down for the 492-mile race.

Here is something that you rarely write as a factual truth in off-road racing. Five rigs entered, and all five were able to finish: four CJs and a lone Bronco. Do you want to take it one step further? In Class 4, three started and all three finished.

Don Adams teamed up with Larry Olsen to replace Myers. Adams looked for redemption from a disastrous Mint 400 and a win to dedicate to Myers. Heading out of Ensenada and toward the first checkpoint, Don Coffland and Buck Griffin were within a minute of the Cherokee, with David Bryan and Darren York minutes behind the leaders.

In the second leg of the race, Coffland and Schwellinger faded with mechanical issues, which allowed Bryan into second place. As the race came around towards Mike's Sky Ranch and San Felipe, it was Bryan's turn to have an issue in his CJ-6, which allowed Coffland back into second place. Schwellinger got around Bryan as well. At the finish, Adams got his win followed by Coffland, Schwellinger, and Bryan.

Rod Hall and Jim Fricker snatched victory from the jaws of defeat for the second race in a row. Heading up a rocky trail, Hall snagged a boulder and damaged the front end. Luckily, the crew was nearby and made repairs that took more than an hour.

David Bryan ran well early and held second place for quite a while before issues arose in the CJ-6 and he dropped to fourth place. (Photo Courtesy tracksidephoto.com)

Don Adams and Larry Olsen paid homage to their fallen friend, Jason Myers, with a win in Baja. The duo ran like clockwork. (Photo Courtesy tracksidephoto.com)

It was a heartbreaker of a finish. Early in the race, the Dodge made an uncharacteristic mistake and lost time. Don Yosten and Bill Donahoe had the lead for hundreds of miles until a late problem allowed the Dodge to slip past them and win the race. (Photo Courtesy tracksidephoto.com)

For a long while, Don Yosten and Bill Donahoe led by nearly an hour. Near Checkpoint 9, Yosten and Donahoe had an issue and fell back into second place.

Barstow Fireworks 250

The HDRA's race at Barstow took place over the Fourth of July weekend. It featured a record-breaking 293 entries.

A dozen rigs showed up for the short-wheelbase battle. Don Adams and Larry Olsen had a terrible first lap and fixed electrical issues throughout the 77-mile course, which cost them an hour in the Cherokee. Eric Heiden and Peter Calaci had a solid first lap, setting the fastest time. They were closely followed by Buck Griffin and Don Coffland as well as J. M. Bragg. Both faded in the middle laps. Griffin took fifth place, and Bragg finished outside the top five.

Eric Heiden put it all together and came away with the win against stiff competition. Heiden only made one unscheduled stop, which was for clean goggles.

With his homebuilt racer down for major repairs, Rock Bradford borrowed the T&J Off-Road Center Commando. He only needed two of the four laps before he found out that no one was left running in his class. (Photo Courtesy tracksidephoto.com)

Adams and Olsen ran strong in the second lap and set their sights on Heiden's CJ-8. July 5, 1986, was Heiden's day, as the only issue that he reported was one extra stop for clean goggles on his way to his first win. Adams finished 1 hour and 20 minutes behind Heiden and took second place.

Typically, Rock Bradford runs a rear-engine creation. However, the homebuilt vehicle was sidelined for Barstow, so T&J Off-Road's George Barnett rented them their Jeep Commando to run in the modified class. After two laps, they found out that they were the only one left running and parked the Commando.

Crossing the finish line with a busted radiator was of little worry for Mike Schwellinger when he took second place in a Nevada race. He was learning quickly and improved with every event.

Frontier 500

This year, it was apparent early that HDRA would not be able to get the Frontier 500 back to a point-to-point format headed towards Reno. Walt Lott devised a 111-mile lap that shared some of the same roads as the Mint 400, but it wasn't an exact copy. Lott found more rocks and silt, and four laps that totaled 444-miles would be enough for anyone.

The rough trails were not kind to the entries in the class regardless of the vehicle being driven. Several took turns in the lead only to come to grief in a silt bed or on a refrigerator-sized rock. Five were close together on the first lap with two stragglers. Two Broncos, a Ramcharger, and four Jeeps went into the second lap. Adams and Olsen had more issues with the powerful Cherokee but kept plugging along. Only four vehicles finished the second lap.

At the halfway point, an ancient Bronco led the way with Mike Schwellinger and Victor Hernadez only 13 minutes behind. In Lap 4, the Bronco stretched the

Don Yosten and Bill Donahoe were smooth, steady, quick, and first across the finish line to take a win away from the Dodge!

lead to over 20 minutes because Schwellinger had overheating issues. Ford took the day, but Schwellinger came home with a well-deserved second place and steam billowing from his radiator. It was his best finish to date. Adams never showed up at the finish.

September 6, 1986, went down in Jeep history as the day the streak ended. There is no proof that some still celebrate it to this day, but it wouldn't be a surprise if it were true. The Dodge failed to complete the entire course. On the first lap, in heavy dust, Rod Hall missed a turn and slammed into a sizeable boulder or two and took out the transfer case, transmission, and various suspension pieces. It took 8.5 hours for Hall to complete the first lap.

Meanwhile, up front, Don Yosten and Bill Donahoe led every lap and were the only vehicle to finish all four laps.

Baja 1000

The year 1986 brought a true Baja 1000 to the racers with an Ensenada to La Paz course. The course was 1,013 miles in total. It was a fast course, except for a few silty areas.

It was a pleasant surprise to see seven rigs entered. At Santa Inez, about one-third of the way into the race, all but one entry were within 1 hour of each other. Buck Griffin and Don Coffland were first and were followed by Adams. Schwellinger, who was having a good race, followed Adams and was being followed by Eric Heiden's CJ-8.

Shortly after this point, the Adams and Olsen Jeep Cherokee blew a head gasket and was reduced to four out of six cylinders. There was no quit in this team, as by San Ignacio, Adams still had the lead despite the gasket issue. A Ramcharger was in second place and within 6 minutes, and Schwellinger was in third place and

During the second half of the race, Don Adams and Larry Olsen were running out of working cylinders. The Jeep finished with half of its original six. Still, the team had built up enough of a cushion that it managed second place. (Photo Courtesy tracksidephoto.com)

Mike Schwellinger fought hard to beat the field, but it did not go entirely his way. He managed a third-place finish that was only 12 minutes behind Don Adams. (Photo Courtesy tracksidephoto.com)

Eric Heiden and his brother Mark were Good Samaritans to their competitors after lengthy repairs killed their chances of winning. They stopped to help everyone they met, which allowed some competitors to see the finish line who otherwise may not have been able to. (Photo Courtesy tracksidephoto.com)

within striking distance. Griffin and Coffland were nowhere to be found, and Heiden had big problems but soldiered onward and pulled out stuck vehicles in the silt.

At La Purisima, the Adams and Olsen Cherokee lost another cylinder, which left them with half as many as they started with. The Ramcharger took advantage and took first place 42 minutes ahead of the Jeep. Schwellinger fell 12 minutes short of catching Adams. Eric and Mark Heiden came into La Paz 4 hours later but were happy to have helped others out along the way.

By 1986, it was probably safe to say that Rod Hall knew his way to La Paz better than anyone. That knowledge helped him finish an amazing 9th overall and first in class by 6 hours.

Don Yosten and Bill Donahoe had many problems. It began when Donahoe rolled the Honcho early in the race to avoid a civilian car that was parked in the middle of the racecourse. After that, it was a series of stops to weld this, replace that, and rewire the other thing. It took 30 hours (9.5 hours longer than the winner), but they arrived in La Paz happy to be there and put a Jeep on the podium in third.

The Wrangler had big shoes to fill by replacing the CJ. The CJ had built a fiercely loyal following during its 41 years in civilian trim.

1987

It was the late 1980s, and music filled the air at most pit locations and in race shops. The Bangles wanted you to "Walk Like An Egyptian." Starship told us that "Nothing's Going to Stop Us Now," and Bruce Hornsby told us all about "The Way It Is" on his way to a best new artist Grammy award.

Jeep Changes Hands Again

Lee Iacocca was on a tear in 1987. After he saved Chrysler, he got busy and rebranded and redesigned everything. When the opportunity came to purchase AMC for a measly $1.5 billion, he jumped on it and made no secret that the Jeep name was the prize in that deal.

This meant several things for off-road racing, including the return of contingency money to the 4x4 and mini truck classes. Chrysler wanted the Comanche to race more. Several had raced in 1986 but with little success and no podiums.

Farewell to the CJ

Before the Chrysler takeover, Jeep had already designed the YJ (Wrangler) as the replacement to the beloved CJ line. With the success of the Comanche, AMC had already killed production on the Scrambler. Don Adams continued to run the Cherokee until the Wrangler was ready for the Baja 1000.

Parker 400

Every year, the local Bureau of Land Management (BLM) office made more demands to SCORE. The BLM imposed

Don Adams brought the Cherokee to Parker and laid waste to the field with a clean run. (Photo Courtesy tracksidephoto.com)

Buck Griffin was a driver of record now, but that was the only change. He and Don Coffland drove a smart race and finished second. (Photo Courtesy tracksidephoto.com)

General Tire motorsports boss Olga Vernon was able to see what off-road racing was all about, as Mike Schwellinger took her for a ride that she has not forgotten to this day. They came out of the weekend with a third-place finish. (Photo Courtesy tracksidephoto.com)

a 30 mph speed limit when pre-running the course. They were also out in force all week and wrote some very expensive tickets with the California Highway Patrol.

Don Adams and Larry Olsen brought out the Cherokee for this race. The gremlins must have finally been exorcised, as the duo had a clean run and led the entire way.

Buck Griffin and Don Coffland chased the Cherokee and eventually finished in second place (18 minutes behind Adams and Olson). Mike Schwellinger took General Tire executive Olga Vernon along for a ride to third place. David Bryan and his sister Debbie nabbed the sixth spot.

Jeep saw better days in Parker, but it was satisfied with a Herculean effort by John Dyck and Al Baker, who kept repairing the Honcho to nab the third spot.

Mike Lesle had a new Class 7 4x4 build on the start line. It was a Comanche built by off-road racing legend John Johnson. The new entry came to Parker with zero testing time, so expectations were low. The plan was for Leslie to drive the California

loop and that Johnson would do the rest.

The class was diverse, with two Jeeps, one Ford, one Chevy, one Nissan, and one Toyota. The Chevy was the defending champion and it led in California by 11 minutes as teams transferred to the Arizona side. Leslie was second with the Nissan just 4 minutes behind.

Heading into Arizona, Leslie moved over to the passenger seat so that he could learn from Johnson—and

With his sister Debbie Keefe riding along, David Bryan had some issues throughout the race but secured sixth place. (Photo Courtesy David Bryan)

John Dyck's Honcho flies through the air. He mounted a hard charge and took third place. (Photo Courtesy trackside-photo.com)

learn he would. By the end of the first lap, Johnson caught the Chevy and put the Comanche in the lead on corrected time. In the Arizona pit, the Chevy lost 45 minutes, and no one was even close.

On the final lap, a rock kicked up and bent a fan blade. Johnson stopped at the next pit, grabbed a torch to trim and reshape the bent blade, trimmed all of the other blades to match, and continued. It was clear sailing from there, as Johnson brought home a maiden-voyage win by 56 minutes. The Jeep Comanche of Mike Randall and Bob Bower placed fourth.

The debut for the new Mike Lesle Comanche could not have gone better. He and John Johnson grabbed the lead in the first Arizona loop. Despite fixing a broken fan blade in the second loop, they gave the Comanche a win in its maiden voyage. (Photo Courtesy tracksidephoto.com)

Mint 400

For the first time in the 20-year history of the Mint 400, the Mint hotel and casino looked for a sponsor. Nissan wasted no time and became the sponsor. Thus, it was the first year of the Nissan Mint 400.

Several teams migrated from Class 3 and Class 4, which made for a sizeable field of 10 in the modified class.

Most of the class finished the first lap, with a home-built entry leading the way, followed by Emil Downey

The old CJ-7 did not make it easy on Don Adams and Larry Olson. In the final two laps, the pit crews were busy fixing suspension and electrical issues. However, the well-seasoned CJ-7 still found its way into the winner's circle.

and Joe Janis in their CJ-8, which was within 2 minutes of the leader. Carl Cook and Glenn Emery Jr., in the rear-engine Jeep CJ-2A, were 7 minutes back, and David Bryan and his sister Debbie Keefe were glued to Cook's exhaust pipes.

By the end of Lap 2, the Downey CJ-8 was out of the race along with three others. Cook moved to the front with a Toyota close behind. Bryan and Keefe made a pit stop to replace a broken front leaf-spring shackle and lost just a few minutes. Heading out into Lap 3, Bryan's seat broke, and a piece of the steel frame poked him in the hip. Cook still led as an uncomfortable David Bryan passed the broken Toyota to move into third place. Besieged with problems earlier in the race, Eric Heiden and Russ Pignon moved into fourth place in the CJ-8.

Cook and Emery maintained the lead all the way to the finish. Bryan and Keefe tried everything to close the gap, but they crossed the finish line 36 minutes after. The broken seat had rubbed Bryan's hip raw to the point that it was bleeding. Nevada likes to extract its pound of flesh. Heiden made the finish line with just 7 minutes left in the time limit to be the last official finisher.

Eight Class 3 entries came to the Mint, and five of those were Jeeps. Adams and Olsen were without the Cherokee because of repairs that it needed, so Adams unretired the CJ-7 for this race. A hearty seven of the rigs made the first lap, with Mike Schwellinger and Les Erickson leading in the CJ-7. A Bronco was next, just 1 minute behind the leader, and Adams was 6 minutes behind the Bronco.

Schwellinger snapped a front axle housing in Lap 2 and lost 3.5 hours due to repairs. Adams moved into the lead with the well-worn CJ-7, followed by a Ramcharger and a Bronco. The Ramcharger didn't complete another lap.

Now repaired, Schwellinger set the fastest lap in class on the third loop, but he was 2 hours behind Adams. The old Jeep did not make it easy on Adams and Olsen. In the last half of the race, they had to replace shocks and a front leaf-spring shackle, and they had a battery issue. However, they held the lead despite the issues and notched another win for the CJ-7. Schwellinger finished in second place, despite losing an hour on the last lap.

While the Dodge ran away with yet another race, a few Class 4 Jeeps and a Chevy fought over the scraps. There was an early tussle involving John Dyck, Don Yosten, and a Dodge and a Chevy, but the Dodge slowed on Lap 2. Dyck stepped out in front of the crowd, and aside from a broken air filter repair and five flat tires, he finished in second place. A 5-hour final lap dropped Yosten down to fifth place.

Mike Lesle and John Johnson had a dream race and led Class 7 4x4 from the start. It wasn't entirely comfortable, as a Chevy S-10 was about 15 minutes behind them lap after lap. Wherever the Comanche was, the S-10 was not far behind. Heading into the final lap, the Jeep had engine troubles that cost more than 5 hours of downtime, and they dropped to third place at the end.

Baja Internacional

In early summer, off-road racers migrate south to Ensenada for the SCORE Baja Internacional. The course was laid out to keep the race on the hotter east side of Baja Norte to a minimum.

Through four checkpoints, Don Adams and Larry Olsen held a 20-minute advantage over Mike Schwellinger and Les Erickson. After the climb up the mountains to Mike's Sky Ranch, Schwellinger turned up the wick on the CJ-7 and led by 13 minutes.

Heading into the final checkpoint just 50 miles from the finish in Ensenada, Schwellinger was 9 minutes ahead of Adams. Schwellinger started the race 1 minute ahead of Adams, so when Adams appeared on his bumper heading into Ensenada, Schwellinger knew that he was in second place. Adams won by 35 seconds.

John Dyck and Jerry Sterling fell behind by 26 minutes early in the race. The Honcho was plagued with a rash of flat tires throughout the race and the engine overheated. In the end, they salvaged a respectable third place.

In a great midseason result for Jeep, two Comanches placed in the top four. A Chevy S-10 driven by Jerry McDonald and Joe McPherson had a flawless race and took the win by a large margin. However, Mike Randall and Bob Bower seemed to have their Comanche well sorted as they were within 7 minutes of the leader early on.

By San Felipe, Randall was in third place (4 minutes behind second place) when on the beach run north of town, they experienced fuel-pressure issues and then a ring and pinion broke. The crew was on scene and quickly made repairs. Meanwhile, Mike Lesle and Jack Ramsey had trouble early with leaking differential seals, but they tried to reel in the leaders and made it as high as third place heading back toward Ensenada.

With repairs made, the Randall Comanche looked to catch a Toyota that passed them while they buttoned up the Comanche. Since the Toyota started 2 minutes ahead of them, they

A disappointing second-place finish sounds odd, but for Mike Schwellinger to see Don Adams pull up on his bumper coming into Ensenada, Schwellinger knew that he was in second place because Adams started 1 minute behind him. (Photo Courtesy tracksidephoto.com)

Despite a fuel delivery issue and broken rear pinion (all repaired by the Randall pit crew), Mike Randall and Bob Bower had the speed to win a hard-fought battle in Class 7 4x4 for second place. (Photo Courtesy tracksidephoto. com)

It was one of those days when leaky differential seals and other ills dropped the fast Comanche to an eventual fourth-place finish. (Photo Courtesy tracksidephoto.com)

knew that if they could get him in sight, they would take the position by elapsed time. Heading into the last 50 miles, Leslie was second in his Comanche, then the Toyota, and then Randall and Bower. Leslie had unknown ills and lost over an 1.5 hours. The battle for second place was between the Toyota and Randall. On the pavement heading into Ensenada, Randall caught the Toyota and passed it to take a well-earned second place. Leslie made repairs and still nabbed the fourth position.

Fall Mix-Up

For Jeep and the off-road racing world, the fall of 1987 saw a shake-up of the usual schedule. The annual Riverside event was forgettable, except for two performances. Don Adams won Class 3 in the CJ-7 and was the only finisher. Al Unser Jr. managed to take fifth place in a short-course-built Jeep Comanche.

The Frontier 500 was placed on the backburner while course issues were handled with government agencies. Not one to let grass grow under his feet, Walt Lott dreamt of an off-road event in Colorado that was not short-course based.

Baja 1000

SCORE made a compact (by Baja 1000 standards) 900-mile course that crisscrossed Baja Norte. Mother Nature had other ideas. Constant storms battered the west side of the peninsula the week before the race which, made one part after Mike's Sky Rancho impassable. After some quick re-routing, the course measured 705 miles.

The Don Adams Wrangler finally made its maiden appearance in Baja. It was very clean and carried new sponsorship with Stroh's Beer along with long-time sponsors Jeep and BFGoodrich. The Wrangler was not only pretty but also fast. It led from the start to Cohabuzo Junction, just after the summit where the steering box failed and cost hours of downtime.

Mike Schwellinger and Les Erickson led from there, but it did not last long. As they came into Tres Posos, the transmission and torque converter failed, which necessitated a change, and they lost hours. Jerry Bundy and Ron Zemanek in the CJ-8 now led the class and continued to do so all of the way to the finish. Three hours later, Schwellinger took second place a few hours ahead of a Bronco.

Mike Lesle once again teamed with John Johnson, who started the race and led early. After the drivers switch, Lesle had over 2 hours of downtime in the southern loop of the course, which allowed a Chevy and a Nissan to slip past him before he got going again. The Randall Comanche had trouble and was not seen again. Lesle soldiered on and brought home a third-place finish and the class championship.

The new Don Adams Wrangler finally made its debut. It was fast and led from the start. Steering box issues dropped the team out of contention for a podium finish. (Photo Courtesy tracksidephoto.com)

Jerry Bundy and Ron Zemanek earned a well-deserved win in Class 3 at the 1987 Baja 1000. The East Coast duo was consistent and tidy in driving around the muddy course. (Photo Courtesy tracksidephoto.com)

Just like a month earlier in Colorado, the father-and-son team of Emil and John Downey were dominant in their CJ-8 and won easily.

1988

The year began with the Winter Olympics in Calgary, Alberta, Canada, and the debut of the Jamaican bobsled team. Just a month, later the Soviet Union collapsed and broke apart the block of 15 countries. Former Beatle George Harrison reemerged onto the music scene with his "Cloud 9" album with a little help from friends, including Elton John, Ringo Starr, Jeff Lynne, and Eric Clapton.

The season began on a low note for Jeep, as it recorded no wins at either the Parker 400 or the Gold Coast 300. By the third race of the year, things looked better for Jeep.

Great Mojave 250

SCORE learned from the racers from last year and reworked the course into a 57-mile loop with less silt, some faster roads, and an earlier start time. Teams had 9 hours to complete the four laps, which meant that everyone would be done before 5 p.m. and could drive home that night for Easter Sunday the following day.

Three Jeeps were among the seven starters in Class 3. The CJ-8 of Jerry Bundy started quick to lead the first lap. He was followed by Schwellinger and Erickson and then Don Adams and Larry Olsen in the Wrangler. Adams and Olsen pitted for a leaky rear-end seal and then took off—only to return moments later because the repair did not hold.

Bundy was in a rough spot on the course, had a flat tire, and then had trouble making the change on the

uneven terrain. Schwellinger motored past to take the lead for good. Olsen was able to get the Wrangler back in third place at the end of Lap 2 before handing the driving over to Adams. On Lap 4, Bundy stayed in the hunt and took second place, while Adams encountered trouble that relegated the Wrangler to fourth place.

Class 4 began to get overrun by specially built trucks that had big factory dollar backing. Chevy, Nissan, and Dodge had big advantages in technology over the Honcho teams. However, as former Class 3 driver Eric Heiden was known for saying, "The desert is a great equalizer."

Sometimes, a little slower and tougher truck yields a positive result. Such was the case with John Dyck and David French, who completed Lap 1 in last place. Something happened to one of the fancy trucks during each lap, and the Honcho kept moving forward and gained positions. By the final lap, Dyck and French were third behind a Chevy and that darn Dodge. Just after Checkpoint 4, there was the Dodge sitting by the side of the course with a broken transfer case. Dyck earned second place in the class in the Honcho.

Mike Lesle and Mike Bakholden came around after Lap 1 only 7 seconds out of the lead behind a Nissan and ahead of a pack of Fords and a Toyota. By Lap 2, the Lesle and Bakholden's Comanche took the lead by 2 minutes over the Nissan with the pack a few minutes behind them. After a pit stop for fuel, the Comanche received word that the rest of the pack was imploding all over the course with broken suspensions, rollovers, etc. The Jeep came home victorious.

Mint 400

Unseasonal weather caused the organizer of the 21st edition of the Mint 400 to cut the official time limit short. A storm that was slated for that night brought dangerous conditions, including flash flooding and near hurricane-force winds.

In Class 3, it was an early exit for the Adams Wrangler. It didn't even complete a lap. This left Mike Schwellinger and Les Erickson to literally cruise to the win and be the only finisher of the four laps. Las Vegas residents Ben Emerson and Allison Krueger piloted their CJ-7 to third place and defeated a few Broncos by more than an hour.

John Dyck and Tom Marion played the savior for Jeep in Class 4 for most of the last two years. Here at

Mike Lesle had tough competition early at the Great Mojave 250. The field dwindled due to attrition, and the Stroh's Jeep was the winner.

Sometimes the Mint 400 is not so much about racing but surviving. It is something that most people learn with experience. In this case, the Schwellinger Jeep came home as the only finisher in its class. (Photo Courtesy tracksidephoto.com)

the Mint, they soldiered onward through the wind and dust to nab a hard-earned fourth-place finish in their class as the only Jeep finisher.

Mike Lesle teamed up with Cameron Steele and took the Comanche to a dominating win by almost an hour over 15 other teams. Lesle drove the first two laps and held a 7 minute lead at the driver change. Steele drove Lap 3 to give Lesle a break. He turned an identical time to Lesle and handed the Jeep back with a 45 minute lead. Lesle cruised the last lap to seal the win.

When taking on the Nevada desert, the tough vehicles usually shine through, and what is tougher than a Jeep product? The top four positions in the class (out of 10 starters) were taken by Jeep products, albeit highly modified.

The rear-engine CJ-2 of Carl Cook took the lead after Lap 1 by 10 minutes over Emil and John Downey in their Scrambler, which had a rollover and some shock issues. The Downeys found their pace and came around the second lap and took a slim 54-second lead on Cook. By Lap

Mike Lesle brought Cameron Steele along to give him a break on Lap 3. The plan worked perfectly, as the duo won by over an hour. (Photo Courtesy tracksidephoto.com)

The race was stopped due to rain, and Emil and John Downey were the winners as an incoming storm canceled the final lap. (Photo Courtesy tracksidephoto.com)

3, that lead stretched to 13 minutes. As they came into the start/finish area, officials waved the Downeys aside to tell them that the course was closing early and the class would be timed over three laps. Cook was second, and Jack Marno and Rob Babiuk brought their homebuilt CJ-7 all the way from British Columbia to take third. Marno and Babiuk were the last of the three lap finishers.

Baja Internacional

The course was 479 miles of fast flowing Baja, including 20 miles of highways, which is something that became more common in Baja.

After 479 miles, three entries were mere moments apart after an epic battle from coast to coast and back, with 2 minutes and 42 seconds covering the three. The players were the Jeeps of Don Adams and Mike Schwellinger and a Ramcharger.

Larry Olsen led (on time) for the first half of the race before he handed off the Jeep to Don Adams. Mike Schwellinger and Les Erickson yo-yoed between 4 and 7 minutes behind Adams, with the Ramcharger glued to his bumper. And so it went, through San Felipe, up the bumpy beach road, and into the sand washes.

Heading into Checkpoint 9 late in the race, Adams had a miscue that cost them about 10 minutes. Schwellinger jumped into the lead and was followed by the Ramcharger and then Adams. You could throw a blanket over the leaders as they rocketed into Ensenada nearly within view of each other. Schwellinger arrived at the finish first and claimed the top spot by 49 seconds over the Ramcharger, and Adams took third by an ago-

nizing 53 seconds. Ken Corriea and Keith Robbins took a distant fourth place with their Jeep.

In Class 7S, Walker Evans Racing took over the factory Comanche project from Enduro Racing. The Comanche spent the better part of 1988 getting sorted out. Behind the wheel was Rob McCachren, a young but capable driver from Las Vegas.

By Camalu, McCachren was in third place and was within 6 minutes of second place and 14 minutes of the leader. Heading inland, McCachren came across a rolled over two-seat buggy that belonged to Mike Gaughan, the owner of several hotels in Las Vegas and McCachren's boss and sponsor. He stopped and helped right the buggy before he continued on and maintaining the third spot.

Headed west, the Comanche encountered a tree limb that smashed the windshield. McCachren and Mike Smig stopped to remove the shattered windshield and managed to get going without losing third place. The Jeep wheeled into Ensenada and held the final podium spot to give the new Comanche its first finish.

In the 4x4 class, it was Mike Lesle's job to uphold Jeep's honor. To help with that task, Lesle enlisted help from Jim Wright, who was normally a two-seat buggy driver with his father, Billy, and had a resume of impressive wins.

At Camalu, Lesle was mired in fourth and fought with a Mazda and a few Fords. By Mike's Sky Ranch, he moved past the Mazda to third. Coming down the hill into San Matias, he handed the Comanche over to Wright, who shot off toward San Felipe and the 180-mile loop back to the same pit area. With smart driving, Wright brought

Rob MacCachren took the wheel of the Walker Evans-prepped Comanche and made a fine show of himself for both of his bosses. For Walker Evans, it was a top-three finish, and for his boss, Michael Gaughan, MacCachren helped flip his two-seater back on its wheels. (Photo Courtesy tracksidephoto.com)

the Jeep back in second and handed it off to Lesle. The leader was too far ahead, and second-place points were better than wrapping the Comanche around a rock or tree.

The Last Riverside

It had been rumored for years, and every time off-road racers gathered at Riverside, it was always on people's lips that this could be the last one. By 1988, papers were signed and dates were set for the handover of the property that was once Riverside International Raceway. It affected every motorsport in Southern California and is still missed to this day.

Everything seemed restrained that last weekend—from the crowd to the entry list. Jeep had a few highlights, and Don Adams took the Class 3 win by a lap over the Jeep CJ-7 of Rich Severson.

Nevada 500

Without Frontier Hotel sponsorship, the Frontier 500 race was renamed the Nevada 500. Michael Gaughan offered his Gold Coast Hotel as the race's headquarters. It was the first event without Walt Lott. His widow, Edna, took up the mantle to see every entry off at the start like Walt always did.

Schwellinger took an early lead in his CJ-7 and was first to Beatty, leading a Bronco and Don Adams's Wrangler by a few minutes. Schwellinger pitted in Beatty for an hour and tried to fix his brakes. Shortly after Beatty was a notorious hill that racers had to climb, and it had a history of ending a lot of racers days. One such example was when Don Adams blew his transfer case trying to get over the silty, rocky hill. The Bundy CJ-8 was back in fourth after much downtime with mechanical ills.

Heading out of Beatty, Schwellinger's Jeep coughed up the engine and that was the end of his day. Jerry Bundy took the last podium spot, finishing nearly 4 hours after the winner.

In Class 4, the Honcho of John Dyck was in third place from the start to just before Tonopah before his day ended unexpectedly with a broken Quadratrac unit. Another J-10 moved into third and stayed there all the way home to net a fine third for Don Yosten and Larry Monroe.

Early in the race, Mike Lesle bounced between second and third place through Beatty and up to Tonopah, where he put in relief driver Jim Wright. Wright soldiered onward for a little bit before he rolled the Comanche, but it wasn't bad enough to be out of the race. He righted the

Jerry Bundy had a long day in the desert after early troubles dropped him down the order. However, the desert rewards perseverance, and Bundy finished in third place and was the first Jeep to complete the race.

Don German earned a solo win in his small CJ. The single-seater, center-seated design is popular with racers in Northern California, Nevada, and Oregon, who run with the Valley Off-Road Racing Association. (Photo Courtesy tracksidephoto.com)

truck and was able to keep going in third place.

Wright hustled the wounded Comanche back to Beatty and handed the truck back over to Lesle, who took off in second place. Lesle arrived back in Pahrump in second place and in the lead for the points championship.

This long race starred Petaluma, California, racer Don German. German had a unique narrowed single-seater Jeep with one seat in the center of the vehicle. German primarily ran in the Valley Off-Road Racing Association (VORRA), which races in Northern California and Nevada.

German, running solo, got a great start, and led at the first checkpoint and at every other one after that. Things became exciting in the last 50 miles, as the Jeep lost all brakes and a fatigued German had to back off. Still, he won by 1 hour and 16 minutes.

Baja 1000

This year's Baja race was mostly identical to 1987. It was a loop with all the usual highlights: Ensenada, Valle de Trinidad, San Felipe, the Summit, Mike's Sky Ranch, and Camalu. Jeeps performed well in Class 3 (4x4) and Class 7 (4x4). No Jeeps finished in Class 4, Class 7S, or Class 14.

It was a two-Jeep race for many miles, as Don Adams and Larry Olsen led for the majority of the first half of

the race, with Mike Schwellinger and Les Erickson close behind. Schwellinger took the lead from Mike's Sky Ranch to the Pacific Coast until he had several problems. He lost his lights on the coast road and was stuck for a time in a tidal pool. Adams's Jeep Wrangler cruised the rest of the way for the victory, and Schwellinger and Erickson finished 1 hour and 20 minutes later. Jerry Bundy and Bob Bogdanoff, in their Scrambler, finished 50 minutes behind Schwellinger and Erickson to complete the Jeep Sweep.

Mike Lesle started well and led the pack early by 2 minutes. Shortly thereafter, issues started with a broken

Don Adams and Larry Olsen debuted the long-awaited Wrangler at the Baja 1000. The duo had a fierce battle with the Mike Schwellinger CJ for a while until Adams grabbed the lead on the Pacific side and held on for the win in the new Wrangler. (Photo Courtesy tracksidephoto.com)

Mike Lesle and Jim Wright did not feel lucky early in the Baja 1000, as parts were breaking on the Jeep. A late rally with a magnificent drive by Wright on the southern loop sealed the victory and a season championship in their class. (Photo Courtesy tracksidephoto.com)

driveshaft, which was followed by a broken axle and three flat tires. By Checkpoint 4, with the help of some attrition, Lesle was back in second place, 11 minutes behind a Ford. He handed the truck to Jim Wright to drive the tough southern loop.

Wright drove perfectly, passed the Ford, and held a solid lead of 46 minutes heading into Mike's Sky Ranch. The Comanche was running perfectly when Lesle got back in to do the last third of the race. He drove at a careful pace and won by a slim 7 minutes. More importantly to Jeep, Lesle secured the class points championship.

1989

The year began with George H. W. Bush being sworn into office as the 41st president of the United States. In March, the Exxon Valdez oil tanker made a navigational error and parked itself on Alaska's Bligh Reef. It punctured 8 of the 10 cargo holds and spilled 5.8 million gallons of crude oil. In May, former Formula One driver Emerson Fittipaldi won his first of two Indianapolis 500s in a thrilling battle with Al Unser Jr. and Michael Andretti.

In off-road racing, the lower participation numbers in Class 3 and Class 14 made for low purses, so the two classes were combined with short-wheelbase production rigs and modified rigs to increase prize money. For years, Class 6 was known as the sedan class. Somehow, in a rule change in 1988, compact two-wheel-drive SUVs were allowed in the class, so Jeep had a new place to play.

Parker 400

The United States had a massive outbreak of influenza. SCORE lost quite a few entrants who backed out due to illness. Volunteers, drivers, co-drivers, and crew members were also affected.

Jeep Woes

Jeep and its teams and fans probably do not fondly remember the 1989 Parker 400 for several reasons besides the flu. Mike Lesle tested his brand-new Jeep Comanche the day before the race and lost the engine. His crew looked everywhere for new pistons, but none were found.

Jack Ramsey, new to truck racing after years of competing in limited Volkswagen-powered classes, debuted in the Lesle Class 7 4x4 Comanche only to have a spun rod bearing by race mile 30. John Dyck retired the Honcho at the end of the California loop with shock issues. Jim Bell and Walt Laycock took 6.5 hours to complete California and put the Honcho on the trailer. Dan and Grant Randall finished, but a 3-hour breakdown on the

last lap dropped them way down the order. Jack Schlaman and Chris Robinson, in a Class 7S Comanche, led with the finish not far away but the panhard rod broke and dropped them to fourth place. Evan Evans's debut in the Class 6 Cherokee was spoiled by electrical issues.

Les Erickson

The worst news came from race mile 22 on the California side. Les Erickson started the race last in the class off the line in the Schwellinger CJ-7. Before long, he passed all but a few of the 15 trucks. He started to feel lightheaded and complained about a numb jaw to his co-driver as he started to pull over. Then, Erickson slumped over the steering wheel and became unconscious. Despite the efforts of two nurses that happened to be spectating nearby, he died due to a blood clot that traveled to his heart.

Erickson was a captain for the Ventura County Fire Department. He lived across from Schwellinger and was involved with the team from the start. His funeral was standing-room only as firefighters and off-road racers alike paid their respects.

Great Mojave 250

The second race of the year was more kind to the Jeep brand. Schwellinger was back out with a new co-driver and determined to keep his word to his late co-driver that he would keep racing.

Dick Landfield's team built a new Bronco that proved to be hard to beat for the next four years. Jeep still had the entries and victories, but Landfield and his drivers didn't make it easy. The Bronco grabbed an early lead, and the battle for second place formed between Mike Schwellinger and Steve Kramer in the CJ-7, Carl Cook in his rear-engine CJ-2, a second Bronco, and a Mitsubishi pickup that failed to come around for a second lap. Adams and Olsen had unknown ills with the Wrangler early on and played catch up all day.

The second Bronco disappeared on Lap 3 with a broken transmission, and Cook slowed a little to allow Schwellinger a clear run in second place. Adams drove quickly to make up positions and was just 9 minutes behind the CJ-7 (in second place) going into the final lap. At the end, Schwellinger finished in second place, and Adams took third place 8 minutes after Schwellinger. Wes Banks and Rich Martinez took fourth place in their CJ-7. Cook faded to seventh place behind David Bryan, who broke a driveline close to the finish but made a quick repair and finished sixth.

Mike Lesle's new Jeep was a two-wheel-drive build. He joined fellow Jeep drivers Rob MacCachren and Jack

Jack Schlaman turned a hot lap when it counted. It lifted him from being in the middle of the pack to the final podium spot in Class 7S. (Photo Courtesy tracksidephoto.com)

Schlaman in the class. After the first lap, three Jeep Comanches were nose to tail in second through fourth place, and all chased a fast Nissan. MacCachren and Lesle were 1 second apart and 1 minute and 40 seconds behind the leader. Jack Schlaman was fourth.

On Lap 2, MacCachren cut the lead to 37 seconds. Lesle had 50 minutes of downtime. By the end of Lap 3, things shifted, as MacCachren lost an hour due to repairs. Schlaman was still in fourth place while Lesle moved back up to sixth. On the fourth lap, things shifted yet again as they headed to the finish. Schlaman turned a wicked lap, was the first Jeep to finish, and took third place. MacCachren recovered from repairs and nabbed fifth place. Lesle's charge fizzled and he came home in a distant eighth place.

Jack Ramsey came around in second place on Lap 1 and chased a Ranger who was 51 seconds ahead. A few Toyotas and Fords were in between Ramsey and the other two Comanches of Sebelius and Randall. By halfway, the Ranger was ahead by 10 minutes. In the third lap, the Ranger had 10 minutes of downtime, which allowed Ramsey to slip into the lead.

In the final lap, the chasing Ranger had ignition problems that cost him an hour and dropped him out of the top five. Ramsey soldiered onward and set a nice pace all the way to the

end. Bud Sebilius and Mark Johnson were able to take the fourth spot. They were followed 12 minutes later by Mike Randall and Bob Grumbein.

Nevada 400

There were big changes for the 1989 version of the Mint 400, which was what the racers still called it, even though Binion's purchased Del Webb and absorbed the Mint into Binion's Horseshoe next door. The name changed to the Nevada 400, and Binion's was the sponsor. The other big change was that the race was back in the Speedrome and featured 105 miles of what veterans said was the "rockiest race ever up here." A total of 373 entries took on the Nevada desert, and only 94 finished (a measly 25-percent finish rate).

The Class 3 Bronco of David Ashley took off and led the field for a lap before the front-end broke and cost him more than 4 hours. Adams and Olsen took the lead and checked their mirrors for Mike Schwellinger, but he broke a tie-rod end in a difficult place for the crew to get to and lost almost 3 hours. It got worse for Schwellinger. After almost 18 hours in the desert and only 9 miles from the finish line, a leaf spring broke, punched a hole in the Quadratrac housing, and resulted in all of the oil draining. Game over.

Adams had a somewhat-clean run, aside from getting

Rob MacCachren earned a big win for Walker Evans Racing at the Mint 400 with a steady drive around the treacherous course.

Mike Schwellinger and Steve Kramer ran a tough race and never gave up trying to win for their late teammate Les Erickson. The duo pressed onward through adversity to get win the Baja 500.

stuck on Lap 2 for a few minutes and having to cure some electrical gremlins on Lap 3. Marshall and Michael Mahr had a good run and took third place in their Jeepster.

In Class 7S, Rob MacCachren found his groove on home turf as the Las Vegas driver, and co-rider Mike Smigulec gained the lead right away and never let go. They brought home the win by 22 minutes. This was the first "Mint" 400 win for MacCachren, who took just 13 hours to complete the course.

Baja Internacional

The 1989 version of the race turned into three 142-mile laps. The start was moved from Ensenada to San Felipe.

The Bronco of David Ashley rocketed into an early lead on Lap 1. Larry Olsen never came back around after he started the race. Mike Schwellinger was third at the end of the first 142 miles and installed Steve Kramer into the left seat for the second lap. Word quickly spread that the Bronco was down with mechanical issues. Kramer now had the lead and hustled to get the CJ-7 back to Schwellinger.

Back in the pits to start the last lap, word came the Bronco was moving again, so Schwellinger put the pedal down. About halfway around the lap, the water pump seized and sent the fan blades into the radiator. Undaunted, Mike decided since the Bronco was probably closing in on him, he would run it until he either won or broke it. At the next pit, efforts were made to plug the holes the best that they could and add water.

Heading toward the next pit, the transfer case split into two pieces and broke the front driveshaft and wedged it into the floor. The offending driveshaft was removed, two-wheel-drive was all he had, and Schwellinger screamed out of there because he thought the Bronco had to be right on him. What Schwellinger did not know was the Bronco had wedged itself into a ditch and was no longer coming. The CJ-7 held together all the way back to San Felipe. The team took its first win since the loss of Les Erickson at Parker and dedicated the win to his memory.

Rob MacCachren had to stop early because his transmission overheated. He kicked out the windshield of the Comanche to allow more air to flow to the coolers in the bed, instead of depending on a scoop over the cab to deflect air to them. With the windshield out, the temperature was reduced. This move was repeated by several teams in the class. The stop and the high temperatures relegated the Jeep to fifth place on the first lap.

In Lap 2, the engine started to miss and then MacCachren had a flat tire, but others in the class had worse issues. First place was now only 12 minutes in front of the Jeep with one lap to go. The charge for the lead never happened, as the engine issue necessitated a change of spark plugs, which helped, but MacCachren took second place by 14 minutes.

Barstow Fireworks 250

This year, the early morning start was used again, and the weather gods blessed the race with a cool breeze that kept afternoon temps in the 90s, which for Barstow in July is cool.

Don Adams and Larry Olsen give way to Walker Evans on their way to second place in Barstow, California. (Photo Courtesy tracksidephoto.com)

The bad news was that the Bronco had a flawless race. Don Adams and Larry Olsen were in pursuit mode in the Wrangler, which netted them second place at the flag. Mike Schwellinger and Steve Kramer had flat tires every single lap, but their pace while running was good enough for third place. Les Barnett and Harry Palomino brought the T&J Off-Road Scrambler home in fourth place an hour after Schwellinger and Kramer.

John Dyck had the Honcho flying over the Barstow terrain and stayed within striking distance of the higher-tech rigs ahead. In the end, he finished in third place, 12 minutes behind second place and a half hour behind the winner. For a low-tech rig, such as the Honcho, that was a significant accomplishment.

Rob MacCachren was out front in Class 7S after the first lap. Chris Robinson was in the Jack Schlaman Comanche and ran in third place. By the end of Lap 2, Robinson nabbed the lead by a few seconds with MacCachren close behind, and Mike Lesle trailed by 10 minutes in fourth place.

At the end of Lap 3, positions switched again with MacCachren in the lead, Robinson close behind, and Lesle advancing to third place. The Jeeps were the class of the field heading into the final lap, where the lead Jeep (MacCachren) had a unique problem: the fuel pump mount fell off. Using duct tape, they wrapped the pump

back on. The fix never lasted long, so there were several stops to re-tape the pump. One time, they ran out of tape and begged for some from another pit crew.

In the end, Robinson was able to get by and win by 23 minutes over MacCachren. Lesle disappeared on the final lap and fell out of the top five.

Nevada 500

HDRA put together a single-lap course that totaled 441 miles and started in Pahrump. The Pahrump Station Casino was a sponsor, and the town was thrilled to have a big event to bolster the summer economy. Temperatures were around 110°F near the start and cooled to 95°F up north.

By the 50-mile mark around Lathrop Wells, the Bronco was out front but was only leading Adams and Olsen by a few minutes. Schwellinger and Kramer were 2 minutes behind Adams and Olsen. That was as good as it got for Schwellinger, as shortly after Lathrop, the Jeep's left front axle broke. Rather than take the time to make a lengthy repair, the team shifted into two-wheel-drive and soldiered onward. Schwellinger and Kramer also had to make several stops when the engine threw the fan belt off the pulleys.

Toward the north end of the course, the Bronco had a problem that necessitated a long pit stop. Adams stormed

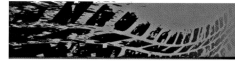

Evan Evans's Long Road to the Start Line

On July 13, 1989, Evan Evans was riding his dirt bike near his home in Riverside, California, as he had done many times before. This time, he was pitched off the bike and suffered injuries that left him paralyzed from the waist down. Not even a week later, Evan prodded his father to look for ways to race an off-road truck with hand controls. Evan needed to start the Baja 1000.

In the July 21, 1989, edition of the *San Bernardino Sun* newspaper, an off-road racing friendly paper since the very beginning, staff writer Katie Castator broke the news that Evan had plans to be at the Baja 1000. Evan was moved from Riverside to Loma Linda Hospital to start his rehabilitation program and learn how to handle life "with his new body," as Evan said.

On November 9, 1989, just 119 days after the accident, Evan Evans was behind the steering wheel with hand controls in his Jeep Cherokee and waited to start the Baja 1000. The original plan was to get from the start line down the 31 miles of pavement to the first turnoff into the dirt, remove the hand controls, and switch drivers. There, Brian Stewart, son of off-road racing legend Ivan Stewart, would take the Cherokee the rest of the way. Stewart had

substituted for Evans in another race a month before, so he had familiarity with the Jeep.

Evans took the starter flag and headed through the streets of Ensenada and onto the highway portion. He started sixth in his class, and by the time he closed in on the exchange point, he had passed all the cars in his class. Evan radioed the crew to move to the next road crossing at race mile 72 for the exchange. Down the dirt road he went and tried to make some time so that Stewart could hopefully retain the lead during the driver swap.

At the road crossing, Evans pulled over and was removed from the Jeep. The crew unhooked the hand controls, and Stewart slid inside. Evans told Stewart that he would stay at the road crossing and radio how far the next in class was behind him. Stewart took off, and Evans noted the time. Ten minutes later, the next car in class went by. Satisfied that everything was under control, Evans was taken back to his hotel in Ensenada, where he took a long soak in the hot tub and spent the next day listening for news from the crew.

Stewart had a dream Baja 1000 and made it to La Paz in 24 hours with no flat tires or downtime for mechanical issues. The team won by 4 hours and 40 minutes.

Only 119 days after he became paralyzed, Evan Evans was back in the Cherokee with hand controls, and he did his part with Brian Stewart to take a big win in class and sew up the class championship for Jeep. (Photo Courtesy tracksidephoto.com)

Rob MacCachren and Mike Smigulec started with some issues and chased the field for a while until they took the lead at Tonopah. (Photo Courtesy tracksidephoto.com)

Bronco was fixed again and ran the Wrangler down close to the finish. Adams watched helplessly as the taillights faded away in front of him. Schwellinger limped home 3 hours later to take third place.

It was a rough start for Rob MacCachren and Mike Smigulec. Right off the start, they threw their power-steering and fan belt off the engine. It was a short fix, but enough to drop them to fifth at Lathrop Wells. By the halfway point, half the trucks in the class were broken, including Mike Lesle, who spun the main bearings. MacCachren was able to run down everyone by Tonopah and cruised home as the winner and sole Jeep finisher.

into the lead and turned south back towards Beatty, but then the radiator picked up a pinhole leak. This meant Adams had to stop at every pit to top off the water. The

In Class 7 4x4, it was a tight group at Lathrop Wells, as the leader, a Nissan, got stuck and broke the transmission.

Larry Olsen charges past David Bryan in the early going of the peninsula run to La Paz. Things slowed down considerably shortly after this photo was taken. (Photo Courtesy tracksidephoto.com)

David Bryan and Gene Hightower go over one of the many cattleguards that dot the Baja landscape. Farmers keep them in good repair to keep their livestock from roaming. Spectators love them because they send the race cars flying. (Photo Courtesy tracksidephoto.com)

A Chevy and a Ford drove past for first and second place, and Jack Ramsey and Mike Lesle were 30 seconds behind them.

Heading north to the halfway point, the Ford behind Ramsey was now in front, as a comedy of errors was beginning for him. He had fewer problems than others, which is saying something, as he climbed to second place at the finish more than an hour behind the Chevy. Ramsey's issues included a broken front axle, broken brake line, broken differential housing, and a broken alternator.

Baja 1000

This year, the Baja 1000 returned to its original roots and was a true 1,000-mile (1,020 miles to be exact) course to La Paz. Jeep vehicles were entered in five classes. One earned a class win, but it was mostly podium finishes for the intrepid Jeepers.

Don Adams and the 1,000 miles of Low RPM

For long races such as this, some teams recruit guest drivers. In this case, Don Adams and Larry Olsen brought Doug Robinson along to help drive.

No matter how good your driver lineup is, Baja has the last say in your race. In the first 100 miles between Ensenada and Valle de Trinidad, the engine acted like it wanted to seize at higher RPM. It seemed okay at lower RPM, so team owner Adams proclaimed to his drivers that 3,000 revs was the limit for the rest of the 920 miles of the race.

Both Robinson and Adams nursed the ailing engine the rest of the way down the peninsula and watched the tachometer for an unbelievable second-place finish in their class.

Gene Hightower's Last Ride

Gene Hightower was at the first Mexican 1000 in 1967 and won the modified four-wheel-drive class with Ed Venable in 32 hours and 2 minutes. In 1989, Hightower was invited by David Bryan to help drive his CJ-6.

David and Gene spent six days pre-running the racecourse. Two guys who have been around the sport from the beginning drove the peninsula and swapped incredible stories. For the race, David started and his sister Debbie rode along from Ensenada to Cataviña (about a third of the way). There, Gene climbed in and drove to San Ignacio with Debbie in the right seat. At San Ignacio, about halfway, Debbie jumped out, Gene moved to the passenger's seat, and David got back in to drive. Hightower stayed in the right seat the rest of the way to La Paz.

It was not a perfect run. There was a broken transmission cooler just past Mission San Javier that needed mending. Down around Constitution, a broken motor mount needed repairs. The pair arrived in La Paz in 32 hours and 13 minutes to take fourth place in class. It was 4 hours ahead of the Bronco that finished in fifth place.

That was a race of closure for both men. Hightower retired from competition after 22 years of racing at the front in Jeeps (and many times with his kids). This was also David Bryan's final race in a Jeep. His team planned to run a Class 8 truck.

The Rest of the Results

Mike Lesle and Jim Wright had a few issues along the way with the Comanche but salvaged third place in Class 7 4x4. Rob MacCachren had problem after problem. From the start, the engine threw the belts, and during that repair, they found a problem with the air filter, which they replaced. Down the course, the Comanche ran into a boulder that broke the rear springs. Farther down the road, the front end hit something and bent the front beam. Another spring broke down the road, and, luckily, Enduro racing was nearby and loaned him one.

Just when things looked better and a top-five finish looked possible, as he neared one of the final pits, the crew found a broken rear differential housing. It took 4 hours to locate a rear end. It was not a perfect fit, as it was 2 inches too narrow and the springs were 2 inches too long. Hence the extra hours for the replacement. They made it to La Paz in a very competitive time for that section and had to settle for seventh place in class.

Mike Lesle and Jim Wright had a few issues along the way that were resolved quickly enough for them to claim third place in Class 7 4x4. (Photo Courtesy tracksidephoto.com)

EPILOGUE

GOODBYE 1980s

When you look back at the jump in technology from 1980 to 1989, it is like going from Fred Flintstone's car to George Jetson's car. The new suspensions imagined by genius level car builders made speeds available to 4x4 drivers that were never previously imagined. Still, you have to give credit to the men who stuck with their production-based Honchos and CJs that represented what made off-road racing great.

Heading into the next decade, Jeep entered into the high-tech world, but the spirit of solid front axles never really died.

TOP: The Russ Wernimont-built Jeep Trophy Truck campaigned by Larry Maddox Racing had some successes in the early days of the Trophy Truck class. It was Jeep's first foray into high-tech off-road racing. (Photo Courtesy tracksidephoto.com)

The second attempt at a Trophy Truck for Jeep came from Mike Lesle Racing with an even more high-tech build that retained the solid front axle. With Lesle and Steve Kelley behind the wheel, the Jeep was in good hands. (Photo Courtesy tracksidephoto.com)

Mike Pearlman poses with his father's original Toyota Land Cruiser that ran in many club events and the first few National Four-Wheel-Drive Grand Prixs. After that, it saw duty as an official vehicle for NORRA. Pearlman brought NORRA back in a big and inventive way that still thrives 24 years later. (Photo Courtesy NORRA Archive)

Expert car builders, such as Russ Wernimont, brought Jeep into the Trophy Truck era. Drivers, such as Curt LeDuc, brought the new long-travel suspension technology many wins in Class 3, Class 6, Class 8, and Trophy Truck. Mike Lesle built his own Trophy Truck in the 1990s. He scored some great finishes and a few wins and shared the driving with wily veteran driver Steve Kelley.

Jeep forged ahead into the 1990s and enjoyed success with the new Comanche mini truck and the venerable Cherokee in Class 6, Class 7, Class 7S, and Class 7 4x4.

Stalwart solid-axle specialist Don Adams continued into 1991 with his Wrangler. He then teamed with Don-A-Vee for a short time in a Class 6 Cherokee before he retired quietly to his buffalo ranch in Colorado.

Wins for the old solid-axle Jeeps mainly came from smaller off-road-racing series, where older technology was still able to compete. These 200-mile events were where the old iron still shined for a time. It is where the old Bronco versus CJ war still raged with the same pride and intensity as it did between Brian Chuchua and Bill Stroppe, J. M. Bragg and Ray Russell, and Mike Schwellinger and David Ashley.

As the new millennium dawned, so did a focus on vintage off-road racing. Mike Pearlman, son of NORRA founder Ed Pearlman, resurrected the name with a rally-formatted off-road competition down the Baja peninsula. The event featured overnight stops and time to repair vehicles every night. Many an old CJ and Honcho found their way out of the corner of the garage or from outside under a tarp to a new life on some familiar old roads.

In its heyday, the CJ and the Commando were the only 4x4s to bring the fight to the Bronco for 25 years. Recently, I traveled to Las Vegas and saw where there was once fierce battles fought in early Mint 400s, there was now industrial parks near Interstate 15 and US 95. I pulled off and parked where the desert met the buildings. I stood and looked out into the sagebrush and could hear the engines of Donnie Beyer, Rod Hall, Ray Russell, J. M. Bragg, Don Adams, the Randalls, Roger Mears, Lowell Arnold, and others echoing through the desert. Maybe it was in my mind, and I wondered if the people working in these stark white buildings knew that under the cement and asphalt was hallowed ground.

Jeep earned its "toughest 4x4" moniker honestly.

My Baja

by Curt LeDuc

There's a place out West that time has forgotten; the sun comes every day.

Rising on the Sea of Cortez to cast shadows of Cactus and Missions on this barren desert.

It's a place I feel comfortable, accepted, vulnerable, and alive. It holds my heart and my tire tracks.

If you get a chance, challenge it.

My soul is in Baja, fueled by the salt rimmed margaritas and lobster burritos.

Sitting comfortably on the cantina's beaches, waiting on the fire-red sunsets on the big blue Pacific swells.

Bad roads bring great people to mix with cruise-ship shoppers, fly-in weekenders and big-catch fishermen dreamers.

The big race to La Paz unites an entire 1000-mile peninsula to come out to cheer on modern day Conquistadors to battle day and night for victory over this unforgiving desert like generations before them.

The Black Diamond is the envy of all, from the very old to the very small. It makes you get up out of your chair, raise up a cold cervesa, and cheer her on!

Pointing those KC lights south, chasing the dream through the dust, silt, and rain, shining through the night, burning fuel at 4 miles to the gallon, crawling at 10, holding your breath at 135, out-driving your lights, trusting the GPS and the fearless co-driver cheating death with every breath staring at the screen watching for the Jets and Cross Bones.

Gambling on beating Mother Earth spinning at 1,000 mph, bringing the rain, fog, and high tides to stop you like wet cement. Never regretting the millions you spent.

The sun will rise and set every day whether we are here or away.

I've seen death and birth and kissed great lips. This is MY Baja, and I am so proud to have shared it with you.

2015 Off-Road Motorsports
Hall of Fame Inductee

If you have been to Baja, you know that Curt LeDuc's words ring true. If you have not been there, then there is something missing from your life. (Photo Courtesy Curt LeDuc)

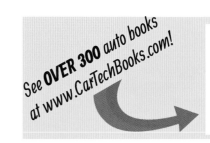

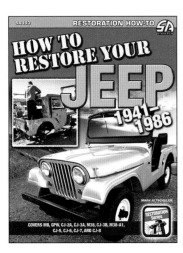
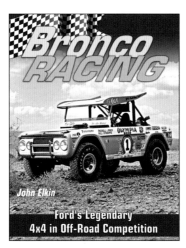
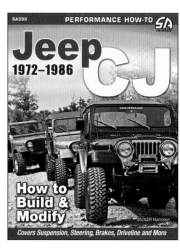